Conversations with
Michael McClure

Literary Conversations Series
Monika Gehlawat
General Editor

Conversations with Michael McClure

Edited by David Stephen Calonne

University Press of Mississippi / Jackson

The University Press of Mississippi is the scholarly publishing agency of
the Mississippi Institutions of Higher Learning: Alcorn State University,
Delta State University, Jackson State University, Mississippi State University,
Mississippi University for Women, Mississippi Valley State University,
University of Mississippi, and University of Southern Mississippi.

www.upress.state.ms.us

The University Press of Mississippi is a member
of the Association of University Presses.

Copyright © 2024 by University Press of Mississippi
All rights reserved

Library of Congress Cataloging-in-Publication Data

Names: Calonne, David Stephen, 1953– editor.
Title: Conversations with Michael McClure / edited by David Stephen Calonne.
Other titles: Literary conversations series.
Description: Jackson : University Press of Mississippi, 2024. |
    Series: Literary conversations series | Includes bibliographical references and index.
Identifiers: LCCN 2024008399 (print) | LCCN 2024008400 (ebook) |
    ISBN 9781496851994 (hardback) | ISBN 9781496852007 (trade paperback) |
    ISBN 9781496852014 (epub) | ISBN 9781496852021 (epub) | ISBN 9781496852038 (pdf) |
    ISBN 9781496852045 (pdf)
Subjects: LCSH: McClure, Michael—Interviews. | Poets, American—Interviews. |
    Beats (Persons)—Interviews. | Beat poetry, American.
Classification: LCC PS3563.A262 Z46 2024 (print) | LCC PS3563.A262 (ebook) |
    DDC 813/.54—dc23/eng/20240311
LC record available at https://lccn.loc.gov/2024008399
LC ebook record available at https://lccn.loc.gov/2024008400

British Library Cataloging-in-Publication Data available

Books by Michael McClure

Passage. Big Sur, CA: Jonathan Williams, 1956.
Peyote Poem. San Francisco: Semina, 1958.
For Artaud, New York: Totem Press, 1959.
Hymns to St. Geryon and Other Poems. San Francisco: Auerhahn Press, 1959 [republished with *Dark Brown* (London: Cape Golliard, 1969; San Francisco: Grey Fox Press, 1979).
!The Feast! San Francisco: The Batman Gallery, 1960.
The New Book/A Book of Torture. New York: Grove, 1961.
Dark Brown. San Francisco: Auerhahn Press, 1961.
Little Odes: Jan.-March 1961. New York: Poets Press, 1961.
Meat Science Essays. San Francisco: City Lights Books, 1963; enlarged edition, 1966.
Two for Bruce Conner. San Francisco: Oyez, 1964.
Ghost Tantras. San Francisco: Privately printed, 1964.
The Blossom, or Billy the Kid, bound with Pour En Finir avec le Jugement de Dieu. New York: American Theatre for Poets, 1964.
13 Mad Sonnets. Milano: East 128, 1964.
The Beard. Berkeley: Oyez, 1965.
Poisoned Wheat. San Francisco: Privately published, 1965; second edition published by Coyote/City Lights, 1966.
Dream Table. San Francisco: Dave Haselwood, 1965.
Unto Caesar. San Francisco: Dave Haselwood, 1965.
Mandalas, with Bruce Conner. San Francisco: Dave Haselwood, 1966.
Love Lion Book. San Francisco: Four Seas Foundation, 1966.
Freewheelin Frank, Secretary of the Angels, with Frank Reynolds. New York: Grove, 1967.
The Blossom, or Billy the Kid. Milwaukee: Great Lake Books, 1967.
The Sermons of Jean Harlow and the Curses of Billy the Kid. San Francisco: Four Seasons Foundation/Dave Haselwood, 1968.
Hail Thee Who Play. Los Angeles: Black Sparrow Press, 1968.
The Shell. London: Cape Goliard, 1968.
Muscled Apple Swift. Topanga, CA: Love Press, 1968.
Love Lion Book. San Francisco: Four Seasons Foundation, 1968.

Little Odes and The Raptors. Los Angeles: Black Sparrow Press, 1969.
Lion Fight. New York: Pierrepont Press, 1969.
Plane Pomes. New York: Phoenix Book Shop, 1969.
The Surge. Columbus, OH: Frontier Press, 1969.
The Cherub. Los Angeles: Black Sparrow Press, 1970.
Star. New York: Grove Press, 1970.
The Mad Cub. New York: Bantam, 1970.
The Adept. New York: Delacorte, 1971.
Wolfnet: Part One. London: Bonefold Imprint, 1971.
Gargoyle Cartoons. New York: Delacorte, 1971.
The Mammals. San Francisco; Cranium Press, 1972.
99 Theses. Lawrence: Kansas: Tansy Press, 1972.
The Book of Joanna. Berkeley: Sand Dollar, 1973.
Solstice Blossom. Berkeley: Arif Press, 1973.
Rare Angel. Los Angeles: Black Sparrow Press, 1974.
A Fist-Full (1956–1957). Los Angeles: Black Sparrow Press, 1974.
Fleas 189–95. New York: Aloe Editions, 1974.
September Blackberries. New York: New Directions, 1974
On Organism. Canton: Institute of Further Studies, 1974.
Man of Moderation: Two Poems. New York: F. Hallman, 1975.
Two Plays. San Francisco: McClure, 1975.
Jaguar Skies. New York: New Directions, 1975.
Gorf; or, Gorf and the Blind Dyke. New York: New Directions, 1976.
Antechamber and Other Poems. Berkeley: Poythress Press, 1977; enlarged as
    Antechamber and Other Poems. New York: New Directions, 1978.
The Grabbing of the Fairy. St. Paul, MN: Truck Press, 1978.
Fragments of Perseus. New York: J. Davies, 1978; expanded edition, New York: New
    Directions, 1983.
Josephine, The Mouse Singer. New York: New Directions, 1980.
Scratching the Beat Surface. San Francisco: North Point Press, 1982.
The Book of Benjamin, with Wesley B. Tanner. Berkeley: Arif Press, 1982.
General Gorgeous. New York: Dramatists Play Service, 1982.
The Beard & VKTMS: Two Plays. New York; Grove Press, 1985.
Specks. Vancouver: Talonbooks, 1985.
Selected Poems. New York: New Directions, 1986.
Adventures of a Novel In Four Chapters, with Bruce Conner. San Francisco: Limestone
    Press, 1991.
Rebel Lions. New York: New Directions, 1991

Lighting the Corners: On Nature, Art and the Visionary: Essays and Interviews. Albuquerque: University of New Mexico Press, 1993.
Simple Eyes and Other Poems. New York: New Directions, 1994.
Three Poems (Incudes "Dark Brown," "Rare Angel," "Dolphin Skull"). New York: Penguin Poets, 1995.
Huge Dreams: San Francisco and Beat Poems. New York: Penguin, 1999.
Rain Mirror: New Poems. New York: New Directions, 1999.
Touching the Edge: Dharma Devotions from the Hummingbird Sangha. Boston: Shambhala, 1999.
The Boobus and the Bunny Duck. San Francisco: Arion Press, 2007.
Deer Boy, with Hung Liu. Oakland: Magnolia Editions, 2009.
Mysteriosos and Other Poems. New York: New Directions, 2010.
Of Indigo and Saffron: New and Selected Poems. Berkeley: University of California Press, 2011.
Mephistos and Other Poems. San Francisco: City Lights, 2016.
Persian Pony. Victoria, BC: Ekstasis Editions, 2017.
Mule Kick Blues and Last Poems. San Francisco: City Lights, 2021.

Contents

Introduction xi

Chronology xix

Michael McClure 3
 David Kherdian / 1969

Gahr, Groooor, Grayohh: For a Meat Poetry—An Interview with Michael McClure 7
 Roland Husson / 1973

Michael McClure Interview 24
 David Rollison / 1976

An Interview with Michael McClure 37
 Stephen Vincent / 1977

A Conversation with Michael McClure 51
 Kevin Power / 1978

Interview with Michael McClure 69
 Inger Thorup Lauridsen and Per Dalgard / 1983

Poetry Wars: An Interview with Michael McClure 75
 Barry Miles / 1986

An Interview with Michael McClure 80
 S. E. Gontarski / 1990

An Interview with Michael McClure   88
Steve Luttrell / 1994

Craft Interview with Michael McClure   96
New York Quarterly / 1995

"What Are Souls?": An Interview with Michael McClure   108
Jack Foley / 2001

Realm Buster: Stan Brakhage   144
Steve Anker / 2001

Artists on the Cutting Edge: Michael McClure Delivers a Passion for Poetry   152
George Varga / 2001

Interview with Michael McClure   155
Sergio Cohn / 2004

A Fierce God and a Fierce War: An Interview with Michael McClure   161
Rod Phillips / 2007

Beat Poet Michael McClure on Jim Morrison, the Doors, Allen Ginsberg, and Jack Kerouac   173
Anis Shivani / 2011

Interview with Poet Michael McClure   182
Jonah Raskin / 2013

Break on Through   186
Garrett Caples / 2013

Poetry Questions: Michael McClure   189
Rebecca Foresman / 2013

Beat Poet Michael McClure Tries New Style at Eighty-Three   192
Sam Whiting / 2015

Index   197

Introduction

Michael McClure was born on October 20, 1932, in Marysville, Kansas, to Thomas McClure and Marian Dixie Johnston. The violent, cyclone-swept, flat and dry Dust Bowl landscape of the Flint Hills of Kansas is a central image in the American collective unconscious due to *The Wizard of Oz* and Dorothy's dramatic transportation through the sky to the Land of Oz, courtesy of a swirling tornado. McClure often recounted the impact of this tumultuous terrain on his imagination. His parents divorced in 1938, precipitating an equally intense interior, psychological, emotional tumult within the young McClure's psyche. As he noted in his interview with Jack Foley, McClure felt as if he "was essentially abandoned" as a boy of five or six (in his recollections he gives both ages) when his mother sent him away to Seattle, Washington, to live with his grandfather, and he "went through the hell that baby primates do—as in the famous experiments on isolating baby monkeys." In this regard, McClure followed the example of several Beat writers who endured troubled childhoods. However, a positive consequence of this emotional upheaval was McClure's enriching relationship with his grandfather, Ellis Johnston, a physician whose love of nature had a profound impact on the impressionable child. Delivering newspapers, McClure was awed by the "ghostly, vast, supernatural, gorgeous brilliance" of Mount Rainier, and while living at 35th Avenue Southwest, he was enthralled by Puget Sound as well as the distant islands and mountains.[1]

The interview was a genre with which McClure was quite comfortable: he himself conducted interviews with poet Robert Duncan and painter Francesco Clemente. As he revealed to Steve Luttrell:

> As a form it's a powerful package of information, because it has ways of being both more formal and less formal than the prose that's written to be read. For instance, when I read a major interview with Francesco Clemente, I understood more about his painting that I had before, and I realized the structure and the shape of the thought behind the painting. . . . I like being interviewed and I also like doing interviews. Mary Caroline Richards visited us and I thought after

asking M. C. what brought her to do the first translation of Artaud into English which was *The Theatre and Its Double*, how much I would like to interview her about her life. Another person to interview would be the painter Jess, who was Robert Duncan's companion.

This volume features interviews from 1969–2015 which chronicle the capacious scope of McClure's creativity. McClure is notable not only for his considerable achievements as poet and prose writer, but also for the many collaborative connections he forged over seven decades—from the 1950s to his death in 2020—with an astonishing range of important figures in the worlds of painting, filmmaking, music, and science. McClure counted among his friends and acquaintances Bruce Conner, Harold Pinter, Amiri Baraka, Richard Brautigan, Wallace Berman, George Herms, Charles Olson, Lawrence Jordan, Dennis Hopper, Bob Dylan, Janis Joplin, Stan Brakhage, Jim Morrison, Ray Manzarek, Robert Duncan, Sterling Bunnell, Francis Crick, Gary Snyder, Francesco Clemente, and Diane di Prima. During his early years in San Francisco—he arrived in 1954—McClure would form significant lifelong friendships, and he attended Kenneth Rexroth's literary evenings. Robert Duncan became a mentor, and McClure also learned much from Charles Olson with whom he corresponded, adopting several features of Olson's concept of "projective verse"—the emphasis on the breath giving birth to the line of verse rather than abiding by strict metrical form, the act of writing poetry as a continuation of the life of the body, and a new typographical freedom—and he became close friends with poet Philip Lamantia and the groundbreaking experimental filmmaker Stan Brakhage. McClure conducted an exchange of letters with Brakhage which lasted for four decades.[2]

McClure came to early prominence when—on October 7, 1955, at the Six Gallery in San Francisco—he read "For the Death of 100 Whales" as well as several other poems, along with Allen Ginsberg, Philip Whalen, Gary Snyder, and Philip Lamantia. McClure had been inspired to write "For the Death of 100 Whales" by an article in an April 1954 issue of *Time* magazine which described seventy-nine bored G.I.s stationed at a NATO base in Iceland who from their powerboats machine-gunned whales for sport. This signaled the beginnings of McClure's lifelong dedication to environmental issues which we will see emphasized in many interviews. Like D. H. Lawrence—one of his favorite authors—McClure evinced a keen sensitivity to birds, beasts, and flowers and made humanity's kinship with the natural world a central theme in his poetry and prose. McClure constantly warns his interlocutors about the dangers of humanity's continual assault on the environment and in his interview with Rod Phillips explains the purpose of his 1965 poem "Poisoned Wheat," which decried the use of exfoliants by the US military during the war in Vietnam. As we have become increasingly aware during the subsequent decades, these destructive chemical agents wreak havoc not only on the health of human beings, but on the delicate balance of the world's ecosystems.

In several of our interviews, McClure tells the story of his early years in Kansas and his friendship with assemblage artist and filmmaker Bruce Conner and early attempts at writing poetry. It is a fascinating byway of literary history that at age seventeen in 1949—a year after Allen Ginsberg's famous Harlem visionary experiences of William Blake in 1948 in faraway New York City—that McClure in Wichita, Kansas, thought he *was* William Blake. In an unpublished 1968 interview with Richard Ogar, McClure recalled:

> Well, I had a dream when I was about seventeen that I was William Blake, and that I lived in the second floor of a giant cuckoo clock and sat in a rocking-chair and rocked. The front of the clock was covered with cyclone wire, and there were lions in there that roared while I rocked. Then a hand reached into the clock and took me up and put me in another place, a dark moonlit scene. It was in front of an Indian palisade, with pointed logs sticking up out of the earth in the moonlight. I turned to a man who was standing there and said, "What am I doing here?" And he said, "Well, the King of England is protecting artists," and I looked and it was Richard Wagner.[3]

The dream is remarkable not only for establishing McClure's early identification with the great British mystical genius Blake, but for the "surreal" details and wild imagination here portrayed, which would become a defining element of McClure's career as poet and playwright. The juxtaposition of a cuckoo clock sporting "cyclone wire"—a compressed image from his Kansas childhood recalling the chain-link fences built to withstand the impact of tornado-force winds—with a rocking chair is a startling surrealist image recalling the paintings of René Magritte or Salvador Dalí. This is followed by roaring lions, a prefiguration of McClure's experiments during the late fifties with "Beast Language" in his play *!The Feast!* As we shall see in several interviews, McClure invented a growling, consonant-rich vocabulary with roots in Old and Middle English composed of words like "GRAAHR" to suggest the "mammal" nature of humanity, culminating in his reading of his *Ghost Tantras* to the lions in the San Francisco Zoo. The dream continues with a hand reaching out to place him next to a Native American "palisade." Of course, shamanism and Native American culture would become central to the Beats, and a few years later McClure would conduct experiments with a central Native American entheogen—peyote. And finally, the astonishing appearance of German composer Richard Wagner lends a vivid, comical, Monty Pythonesque twist to the finale of this wonderful dream-fantasy. The dream provides a fascinating example of the ways artists rely on their unconscious to provide a fecund source of material which they then reshape through the creative act into their poems, novels, paintings and musical compositions.

This allusion to German culture provides yet another prophetic moment, for McClure gleaned several concepts from his familiarity with German language—he had studied German at the University of Arizona—and literature. For example, the notion of the twin nature of the human being was signaled for McClure by the fact that German "has two words, *Geist* for the soul of man and *Odem* for the spirit of beasts. Odem is the undersoul. I was becoming sharply aware of it."[4] And in his interview with Anis Shivani, McClure declares:

> Schlegel the German Romantic wrote, "All art should become science and all science art; poetry and philosophy should be made one." When I gave my first poetry reading in 1955, it was the time to go beyond Existentialism. Reductionism had reached its peak in the sciences and in art. Inspiration and imagination were there to be freed and reflect their presence in nature.

McClure was inspired by another German—Ernst Haeckel—and British philosopher who taught for many years at Harvard, Alfred North Whitehead, for both "believed that the universe is a single organism—that the whole thing is alive and that its existence is its sacredness and its breathing. If all is divine and alive—and if everything is the Uncarved Block of the Taoists—then all of it and any part is beauteous (or possibly hideous) and of enormous value. It is beyond proportion."[5] Ernst Haeckel's *Kunstformen der Natur* [*Art Forms in Nature*] (1889–1904) is an extraordinary collection of the great biologist's precise (and prepsychedelic in their intense, colorful, visionary power) engravings based on his drawings and watercolors of—among many other fauna and flora—jellyfish, hummingbirds, antelopes, spiders, sea anemones, radiolarians, bats, and lizards.[6] McClure continued his engagement with science throughout his life, and we witness in these interviews his wide-ranging reading and personal acquaintance with ornithologist Hans Peeters, ecologist H. T. Odum, biologist Sterling Bunnell—with whom he became close friends and traveled to Mexico in search of mushrooms to be employed in psychological experiments regarding creativity—and botanist Richard Felger, who was indebted to McClure for his research contributions concerning the trees of Sonora.

McClure's scientific fascinations overlapped with his desire to document his interior experiences with entheogens by employing the same phenomenological precision which he admired in Haeckel's arresting and profound artistic renderings of the natural world.[7] Human consciousness was to be explored as another realm of Nature with equal claims to new discoveries. As he told S. E. Gontarski, McClure was motivated to begin chronicling his drug experiences due to his dissatisfaction with the way authors such as Henri Michaux had described the effects of mescaline in *Miserable Miracle* (1956).[8] McClure's "Peyote Poem" would garner the admiration of the codiscoverer with James Watson of DNA, Nobel Prize winner Francis Crick, who included verses from McClure's poem—"THIS IS THE POWERFUL KNOWLEDGE / we smile with it"—in his book *Of Molecules and Men* (1966), as an epigraph to the chapter "The Simplest Living Things."[9] McClure would go on to compose the essays "The Mushroom" and "Drug Notes: Peyote, Heroin, Cocaine," published in 1963 in *Meat Science Essays*. However, McClure's early experiments with peyote and a variety of entheogens led ultimately to a "dark night of the soul"—St. John of the Cross's term for the desolation and sense of solitude and spiritual emptiness which comes when one experiences a total nakedness and vulnerability in the face of the terror of existence. In the author's note to *The New Book/A Book of Torture* (1961), McClure acknowledged: "Reality has opened up with psychedelics. The imagination is projected upon reality in new shapes, and auras, and virtues, and colors, and smiles, and griefs, and pains, and tortures, and agonies, and myths, and heavens. . . . I had gone too far. There was no one to lean on except a few friends and loves."[10] Thus, in these interviews, we witness a remarkable figure in American letters who throughout his career chose to do things in his own way. McClure showed a great deal of courage in taking his positions to wherever they would lead him and accepted the dangers of his pioneering efforts—he realized he "had gone too far" in his drug experimentation—as part of the price of the journey.

Yet another area which these interviews illuminate is McClure's lifelong passion the theater, for films and filmmaking. It is natural that McClure would be attracted to films, since his imagination had been theatrical from the beginning. He wrote many plays, most famously *The Beard*, which was raided by the police for supposed "obscenity," as is chronicled in several interviews. McClure became friends with Stan Brakhage as we have seen above, and in the interview with Steve Anker, we may observe how seriously McClure took film as a new art form and his deep understanding of Brakhage's aims and methods as a pioneering artist. McClure also contributed a laudatory essay about Jayne Mansfield to Jonas Mekas's *Film Culture* (Spring 1964), and appeared in several films, including Lawrence Jordan's *Visions of a City* (1956), *Spectre Mystagogic* (1957), and *Triptych in Four Parts* (1958). McClure also was a participant in documentary *The Maze* (1967), in which he led viewers on a tour of Haight-Ashbury in San Francisco during the height of the hippie movement; Norman Mailer's *Beyond the Law* (1968), playing a wild motorcyclist; and in Peter Fonda's *The Hired Hand* (1971), in the role of a "small town troublemaker."[11] In his interviews with Roland Husson and Anis Shivani, McClure speaks of his close friendship with Jim Morrison and their collaboration on a filmscript to be called *Saint Nicholas*, based on McClure's novel *The Adept* (1971). McClure's relationship with the Doors would continue following Morrison's early death with his collaboration with keyboardist Ray Manzarek. As we see in the later interviews, the poet and musician would frequently perform together throughout the country and also created together several recordings.

McClure's spiritual quest is also on display, as when he tells the *New York Quarterly* concerning the struggle involved in "creating a soul.... The work of soulmaking has to be outside. As Keats said, it's a vale of soulmaking; you've got to be in that vale." The epigraph to McClure's book of plays *Gargoyle Cartoons* (1971) reads, "Call the world if you please 'The Vale of Soul-Making,'" and McClure takes this from the famous John Keats letter of April 21, 1810, which continues:

> Then you will find out the use of the world (I am speaking now in the highest terms for human nature admitting it to be immortal which I will here take for granted for the purpose of showing a thought which has struck me concerning it) I say "Soul making" Soul as distinguished from an Intelligence—There may be intelligences or sparks of the divinity in millions—but they are not Souls till they acquire identities, till each one is personally itself.... Do you not see how necessary a World of Pains and troubles is to school an Intelligence and make it a soul? A Place where the heart must feel and suffer in a thousand diverse ways![12]

McClure returns frequently in these interviews to this theme of the alchemical transformation of the self through the trials of existence into a higher form of consciousness. Commentary on visionary poets such as John Keats, William Blake, and Percy Bysshe Shelley are frequent throughout McClure's conversations, and he conceives of the spiritual, artistic, and literary vocations as being all part of the same search of what C. G. Jung called "individuation," or the opening of the soul to its highest possibilities. McClure had begun studying Kundalini Yoga in the early sixties and continued to explore Hindu and Buddhist thought throughout his career. As we can see from the interviews chronicling his later life, McClure would turn to a deep study of Hua Yen Buddhism and *The Buddhist Teaching of Totality* by Garma C. C. Chang.

McClure emerges in these interviews as a thoughtful, sensitive, and committed artist who bridged the worlds of the Beat fifties and the hippie sixties. McClure employed and extended the techniques of projective verse created by his friend Charles Olson, bringing a fresh eye to the typographical look of the poem on the page. He also was instrumental in battling against censorship and for free speech in his play *The Beard* and advocated that humanity cease refusing its "mammal" nature. McClure was a central figure in the birth of the environmental movement, and along with his friend Gary Snyder, he continued throughout his career to advocate for a sane approach to caring for Planet Earth. McClure made contributions to the fields of ethnobotany through his collection of mushrooms with biologist Sterling Bunnell and studied the trees of the Sonoran Desert. McClure's creative and original contributions to such a wide variety of disciplines and fields of endeavor mark him as a unique contributor to American culture. It is hoped that these interviews will gain him the wide readership his works deserve.

DSC

Notes

1. Paul E. Nelson, *American Prophets: Interviews with Thinkers, Activists, Poets & Visionaries* (Seattle: Seattle Poetics Lab, 2018), 147–48.
2. https://bigbridge.org/BB15/2011_BB_15_FEATURES/Luna_McClure_Brakhage_Feature/THE_FLAME_IS_OURS.pdf
3. Richard Ogar, "Interview with Michael McClure," University of California at Berkeley, Bancroft Library, BANC MSS 80/53 c, 2–3.
4. Michael McClure, *Scratching the Beat Surface: Essays on New Vision from Blake to Kerouac* (New York: Penguin Books, 1982), 26.
5. McClure, *Scratching the Beat Surface*, 27.

6. Ernst Haeckel, *Art Forms in Nature* (Munich/London/New York: Prestel Taschen, 2022).

7. On McClure's scientific and mystical quest, see Stefan Benz, "'Sing[ing] of the Middle Way': Michael McClure's Venture for a New Mode of Thought Between Natural Science and Mysticism," COPAS, *Current Objectives of Postgraduate American Studies* 19, no. 1 (2018), 1–24.

8. Henri Michaux, *Miserable Miracle* (Monaco: Editions du Rocher, 1956).

9. Francis Crick, *Of Molecules and Men* (Seattle and Saint Louis: University of Washington Press, 1966), 29.

10. Michael McClure, *Meat Science Essays* (San Francisco: City Lights, 1963), 15–41; Michael McClure, *The New Book/A Book of Torture* (New York: Grove Press, Inc., 1961), 5.

11. On McClure and film, see Jane Falk, "Michael McClure: A Filmography," *Journal of Beat Studies* 6 (2018), 75–88.

12. John Keats, letter of April 21, 1810.

Chronology

1932   On October 20, Michael McClure born in Marysville, Kansas.

1938   McClure's parents divorce and Michael is sent to Seattle, Washington, to live with Ellis Johnston, his physician grandfather whose love of nature—Ellis raises dahlias and finches—influenced McClure. He enjoys children's books about mammals, fossils, the nature of plants and the earth. McClure works delivering newspapers and on the way to school, contemplates in a pond polliwogs, large crustaceans, shrimp and water beetles.

1942   Returns to Wichita, Kansas with mother and new husband, Joe McCoy, an aeronautical engineer.

1946   In eighth grade at Robinson Junior High School, meets Bruce Conner and Lee Streiff, who gives McClure a copy of his older brother James's science fictional *The Epic of the Martian Empire*. Begins writing poetry and over the next few years reads e.e. cummings—discovering his erotic poems in the high school library—Ezra Pound, Kenneth Patchen, Rainer Maria Rilke, Jacob Boehm, and Emmanuel Swedenborg.

1949   Reads about Jackson Pollock in the August 8 issue of *Life* magazine. Dreams he is William Blake and composes poems in his style. Reads Milton, Yeats, Dylan Thomas, Theodore Roethke. Decides to teach himself poetic meters, stanzaic structure, and forms such as the villanelle and sonnet.

1951   Attends University of Wichita where he takes creative writing course with Joan O'Bryant and composes a small book of villanelles. At the university, along with Conner, Dave Haselwood Lee Streiff, and Eric Ecklor, McClure collects manuscripts for a magazine, *Provincial Review*, inspired by Ezra Pound's Vortex Manifesto. However, the magazine project never came to fruition until 1996 when Conner and Streiff published it. Becomes acquainted with bebop and listens to Charlie Parker, Dizzy Gillespie, Bud Powell, and Thelonious Monk.

1953 In the summer, travels to New York City with Bruce Conner, views paintings by abstract expressionists Jackson Pollock and William Baziotes and meets Robert Motherwell. Attends University of Arizona for one year where he studied German, the short story, anthropology and painting. Meets Joanna Kinnison.

1954 Arrives in San Francisco on December 31 from Tucson to pursue Joanna—whom he marries—and ostensibly to study painting with Clyfford Still and Mark Rothko at the Art Institute, but they had left the previous year. Enrolls at San Francisco State University. Lives on Scott Street in North Beach and meets Robert Duncan in his workshop class at San Francisco State. Meets experimental filmmaker Stan Brakhage with whom he establishes a lifelong friendship.

1955 Encounters Allen Ginsberg at a party for W. H. Auden. Duncan dissuades McClure from composing villanelles, sestinas, Petrarchan sonnets. He works at a produce market at night which provides the inspiration for his poem "The Breech." Meets poet Philip Lamantia who takes him to Kenneth Rexroth's Friday night poetry readings and introduces McClure to translations of Antonin Artaud's *Concerning a Journey to the Land of the Tarahumaras* and research about peyote. On October 7, reads "For the Death of 100 Whales," "Point Lobos: Animism," "Poem (Linked part to part)," "Night Words: The Ravishing," "The Mystery of the Hunt," and "The Breech" at the Six Gallery with Allen Ginsberg, Philip Whalen, Gary Snyder, Philip Lamantia (who reads poems by his friend, poet John Hoffman). Kenneth Rexroth is the emcee and Jack Kerouac attends with a jug of wine, shouting "Go! Go! Go!" to encourage the poets. The next day, Ginsberg brings Kerouac to McClure's place: they smoke marijuana together and become friends. Earns BA at San Francisco State College.

1956 Relocates with Joanna to 2322 Fillmore Street which he calls "Painterland." Duncan and Jess help them move, and Kenneth Rexroth carries their wood stove up the steps. Publishes first poems—dedicated to Theodore Roethke—in *Poetry*. Edits with James Harmon *Ark II/Moby I* in San Francisco, a revival of *Ark*, the anarchist review. Adding "Moby" to the title signaled the beginnings of the new environmental consciousness. First book *Passage* published by Jonathan Williams's Jargon Press. In the spring, drives to Mill Valley to visit Jack Kerouac, who was staying in a shack there. Daughter Jane is born on August 11. Stars in filmmaker Lawrence Jordan's *Visions of a City* which depicts McClure walking the streets of San Francisco. Works in the mail room of the San Francisco Museum of Art operating an addressograph machine. McClure plays the role of "A Boy" in Robert Duncan's "comic masque" *Faust Foutu*. Allen Ginsberg shows McClure stanzas from Kerouac's *Mexico City Blues* that Kerouac was sending to Ginsberg. McClure takes Robert Duncan to meet Kerouac at the Portero Hill housing project where Kerouac had been living with Allen Ginsberg and Duncan becomes appreciative of *Mexico City Blues* due to McClure's recommendation.

1957   McClure attends Charles Olson's—with whom McClure will carry on an extensive correspondence—talks given at Robert Duncan's house where Olson shares his recent fascination with Alfred North Whitehead's *Process and Reality* (1929). Whitehead—through Duncan's influence—will become a major text for McClure. McClure is published in *Evergreen Review* San Francisco Poetry issue. "Poem" and "Palisade" appear in the *Black Mountain Review* 7—the final, so-called "Beat issue"—edited by Robert Creeley and published by Jonathan Williams of Jargon Press. Writes children's story, *Boobus and the BunnyDuck* with crayon illustrations by Jess, not published until 2007. On September 1, Bruce Conner and his new wife Jean Sandstedt move to San Francisco and stay with the McClures at 2322 Fillmore Street. McClure tells Conner that the favorite phrase of his boss at the Vic Tanny gym in San Francisco was "Rat Bastard," and Conner takes the phrase for the name of his Rat Bastard Protective Association, intended "to prevent cruelty to artists in a society indifferent to their work." Members included McClure as well as Wallace Berman, Joan Brown, Jay De Feo, David Haselwood, Wally Hedirck, George Herms, Jess, among others. Takes five peyote buttons given to him by Wallace Berman, and McClure then informs his friend Bruce Conner about the entheogen. Meets naturalist Sterling Bunnell who teaches him "to watch coyotes and foxes and weasels and deer, and walk through savannah country. Hike through the foothills, go over mountains, and to the seashore and look into tide pools."

1958   Filmmaker Lawrence Jordan features McClure in his film *Triptych*, chronicling a trip to Mexico. The third issue of *Semina*—edited by

Wallace Berman—is devoted in its entirety to McClure's "Peyote Poem." Francis Crick purchases a copy of the broadside poem at City Lights. Organizes with Bruce Conner, Dave Haselwood, and others a "Rat Bastard Parade" which includes about two hundred people who proceed through North Beach to arrive at the Spatsa Gallery: here in June and July, there is an exhibition of Rat Bastard Protective Associate art.

1959 Composes his first play, *The Raptors*, and *The Blossom, or Billy the Kid*. "Rant Block" appears in *Yugen 5*. Publishes "Lines from a Peyote Depression" in June issue of *Beatitude*. On August 29, participates with David Meltzer, Lawrence Ferlinghetti, and John Wieners in "Auerhahn Mad Mammoth Monster Poetry Reading and Parade" held in Garibaldi Hall benefit organized by Philip Lamantia and painter Robert LaVigne to raise money for publication of *Hymns to St. Geryon and Other Poems*. Embarks with Philip Whalen on November 6 on a reading tour, appearing at City College, Muhlenberg College, Princeton and Wesleyan. McClure visits Charles Olson in Gloucester and goes to Dogtown for an afternoon. Writes "Foreword" to Charles Olson's *Maximus, From Dogtown I*, published in 1961 by Dave Haselwood's Auerhahn Press. Sends to Charles Olson manuscript of poem beginning "COURAGE COURAGE" containing the verse "I am a Beast a Bulk in the Black Lilly of space. Oh courage," and Olson responds in a letter of January 25, 1960.

1960 Stays with Diane di Prima on the Lower East Side in New York City. His artwork—influenced by experiments with entheogens—is exhibited in San Francisco at SPAATSA Gallery's "Visionary Portraits and Banners." Publishes "Two Poems from a Small Secret Book" in the spring issue of *Big Table*. Contributes "Lines from a Peyote Depression" to *Beatitude Anthology*, edited by John Kelly. Nine of McClure's poems are included in Don Allen's *The New American Poetry*. In August, travels with Lawrence Ferlinghetti and Lew Welch to Big Sur to meet Jack Kerouac, who reads his poem "Sea" aloud next to the ocean. Writes press release for November 3 opening of Bruce Conner's gallery debut *!The Feast!*, dedicated to Ornette Coleman and performed on December 22 at Billy Jahrmarkt's Batman Gallery. The dialogue is partially in "Beast Language" and among the actors are Kirby Doyle, Robert LaVigne, Morton Subotnick, Ron Loewinsohn, David Meltzer, Joanna McClure, and Philip Whalen.

CHRONOLOGY xxiii

1961 From January 8–February 4, McClure has one-man gallery show at Spatsa Gallery in SF: "Meat Science show of Visionary Portraits and Banners." Lives at 264 Downey Street, three blocks from Haight-Ashbury, near the Grateful Dead and Country Joe and the Fish. City Lights publishes *The Journal for the Protection of All Beings: A Visionary and Revolutionary Review*, edited by McClure, Lawrence Ferlinghetti, and David Meltzer, where McClure's essay "Revolt" appears along with Antonin Artaud's "To Have Done with the Judgement of God." In August, Diane di Prima stays with the McClures during her trip to California. *The New Book/A Book of Torture* chronicles McClure's drug experiments/experiences. Sells books in hopes of taking his family to London. They go first to New York to find funds for the remainder of the trip but stay in New York until they are forced to return to San Francisco. *Pillow* is performed on October 29 along with plays by di Prima and LeRoi Jones at the New York Poets Theatre. Studies during this period Sir John Woodroffe's *The Serpent Power* and publishes "Spontaneous Hymn to Kundalini" in Jon and Gypsy Lou Webb's *The Outsider* 1, no. 1 (Fall).

1962 Robert Duncan creates a "Moon Society." Meetings were held on Tuesdays following the new and full moon: McClure and Joanna along with others including Robin Blaser, David and Tina Mletzer and Richard Baker attend. During the early sixties, becomes friends with Richard Brautigan. Begins writing a novel—*The Mad Cub*—which is published three years later in 1965. Jack Kerouac portrays McClure as "Pat McLear" in his novel *Big Sur*. With psychologist Frank Barron at UC Berkeley's Institute of Personality Assessment and Research, McClure and biologist Sterling Bunnell study the effects of entheogens on creativity. McClure works as cameraman, taking films of people who have ingested psilocybin. In June, travels with Bunnell to Oaxaca, Mexico, returning with five species of psychedelic mushrooms. The report of their findings is presented at 1962 American Psychological Association Conference. Works as manager of a Vic Tanny gym. Is appointed associate professor of English and humanities at California College of Arts and Crafts in Oakland. In July issue of *Origin*, publishes "The Held Back Pain: a statement of doubt made in precedent to freedom."

1963 Contributes to *City Lights Journal* no. 1.

1964   In June and July, Diane di Prima produces McClure's *The Blossom, or Billy the Kid* at her New York Poets Theatre: George Herms creates the set. A recording of Antonin Artaud's "Let Us be Done with the Judgement of God," is played during the performance. Publishes "Defense of Jayne Mansfield," in *Film Culture* no. 2, Spring issue. The broadside, "Poetry Is a Muscular Principle" is privately printed in Los Angeles, featuring a photograph by Wallace Berman of a nude McClure with "beast" make-up created by Robert LaVigne. The photograph appears on the cover of *Ghost Tantras* published by City Lights. The final, ninth issue of *Semina* features just one work—McClure's poem "Dallas"—concerning the Kennedy assassination. The cover image is a television screen shot depicting the killing of Lee Harvey Oswald by Jack Ruby. McClure reads Herbert Marcuse's *One-Dimensional Man* and corresponds with Marcuse.

1965   Stan Brakhage creates a 16mm, color, silent film, *Two: Creeley/McClure*, featuring the two poets. According to Brakhage, during the mid-sixties, Sterling Bunnell offered McClure several "exotic creatures, including a boa constrictor." On December 5, Larry Keenan takes famous photograph of McClure, Bob Dylan, and Allen Ginsberg in the alley behind City Lights Bookstore. That evening, Dylan performs at the Masonic Memorial Auditorium in San Francisco and McClure is invited by Allen Ginsberg to see the concert where he meets Hells Angel Freewheelin Frank. After his concerts in the Bay Area, Dylan invites McClure and Ginsberg to go with him to Southern California, which they do—in Ginsberg's VW van. Publishes "Poisoned Wheat," a polemical poem against America's defoliation campaign in Vietnam and Bob Dylan reads the poem. *The Beard* is performed at Encore Theatre San Francisco Actor's Workshop on December 18. The performance—and another which took place on July 24, 1966, at the Fillmore Auditorium—is secretly tape recorded by the San Francisco Police Department and is prosecuted for obscenity.

1966   Dylan gives McClure an autoharp which "sat on the mantelpiece for six weeks before I picked it up and strummed it." McClure spends a year-and-a-half learning the instrument and composes several songs including "The Blue Lyon Laughs," "The Allen Ginsberg for President Waltz," and "Come on God, and Buy Me a Mercedes Benz." In 1970, Janis Joplin recorded "Mercedes Benz," inspired by McClure's lyrics. Meets George Montana, and with Freewheelin Frank, McClure plays music featuring two autoharps, a harmonica and tambourine. Reads to the lions at San Francisco Zoo for the public television film *USA: Poetry Michael McClure and Brother Antoninus*. On May 19, reads at the Straight Theatre with the Grateful Dead and the Wildflower at the Avalon Ballroom. Codiscoverer of DNA with James Watson Francis Crick includes lines from McClure's "Peyote Poem" in his book *Of Molecules and Men*. *The Beard* is staged on July 24 at Phil Graham's Fillmore Auditorium. On August 8, following three performances at the Committee in North Beach, the police arrest actors Billie Dixon and Richard Bright. The charges are ultimately dropped, but *The Beard* is prohibited from being performed in San Francisco. Creates "Mandala Deck" with Bruce Conner. McClure learns that Andy Warhol had made a film of *The Beard* and writes to filmmaker Stan Brakhage on June 6 concerning his displeasure concerning its quality and that Warhol had not asked his permission. Participates in a "Teach-On LSD," a benefit for the Timothy Leary Defense Fund. Participants include Big Brother and the Holding Company, Allen Ginsberg, David Meltzer, Timothy Leary, and Richard Alpert. Wildflower releases song "Baby Dear" with lyrics by McClure. On July 29, sends Dylan telegram inquiring if he would like to stay with the McClures while recuperating from his motorcycle accident. Contributes to *City Lights Journal* no. 3.

1967   *The Blossom, or Billy the Kid*—"for James Douglas Morrison"—is performed on January 10 at the University of Wisconsin, Milwaukee, directed by Robert Cordier. The Regents of the University close it after one performance. Receives National Endowment for the Arts grant. The ACLU wins a decision from the San Francisco Superior Court preventing criminal proceedings against *The Beard*. On January 14, sings his poem "The God I Worship is a Lion" with the autoharp Bob Dylan gave him, at the Human Be-In—the event is planned at McClure's apartment—at Golden Gate Park. The poem was published in the *San Francisco Oracle #5 Human Be-In Issue*, "Gathering of the Tribes." Gary Snyder, Allen Ginsberg, Lawrence Ferlinghetti, Lenore Kandel, Timothy Leary, Richard Alpert, and Shunryū Suzuki of the San Francisco Zen Center are present. On April 19, *The Beard* is performed at

Stanford University and at University of California at Davis on May 4. In October, *The Beard* opens at the Evergreen Theatre on Off Broadway in New York, directed by Rip Torn. Publishes *Freewheelin Frank, Secretary of the Angels*. KPIX channel 5 in San Francisco airs *The Maze*, a film in which McClure leads a tour of the Haight-Ashbury. McClure visits the Psychedelic Bookshop, and The Straight Theatre and the film also features views of the Grateful Dead and McClure with Richard Brautigan. On November 15, *The Beard* is performed at California State University at Fullerton. McClure takes Robert Lowell to hear rock 'n' roll which was not to Lowell's liking. "Poisoned Wheat" published as centerspread in August issue of the *San Francisco Oracle*.

1968   In January, McClure and Dennis Hopper discuss with director Bob Rafelson the possibility of making a brief film based on McClure's short story "The Queen." McClure visits Hopper in the fall during as well as after the filming of *Easy Rider*. The literary agent Michael Hamilburg arranges a meeting between McClure and Jim Morrison in New York while *The Beard* was playing. They explore the idea of Morrison starring in a film version of *The Beard*. In February, *The Beard* opens at the Warner Theatre in Los Angeles, where it is closed fourteen times. On June 8, reads with Ferlinghetti, John Wieners, David Meltzer, Philip Whalen, Lew Welch, and Allen Ginsberg at Nourse Auditorium in San Francisco. Appears in Norman Mailer's *Beyond the Law* as an outlaw motorcyclist. In mid-October, spends time with Jim Morrison in London. Poet Christopher Logue takes them to visit the place where William Blake's house existed, to the Tate and to the Lake Country. McClure and Jim Morrison meet with film producer Elliot Kastner to discuss the possibility of Morrison starring as Billy the Kid in a film version of *The Beard*; however, it was agreed that the play was considered too controversial to film without extensive censorship. Instead, they offer to make a film version of McClure's not-yet-published novel *The Adept*, but Kastner passes on the offer. In November, Rip Torn brings *The Beard* to London. McClure goes to Paris where he discusses environmental issues with students. On November 4, *The Beard* opens in London. Beatle George Harrison sees one of the performances and quotes lines from it to Paul McCartney. McClure has his attorney Melvin Belli confiscate Andy Warhol's 1966 filmed version of *The*

Beard. Contributes "For Anger" and "Poisoned Wheat" to *War Poems*, edited by Diane di Prima. Reads *The Anatomy of the Cell* by Björn Afzelius, a Swedish electromicroscopist, which makes him aware that "the inside of the cell is as complex a structure as we can conceive of." He also reads Samuel Butler's *The Way of All Flesh* (1903) and believes that "to see into Victorian society and to see into the interior of the cell are two really great sights." Jerome Rothenberg includes poems 1, 49, and 51 from Ghost *Tantras* in *Technicians of the Sacred*.

1969   Brings Jim Morrison to performances by the Living Theater in San Francisco. Publishes *Fleas 1–9*—the first of two hundred and fifty—in *Caterpillar 8/9*, which McClure explained "are childhood memories. They are an obsession, like Billy the Kid and Jean Harlow are obsessions." In February, attends the Living Theater's production of *Paradise Lost* at San Francisco's Civic Auditorium. Creates "Lion Fight" poetry deck. On May 1, gives poetry reading with Jim Morrison and D. R. Wagner at the Sacramento State College Gallery. The poster for the event announces: "Concrete poetry by Michael McClure, author of *The Beard*, and D. R. Wagner will go on display Thursday in the gallery of Sacramento State College. McClure will read from his poetry at a reception at 8:30 p.m. Thursday. The show will continue through May 9." In May, McClure's play *The Cherub* opens in John Lion's Magic Theatre. On May 15, during the People's Park protests in Berkeley, James B. Rector is killed and McClure dedicates a poem to him. In June, McClure moves into the Alta Cienega motel in West Hollywood and spends several weeks working with Jim Morrison on a film script based on his not-yet-published novel *The Adept* to be called *Saint Nicholas*. Begins writing *Gargoyle Cartoons* which he will continue until 1971. McClure's essay "Tear Gas" is published in Diane di Prima's *The Floating Bear*, issue 37: "It's time that the political platitudes of Left, Right, and Middle were dissolved and people found a new Biological basis for living together and with other living creatures .... Man's environment is other men—and their structures, media, and transport. A man's ideals are prefabricated and preconstructed by the Society." McClure was ahead of his time in his "Tear Gas" commentary on Thomas Jefferson: "One can imagine Thomas Jefferson walking in the halls and walls of his own creation and design. He can be imagined, perhaps as he saw himself, as a free spirit, as a healthy animal, perhaps even like a Greek or Roman as he deliberately opts for sophistication, for the choice of the virtues of Society. But free, and yes, a slave owner at the same time.... WHAT IS HE DOING THERE? What is Jefferson doing there?" Contributes to *Green Flag* [*Journal for the Protection of All Beings* no. 3].

1970 Begins intense reading of books on ecology, biophysics, and biology, including H. T. Odum, Harold Morowitz, and Ramon Margalef. McClure is introduced by Gary Snyder to Hua Yen Buddhism and Garma C. C. Chang's *The Buddhist Teaching of Totality*. Novel *The Mad Cub* published.

1971 In June, McClure participates in Robert Duncan's residency at the University of California at San Diego where Duncan held discussions on the topic of "Sight, Vision and Imagination." For release on July 14, "Bastille Day," signs "Declaration of Independence for Dr. Timothy Leary" proposed by the San Francisco Bay Area Prose Poets' Phalanx. Other signatories included Allen Ginsberg, Ken Kesey, Lawrence Ferlinghetti, Robert Creeley, Lenore Kandel, Anaïs Nin, Diane di Prima, Ted Berrigan, Paull Krassner, and Laura Huxley. Acts in Peter Fonda's film *The Hired Hand*. In October, returns to Kansas where he feels the same sense of exaltation he experienced as a child. Earns Guggenheim Fellowship. Contributes essay on the death of Jim Morrison to the August 5 edition of *Rolling Stone*. On August 19, reads with Diane di Prima, Allen Ginsberg, and Lawrence Ferlinghetti at benefit reading at UC Berkeley for defense fund in support of Judith Malina and Julian Beck's Living Theater.

1972 Attends United Nations Environmental Conference in Stockholm with Gary Snyder, Sterling Bunnell and Stewart Brand. Hopi Navaho and Mohawk Indigenous leaders attend. McClure writes about the event for *Rolling Stone* magazine. Returning to San Francisco, he participates in a pro-whale demonstration. John Coney at KQED makes television production of *September Blackberries*.

1973 "Phi Upsilon Kappa" and "Revolt" are published in Donald Allen's *The Poetics of the New American Poetry*. On April 16, gives poetry reading at Kent State University in Ohio. At the University Bookstore, McClure purchases a copy of Alfred North Whitehead's *The Function of Reason* which he declares "was the most difficult thing I've ever read in my life.... and through that book I found out that any point in the universe is the center of the universe, and is the point that the universe is experiencing itself at, prehending itself at, at that moment. And I said, 'Oh, I get it.'" Travels to Asia, East Africa, and Peru. Receives Guggenheim Fellowship.

1974 Receives National Endowment for the Arts grant. *Gorf* is produced successfully by the Magic Theatre. Publishes "Wolf Net," a long essay in *Io 20*. Publishes essay on Bob Dylan, "The Poet's Poet," in the March 14 issue of *Rolling Stone*.

1975 Rockefeller Fellowship for Drama. Begins working with Bruce Conner on a deck of cards for creating poetry from random strings of words. *Margins* "Symposium on McClure" published with appreciation by Francis Crick. Contributes a brief introduction to the Spanish biologist Ramon Margalef to *CoEvolution Quarterly* 6 (Summer). On April 19, McClure reads at Graham Pond at the University of Florida along with Allen Ginsberg and Gary Snyder to honor ecologist H. T. Odum.

1976 Forms "The Elegant Buffoons," a musical group in the tradition of Taiwanese bands which includes participants Philip Whalen, Robert Duncan, Michael Palmer, and Chris Gaynor. They meet at Kathie Bunnell's place in Mill Valley or at McClure's in the Haight Ashbury in the evenings and play instruments such as bronze bells, violin, brass cups, tin pans, koto, erhu, and saranghi. On July 17, delivers lecture "Cinnamon Turquoise Leather: (A Personal Universe Deck)" at Naropa University in Boulder, Colorado. Participates in Proposition 15 rally in Union Square Park regarding safeguards for nuclear energy plants in California. On November 25, Thanksgiving Day, at Bill Graham's Winterland Auditorium. Recites from Chaucer's "Prologue" to *The Canterbury Tales*, appearing with Duncan, Ferlinghetti, and di Prima at the final concert of The Band, memorialized by Martin Scorsese's *The Last Waltz*, Play *General Gorgeous* performed in spring repertory at the Yale Repertory Theater.

1977 Becomes full professor at California College of Arts and Crafts in Oakland. Writes *Josephine, The Mouse Singer*.

1978 Edits with Lawrence Ferlinghetti, David Melrzer and Gary Snyder, *Journal for the Protection of All Beings* no. 4. On May 9, appears with Robert Duncan and Diane di Prima at a symposium in the East Bay commemorating the 1965 Berkeley Poetry Conference. On October 1, reads at the Tribal Stomp at the Greek Theatre in

Berkeley with Diane di Prima, Allen Ginsberg, Lenore Kandel, and Wavy Gravy. *Josephine the Mouse Singer* produced at the WPA Theatre in New York. On November 4, participates with—among others—Ishmael Reed, Thom Gunn, Lawrence Ferlinghetti, William S. Burroughs, Gregory Corso, and Audre Lorde in the Third San Francisco International Poetry Festival. The Magic Theatre stages *The Red Snake*, McClure's version of a James Shirley revenge tragedy.

1979   Wins the Obie Award for *Josephine, The Mouse Singer*, Best New American Play of the Year. The presentation took place at the Bottom Line and was televised on Channel 13's "Skyline." Lecturer at State University of New York. In August, composes "Afterword" for a biography of Jim Morrison, *No One Here Gets Out Alive* by Jerry Hopkins and Daniel Sugerman.

1980   Wins the California Arts Council Berkeley Stage Company Ward. Gives lectures on Charles Olson at the State University of New York at Buffalo.

1982   Four poems are included in Donald Allen's *The Postmoderns: The New American Poetry Revised*. On February 10, participates with Robert Duncan, Michael Davidson, and David Meltzer in a panel at the University of California, "The Various Arts of the San Francisco Renaissance." Associate Fellow of Pierson College, Yale University. Reads poem "Listen Lawrence"—addressed to Lawrence Ferlinghetti—at the University of California at Berkeley with Denise Levertov for the nuclear freeze movement. The following week McClure gives reading to raise money to assist the Salvadoran guerillas with medical supplies. Publishes *The Book of Benjamin* about his pet rabbit of eight years, Benjamin. McClure is featured in Robert Frank's documentary *This Song for Jack*, filmed in Boulder, Colorado, during "On the Road: The Jack Kerouac Conference," held to commemorate the twenty-fifth anniversary of the publication of Kerouac's 1957 novel.

1983   Contributes "Action Philosophy" to *Peace or Perish: A Crisis Anthology*—"The poets' mobilization against nuclear holocaust."

1984   On September 16, attends wake for the death of his friend Richard Brautigan at Enrico's in San Francisco.

1985   McClure's interview with Robert Duncan is published in *Conjunctions* 7 and he contributes to the fall issue of *Sagetrieb* 4, nos. 2–3, a special issue devoted to Robert Duncan.

1986 Meets Amy Evans, sculptor and artist. Contributes to *Practising Angels: A Contemporary Anthology of San Francisco Bay Area Poetry* and an essay to Dennis Hopper's book of photographs *Out of the Sixties*. Hears Ray Manzarek, keyboardist for the Doors, performing with Michael C. Ford at McCabe's Guitar Shop & Music Club in Santa Monica and discusses with Manzarek the possibility of performing his poetry with him. McClure had met Manzarek previously at the third recording session of the Doors.

1987 At the State University of New York at Brockport, McClure and Mazarek play together and decide to continue doing so. From September 7–13, takes part in "River City Reunion Week" in Lawrence, Kansas, with Burroughs, Ed Sanders, Anne Waldman, Robert Creeley, and Allen Ginsberg. Receives Lifetime Achievement Award from the National Poetry Association.

1988 On June 24, performs with Ray Manzarek at the Smith Center in Lowell, Massachusetts, with Lawrence Ferlinghetti and Allen Ginsberg. In December, in New York, Judith Malina directs Theatre for the New City in McClure's *VKTMS: Orestes in Scenes*.

1989 Performs prose poem "Sixty-Six Things about the California Assemblage Movement" at the Wight Gallery at UCLA. On March 13, introduces Diane di Prima reading at California College of Arts and Crafts.

1991 Publishes his interview with Italian artist Francesco Clemente in *Francesco Clemente: Testa Coda*. Performs "For Monk" on *JazzSpeak: A Word Collection*, a CD released by New Alliance in Los Angeles.

1993 Wins award for Lifetime Achievement in Poetry from the National Poetry Association. On August 29, performs with Ray Manzarek, Robert Hunter and di Prima at the Great American Music Hall in San Francisco. Releases *Love Lion* album with Manzarek. Contributes a preface to Jack Kerouac's *Old Angel Midnight*.

1996 Publishes essay "Poetry of the 6" in *The Beat Generation: Galleries and Beyond*.

1997 Marries sculptor Amy Evans. Becomes increasingly immersed in Zen Buddhist studies. Contributes to *Hey Lew: Homage to Lew Welch*.

1998 On February 9, delivers lecture "Thoughts on *Rivers and Mountains Without End*" at Stanford Humanities Center, a research workshop convened to explore Gary Snyder's eponymous poem. Is involved in near-fatal airplane crash.

1999 *Rain Mirror: New Poems* is published, which contains "Crisis Blossom," recounting his airline accident as well as McClure's time in Bali with his wife Amy during which he experienced "a series of unexpected, intense, and vividly real childhood memories." Following this trip, he experienced a "psychophysical breakdown" and spent time hospitalized. With Amy, he studies the works of Aitken Roshi and Suzuki Roshi, and "was receiving advice from Phil Whalen and Gary Snyder." He also begins a serious reading of Dōgen—Amy reads to him from *Moon in the Dewdrop*, translated by Kazuaki Tanahashi—the "thirteenth-century mystical, visionary Japanese founder of Soto Zen," and McClure declares: "When I was fifteen or so, I discovered William Blake, and at sixty-five I discovered Dōgen—or, more accurately, Dōgen discovered me." Contributes to *Ragged Lion: A Tribute to Jack Micheline* and *The Outlaw Bible of American Poetry*.

2000 On April 27, is at Washington State, Pullman, with Ray Manzarek.

2001 *The Trees of Sonora* by Richard Felger is published, and McClure is thanked in the acknowledgments for his botanical "fieldwork in Sonora, Mexico." Reads "The Sea," the concluding section of Kerouac's *Big Sur*, at marathon reading of the novel. McClure recalls that he heard Kerouac read the poem.

2002 On September 1, speaks at the funeral of his close friend Philip Whalen. Contributes to *An Eye for an Eye Makes the Whole World Blind: Poets on 9/11*. On October 11–13, participates in the First Annual Beat Generation and Beyond Conference at the John Natsoulas Gallery in Davis.

2003 Gives reading with Diane di Prima at City Lights Bookstore in San Francisco.

2004 *I Like Your Eyes Liberty*, collaboration with Terry Riley, recorded at Sri Moonshine Ranch (2003–4). Kurt Hemmer and Tom Knoff produce McClure documentary *Rebel Roar: The Sound of Michael McClure*.

2005 Contributes to *The Wisdom Anthology of North American Buddhist Poetry*. Verse Theater Manhattan presents *VKTMS* at the Medicine Show Theatre on 52nd Street.

2008 On October 22, gives reading at Holloway Series in Poetry. UC Berkeley. Participates in Beat Generation Symposium at Columbia College, Chicago.

2009 Composes poems in a collaboration—*Deer Boy*—with artist Hung Liu, who painted images of dead deer she encountered during her walks in the Oakland Hills.
2010 "Double Moire for Francis Crick" is published. On July 8, gives reading introduced by Iain Sinclair at the London Review Bookshop.
2011 On March 8, reads at the Sherwood Auditorium in La Jolla, California. On August 7, reads with Diane di Prima at Mythos Fine Art in Berkeley. On October 20, reads with Michael C. Ford at Beyond Baroque, Venice, California.
2012 *Piano Poems: Live in San Francisco* CD with Ray Manzarek, is released by Oglio.
2013 On October 25, *Abstract Alchemist of Flesh*, a documentary about McClure by Colin Still and Optic Nerve of Great Britain is shown at the 22nd Berkeley Video and Film Festival.
2015 On October 3, gives the Sixth Annual Charles Olson Lecture at the Cape Ann Museum, Gloucester. Reads on November 7 in Palo Alto, California, reciting poetry in conjunction with an exhibition of his wife Amy Evans McClure's art works.
2016 On April 30, McClure reads at the Winchester Cultural Center in Las Vegas and on May 1, conducts a writer's workshop at the Flamingo branch of the Las Vegas-Clark County Library District. On November 17, McClure reads from his book *Mephistos and Other Poems*.
2020 Michael McClure dies on May 4. His "Life's Triumph: A Lecture on Shelley"—originally delivered at the New College of California—is published in *Roots and Routes: Poetics at New College of California*.

Conversations with
Michael McClure

Michael McClure

David Kherdian / 1969

From *Six San Francisco Poets: Snyder, Whalen, McClure, Meltzer, Ferlinghetti, Antoninus* (Fresno: The Giligia Press, 1969), 37–40. Reprinted by permission.

Michael McClure is that rarity, a writer who invites the reader to seek *pleasure* as the antidote to depression and ennui. He believes we are warm-blooded sensory creatures whose personal revelations lie in understanding and gratifying this "spiritmeat" or body-and-mind. This new concept of self-involvement has begun with the *Ghost Tantras*, which are exercises in learning, in becoming the man unafraid of the personal totalities of his spiritmeat. His enemy here is repression and the unconscious; and his intention is for the making of a new romantic: *mammal*. For McClure the old notion of *man* is no longer pleasing. The sensory images of his poetry concern the creatures with which he aligns himself because of their "warm-bloodedness": the falcon, eagle, and gyrfalcon; and the warm-tempered salmon and kraken. To become, he feels, we must dare to become: man is not a cool cat, he is a warm-blooded-loving-balling-ape-mammal-bird-beast-fish. He must push out to the extreme limits of his being if he is to be free, unconquered, and capable of his own conquest and release. For McClure there can be no distinction between the man and the writer—one being condemned to serve the other—nor can there be a differentiation between the mind and the body; for if the mind is in error it will be reflected by a gesture of the body. The poise he is concerned with in the stance he strikes is determined by the position and balance of the mind: a man's walk being determined by the movement of his thought.

It is this fusion of mind and body as a single principle that is the particular stamp of the man, and it is this concept that has determined the flow of his work, which is of constant change, growth, and expansion. Unfortunately, the growing social concern of his poetry has entailed work in areas that no longer require a lyric quality, which is his finest poetic gift.

The concept that determined *Ghost Tantras*, for example, he could have been compressed into one poem, but to convey the idea with the force it required—if it were to have the impact on the public he intended—an entire book of poems had to be published.

McClure's best performances are often those in which he yields to a creative urge, and in the mysterious process of creation produces a work of which the eventual meanings can only be half-known to the artist. Outwardly, his Billy the Kid, Jean Harlow plays appear as casual Pop Art performances in which the hero and heroine are displayed and allowed to prance and strike familiar poses. There is an objectivity here, however, that saves McClure, for while these two are truly folk-heroes he is never unaware of their psychic disorders—which are the disorders of an entire civilization that lives in sexual catatonia—who, unable to live joyously and sensually with their bodies, erect heroes who are so psychically corrupted they are actually able to caricaturize what they cannot do. McClure has the courage to write of the disease with the personality of one who is infected, but who wishes to cure and be cured. The aim of McClure is to undo and destroy, to kill the childhood daemons that haunt his adult life; even though in so doing the art he creates can only be transitory: even though he must kill his own heroes. To achieve an understanding and with this knowledge to transform thinking is what is needed—for it is only by being free of the myth of America that one can begin to understand the truth of this country. It is this awareness, this growing concern of contemporary values and concerns, that has broadened McClure's art and sharpened his ability to communicate— often in new forms—for the danger, as he well knows, is that we are losing one another and that only by direct and personal communication—even if only one hand reaching out to touch another—can art arrest and heal. There is no longer time for gentility and tradition in literature. The poet cannot afford to talk from inside closed walls, either of the work room or the flesh; he must be willing to expose and dare all. This new awareness and responsibility has demanded new forms. For Bill Wilson, who is reluctant to publish, a new form of letter writing to friends; for the artist, Ray Johnson, who rarely exhibits, envelope-sized collages mailed to a circulating library of correspondents, and for Michael McClure, anonymous greeting cards with personal inscriptions, such as his exquisite and strikingly beautiful *Fuck Death* card.

Michael McClure is young and handsome, with brown wavy hair that runs down his neck and stops just teasingly short of his shoulders. His face tapers gently from a broad handsome forehead to a delicate chin. His eyes seem to carry one expression, which is a cross between glint and gleam, and together with his hands and feet are continuously busy: his feet, always within plain black Spanish boots; his hands never still, never exactly in gesture, are almost never without a cigarette, almost a sixth finger—straight and lean—that counterbalance thick, fleshy hands. His dress is stylized: either a mustard-yellow cardigan sweater buttoned from top to bottom, or a suit coat and tie with the collar turned up. His pants: black denim; his boots: black high tops. His work is individual and changing, his dress individual and rigid: the purposeful design of a man obsessed with his image and role. For McClure it is this dividing of the juices between creativity and performance that have so often given his work the facility that is easy to respond to but also easy to forget. The indispensable legerdemain in performing for a fickle public is constant production, constant change—to anticipate and guide, to control and lead. This passion for swift and easy production occasionally finds McClure walking so furiously within the circle of his own talent he sometimes seems in danger of colliding with himself.

Our first meeting took place in Berkeley at the Oyez publishing offices where I tuned in the manuscript of my monograph on David Meltzer, and McClure had stopped by to see the advance sheets of his play, *The Beard*. He knew of my intention to do a prose sketch and checklist on him and he was eager to talk and learn of my intentions and the point of view I was establishing for the series. We chatted about the Midwest, where we were both born and raised—about the rain and snow, the smells and sounds, and how they differed from California. More than anything he seemed to remember and miss the icy chill of winter that remained in the shoulders on into spring, and he came to understand that this became the symbol of remembrance and longing for him. The conversation moved on to new forms in painting, the pleasure of living in San Francisco (and that, as he said, the so-called *San Francisco Poets* were only those individuals who wanted to write poetry and to do so in the best city in America—San Francisco; and he couldn't understand why this was given a group-movement label). Before going to lunch we went out to put money in our parking meters, my car a Volkswagen, Mike's a red Triumph. Walking back upstairs I remarked that no matter how long one owns a Volkswagen it remains totally and miserably unchanged, at no moment taking on the properties of the owner. He agreed excitedly and told me of the Volkswagen he had owned before his present car and how, after two years, he had given it up as hopeless. Later, the four of us—Robert Hawley, Oyez publisher; Graham Mackintosh, freelance printer; McClure and I—went to lunch. Earlier Mike and I had discussed the school where he teaches English and Drama. He had begun what he termed Chance Drama in which the dialogue for the play, in the present case, *The Last Christian*, was written on individual cards as poems by the members of the class. The students would take roles and perform the parts with their own decks or exchanging decks. The movement and meaning in the play would be determined by the ability of the students to make their lines enter into the plot and design of the drama. McClure felt that such improvisatory exercises would be liberating for his students and would allow a further range of expression than in normal drama. After lunch, walking back four abreast, McClure, rather than return upstairs with the rest of us as I had expected, suddenly flanked-off and was, when I looked up, halfway across the street turning three-quarters with a wave of farewell with one hand, the other in the front pocket of his black denims. By the time we reached the office door he was already part way down the street in his ground-hugging red sportscar—and with his collar upturned and his hair brushing his shoulders, it didn't seem impossible that he *would* change reality (for himself)—and possibly for others.

Gahr, Groooor, Grayohh: For a Meat Poetry—An Interview with Michael McClure

Roland Husson / 1973

From *Entretions 34: Beat Generation*, edited by Yves Pellec (Rodez: Editions Subervie, 1975), 207–20. Translated by David Stephen Calonne.

Roland Husson: What experience of your childhood had lasting consequences for the poet that you have become?
Michael McClure: The sense of space. I was born in Kansas—in the heart of the great plains swept by the wind. Kansas is also known for its oil, for its wheat and for its corn, and during the second World War for its airplane factories. At six years of age, I was sent to my grandparents in Seattle. At this time, the city was still surrounded by thick forests. The ocean was very near and I often went to watch the ocean crashing on the black rocks, to contemplate the mysterious islands scattered in the bay. Later, I returned to Kansas. I was taken back to the sense of immensity, this region of tornadoes whose damage we used to measure during weekend walks. The wind blew constantly and the particles of organic material—perpetually agitated—gave the sun a high degree of static electricity. I was very early curious about nature, in the sense of natural history as one called it in the nineteenth century, and an exaltation before the immensity of American space.
RH: What was your relationship like with your parents?
MM: My father was an automobile salesman. He had to sell his garage during the Depression. His relations with my mother had deteriorated. They divorced in 1938 and I went to live with my grandfather who was a doctor in Seattle. After the remarriage of my mother, I returned to Kansas and I stayed there until the age of seventeen.

I only returned once, in October 1971. In spite of all the fences which enclose other fences which enclose the fields, in spite of all the damned owners who seek to cage this living being—the Great Plains—I felt the same exaltation—the same vital presence of the earth—a little like this summer in Iceland. When I saw *The Last Movie* by Dennis Hopper, who like me is from Kansas, I asked myself for a long time why the critics demolished this film. They did not note that the principal hero was called Kansas and that Dennis sought to express the caging of an innocent energy. I would like very much to see this film again and to write an article to show what its true meaning is

RH: When did you start writing?

MM: At the beginning of adolescence, I took pleasure in playing with words. I constantly created "word games," free compositions which I did not perceive as poems but which I recited to myself. At the same time, I was interested in surrealism and anthropology. And then, thanks to Bruce Connor who was a painter before becoming a filmmaker, I discovered Motherwell, de Kooning, Pollock, and the abstract expressionists. I felt a close affinity between what they were painting and what I was writing. Their paintings were a spiritual autobiography, an extension of their being on the canvas—and my poetry represents an increasing of my capacity to experience the world and to share with others. This is also what I love so much in Kerouac. I am at the opposite of most of his ideas, but when I read one of his novels, I saw with his eyes, I tasted with his mouth, I perceive the world through his sensorial apparatus. For me, this is the essential, this is what I try to do.

RH: In separating the opinions of a writer and the way he makes us feel the world, this doesn't bother you?

MM: No, the opinions are without importance.

RH: It is an attitude which places you at the opposite of Sartre.

MM: Yes, but Sartre is limited by the little he knew about contemporary science. I have a great admiration for Sartre, but I believe that he has an intellectualist conception of science and that we have an organic one. Sartre did not fully take into account the consequences of the discovery of the genetic code and recent theories on the cell.

RH: What scientific background do you have?

MM: I studied natural history and biology in high school and a little at the university. I always had a great interest in the natural sciences. Currently I have established a five-year plan to deepen my knowledge of biology. I studied with a biologist friend who like me taught at the College of Arts and Crafts in Oakland. I read a very large number of works devoted to nature, from the way to organize a ranch to the extinction of the animals of the Pleistocene and the origin of nuclear cells. Finally, I spend a large part of my time walking in the countryside and observing the nature of California and of Scandinavia. Next year, I plan to take a course in biochemistry given by one of my friends.... In brief I keep myself informed.

RH: You don't have the feeling that there exist two separate cultures: one scientific and the other literary.

MM: There isn't the same impermeability as in Europe. Scientific discoveries influence my poetry or that of Gary Snyder. Conversely, Francis Crick has cited one of my poems in a recent work. I am amazed by biology, and I believe that it represents the alchemy we've been talking about for so long.

I don't believe in progress and especially not in technological progress. The alchemy I am talking about allows a better knowledge of living matter.

RH: Even if it is spreading to the United States, the refusal of progress is not a popular idea in the most primitive countries.

MM: I realized this at the conference at Stockholm on the environment. No one dared to warn the countries of the Third World against the dangers of our society because if that had been done, we could have become aware of what threatens us. But it is necessary above all to keep ourselves in ignorance, isn't it? A more serious thing, the so-called delegates of the Third World were most often members of the local castes, formed in the American universities, incapable and moreover not willing to react to the bullshit they were fed. In fact, there was no one to represent the Third World, the civilizations not supported by a galloping technology.

McCarthy, Screw You

RH: Shall we talk about your arrival in San Francisco? What does this city mean to you?

MM: Kenneth Rexroth has correctly said that San Francisco was like Barcelona in the thirties: a refuge for anarchists of the idea. I am thinking of Rexroth, of Kenneth Patchen, of Robert Duncan, of Philip Lamantia, and of William Everson. With Miller in Big Sur, they represented a nucleus of subversive thought. San Francisco also became a pole of attraction for conscientious objectors who—once out of the camps—regrouped in the Bay Area.

Another advantage of San Francisco is that is not a commercial city like New York or Los Angeles, nor a place where one is obsessed by political pettiness. It is a cosmopolitan and tolerant city like Hong Kong in the fifties.

Last but not least, it is a very beautiful city and close to a very diverse nature: near Big Sur, the Central Valley, Mount Tamalpais, and the Sierra Nevada.

RH: When did you take part in the literary life of San Francisco?

MM: I read my poems in public for the first time in 1955 at the Six Gallery—the same day when Ginsberg read "Howl." The other poets who read that night were: K. Rexroth, Ph. Lamantia, G. Snyder, Ph. Whalen. As for Kerouac, he was in the room, drinking and yelling. The audience was extraordinary, ripe to receive this new poetry.

RH: What audience frequented the Six Gallery?

MM: Men and women between twenty and forty years old: artists, students, carpenters, masons, housewives, etc. You have to realize that San Francisco is perhaps with Greenwich Village the only part of the USA where there is a tradition of the worker-bohemian who plies a manual trade to support himself and passes the rest of his time making love, enjoying life, and backpacking. It is very different than working conditions in Europe where a guy works six days a week without hope of escaping.

RH: Wasn't that the era of McCarthyism?

MM: Yes. But still, San Francisco—and in any case, North Beach—was one of the rare places where one could say in a quiet voice: "McCarthy, go screw yourself." Elsewhere, one felt a climate of agonizing political repression. People looked at each other suspiciously in the elevators and did not dare to say what they were thinking. At that time, I was so disgusted that I was not only apolitical, I was antipolitical.

RH: Why have you refused to be included in the Beat group?

MM: For many reasons. At first, the people who were called Beat were all older than I was and I felt like another generation. I was friends with Allen, with Gregory, with Gary, but I did not want to be labelled once and for all. It seemed important to preserve the creative originality of each poet. Next, the term Beat is ambiguous. It is a little like the word "surrealism." In France, it designates the poets grouped around Breton. Here, the word surrealism has a larger meaning: it signifies a new way of perceiving reality and we include in this movement many people, from Alfred Jarry to Jackson Pollock.

If one means by "the Beat movement" a new way to perceive the world, then I feel like a member of the Beat Generation. Besides, I have grown older and the age difference with separates me from the other poets has tended to diminish.

RH: What has the Beat movement brought that is new?

MM: A feeling of liberation and a very clear break with the poetry which preceded us. We changed our perception of sexuality, our idea of honesty, and the relations which exist between people. We accepted contradictions: for example, to feel part of the universe and to perceive it only in a fragmentary way. We have shown that the contradictions come from the artificial divisions of history and sociology. There are historians and sociologists who are bothered by these contradictions, not by our noses, our ears and our fingers.

RH: What role did drugs play at this time?

MM: I tried practically all the available drugs, and I traversed "the dark night of the soul"—a night which lasted for years. Drugs increased my possibilities of perception, and I would not be what I am without having taken them. But now I no longer use any drugs, not even alcohol or tobacco.

For a long time, San Francisco possessed a culture which included drugs, in particular peyote. Every year, people left for two or three days to Pyramid Lake and embarked for a "trip." It was very romantic and very mysterious.

RH: Did you renounce drugs because they were a dead end, a little like Michaux?

MM: I rejected neither mescaline nor peyote, but I do not feel the need to take them at this time. The reaction of Michaux in *Miserable Miracle* seems to me excessive and typically European. What Michaux finds as demoniac in the drug is more in his head than in the drug. I also don't believe that drugs only reveal what is already in us. When you take mescaline, the outlines that delineate objects disappear: it is like a flow of forms. Without the drug, this experience is unimaginable, because it is the rupture of a biological phenomenon in vision.

RH: Do you see a continuity between the Beat movement and the more directly politicized debates of today?

MM: Yes, thanks above all to Allen Ginsberg. Allen has been the common denominator and the saint of the movement. And the movement has been as noble as Allen himself. My own position is probiological rather than political, but under the influence of Ginsberg I have taken political positions more frequently. The trouble with politics is we don't care enough about humanity as a whole. There have been very important events like the trial of the Chicago Seven, but now the movement is politically dead. People have returned to their ivory tower. The great problem is to make the young aware of the degradation of our planet by pollution and by overpopulation. All the "isms" and all the parties are so off the mark that their supporters who congratulate each other for their "engagement" are profoundly ridiculous. Besides the political pseudosolutions are on the first page of newspapers and nobody pays attention to them.

RH: This is a difficult position to make Europeans accept.

MM: I know this very well. When I was in Paris in 1968, I spoke to students about the environment. Nobody cared, and academics accused me of being an "elitist." Elitist my ass! I found them unaware of clinging to inherited ideas from the nineteenth century. . . .

My only hope is that the young see with their own eyes what is happening. That said, it is still necessary even so to act politically but by getting rid of the good conscience. It is nevertheless curious to hear the working class claim to be on the left in Europe and to see that they continue to vote for conservative regimes.

Poetic Itinerary

RH: In a rather long literary career, do you perceive any changes?

MM: Yes, the big change is that I learned about the value of theater. The ego of the poet is valued and protected as the source of poetry. The dramatic author uses his ego as a test instrument and the theater permits him to extend considerably the possibilities of poetry. Besides, I have not renounced poetry and I probably write much more poetry than plays but I take a great joy in working on the scene.

RH: What relationship do you have with the directors?

MM: Excellent, particularly with John Lion.[1] I give him the text of my play and I do not attend the first rehearsals so as not to hinder the actors in their quest for meaning. As soon as the tone is found, I am very attentive to the work of the director. The work produced is the result of the combined efforts of the writer, the director, the actors and the technicians: it is the birth of a new organism.

I place complete confidence in the director, and it is to him alone that I address critiques and suggestions. I also agree to edit my text to give it greater dramatic effectiveness. On the advice of John, I lengthened the too abrupt denouement of *The Button*. In another play, I also incorporated an introductory dance which had been presented to me by the director. But overall, I am surprised that I edit my texts so little.

RH: After the scandal of *The Beard* in Los Angles, Antoine Bourseiller staged a French version of the play in Paris. What were your reactions?

MM: I found that his staging to be very spirited, full of athletic qualities. The difficulty for Bourseiller was to transpose the shock value of the obscenities and to find the equivalent of the slang used by Jean Harlow. Due to the impossibility of respecting all the nuances, he reinforced the physical aspect. The actors compete like two magnificent snow leopards and I really liked that.

My play had been well received by the leftist critics but was not a play for France. You don't have the same obsession that we do for Billy the Kid and Jean Harlow. The English appreciated it more because they feel the play as profoundly American—therefore foreign—while listening to it in the original version.

RH: Do you plan to present another of your plays in France?

MM: Antoine has been asking me for a long time, and I hope to send him a text in the not-too-distant future.

RH: How do you perceive your evolution as a poet?

MM: My first poems were published in 1956. In a very free form, they tried to portray romantically the experience I had of myself in the city or in nature. They came after other poems in fixed forms (sonnets, villanelles) and constituted an intentional rupture in order to render without formal limitation my sensorial and hallucinatory experiences. At the beginning of the sixties, I believe I enlarged my poetic field in order to reflect the present reality.

On the formal plane, I tried to develop myself in the greatest numbers of directions. I wrote some plays, two novels—one took a lot of work and the other more spontaneous—and a number of essays laboriously composed. I even have a collection of two hundred and fifty stanzas on my childhood. But this is an unpublishable book because the tone situates itself at the meeting place between Lord Byron and Walt Disney.

I don't have a unique method of working. Each poem is for me an autonomous world, a small biological being with silky fur and brilliant eyes. Thanks to my poems I broaden the conscience of the world. The main thing is to keep this spirit of adventure, not lock oneself into models defined once and for all.

I just wrote a long poem of fifty pages, *Rare Angel*, which developed voluntarily in an incoherent way. By contrast, I paid particular attention to the coherence of expression and the punctuation. In a collection, I can easily follow a well-worked poem by a poem written in a few days.

RH: In your work are you aware of obsessive images which return in spite of yourself? On what themes?

MM: I don't think one can be a creator without being inhabited by obsessions. I am obsessed with enlarging myself, increasing my possibilities of perception. I am obsessed by Billy the Kid and Jean Harlow, or rather I obsess them! And if it is true that thought is a muscular energy, then I am obsessed by the theater which allows me to embody my thoughts, to present them athletically.

RH: That is not what I wanted to say. I speak about the source of images: parts of the body, forms, privileged objects, natural elements, etc.

MM: All my poetry is made from obsessions, and that is why it is difficult for me to speak of it. I am obsessed by the human body, by blood, by violence and sexuality. In this sense, I am typical of my generation. I am fascinated by films like *The French Connection* and *Clockwork Orange* without being able to say if I like them or if I detest them.

RH: How do you work?

MM: I write every day. I stop before I have exhausted all the creative energy in me because I can start more easily the next day. Writing is a little like the training of an athlete. How many laps of the track without an audience! How many pages written and never published!

In the past, I relied exclusively on creative energy. I wrote my first *Gargoyle Cartoons* all at once. They came out directly from my dreams, and I was afraid to stop and lose the thread. I felt relived—more the master of myself—when I spent two days to write one of these "dreams." The fact remains that I strive to find within myself the creative vibration and to follow its movement without "forcing."

Frisco 73

RH: Do you currently feel—like Gary Snyder—closer to Asia than to Europe?

MM: In a sense, yes. Of course, San Francisco is a western city. My culture is western and my ancestors—for four or five generations—came from Scotland and Ireland. But the originality of San Francisco is to be turned towards Asia. Here, I am so accustomed to Asia, to oriental cuisine—whether it is Chinese, Japanese, or Korean—that it is French cuisine which seems exotic and really distant to me.

In the literary area, the Japanese poet Matsuo Bashō (1644–94) is in my opinion the foreign writer who has the greatest influence on the Bay poets. The haiku is a form of poetry often taught in American schools; it is valued due to its brevity and speed to unite two levels of reality.

RH: What does it mean to you to be an American in 1973?

MM: I don't feel myself to be an American citizen but an American poet, and in addition still a mammal full of life existing in 1973. Sometimes, I see myself as a privileged child leading a life of luxurious comfort, sometimes I am at the edge of a cliff contemplating Asia destroyed for my own pleasure, sometimes I am an ogre among ogres, sometimes a fairy with transparent wings watching the monsters evolve, sometimes finally I feel almost like everyone else, like the father of a sixteen-year-old girl helplessly watching the destruction of our environment.

But what dominates in me is the joy of being alive, of enjoying my faculties, and of never having had to serve in a war. I have a strong belief that I am one of the few deeply happy beings on this earth.

RH: What role does San Francisco play now for you?

MM: About the same as at the beginning. Now I have roots there. Which doesn't mean that I won't leave if we continue to degrade nature. Currently, it is here that the concern for the environment is greatest. In Stockholm, the largest delegation came from the Bay. You couldn't walk a hundred yards without meeting someone from San Francisco.

I am attached to this city but I leave it often. In addition to long trips, lecture tours, I go to LA very often. Every weekend I take long walks in the area or retreat to the Zen Center—the Los Padres Mountains—two hours from Carmel.

Explosions and Ecology

RH: What meaning do your first poems have for you?

MM: My first poems, I mean my first published poems, written in 1954–55, correspond to my desire to create a new lyrical form. I wanted to go off the beaten track—spring, autumn, shared love, love misunderstood—I wanted to expand the poetic possibilities. At this time, I was very influenced by Blake, by Shelley, and I had just discovered Artaud. Without being a painter, I felt myself to be very close to the abstract expressionists, to their desire to project themselves spiritually onto the canvas of their paintings, to give a primordial aesthetic reality to their emotions and their feelings. There was a kind of surprising convergence for me between their discoveries and, mine, the jazz played in Kansas City and in New York, the first writings of Ginsberg, Snyder, Corso, Creeley, Lamantia, Denise Levertov. Finally, I already knew the works of Rexroth, of Patchen, and of Duncan, but I was very influenced by the conversations that I had with them at this time.

I wanted to paint the city itself, the feeling that I experienced before a street corner, the ceiling of my room, my worktable. I wanted to convey explosive meaning of what is happening at each instant, the luminous intensity which colors each thing and which, in fact, emanates from myself. I wanted to create a lyrical form expressing my astonishment before each piece of reality and my amazement at every bit of reality and at the same time the kind of inner peace that follows this perception. At least that is what I tried to do in poems such as "The Breech," "The Rug," "The Rope," "Canticle."

RH: What's in the title *Hymn to St. Geryon*?

MM: Geryon was the strange guide of Dante and Virgil, a mythical helicopter permitting them to descend to the seventh and eighth circle of Hell. Geryon was this creature with the body of a dragon covered in scales, with broken spears stuck in him, swords, fragments of armor, two black wings, and a long satanic tail. And this monstrous body was surmounted with a splendid and smiling face. For Dante, he incarnated falsehood. He was the one who seduces you with his gaze while stripping you of your most precious possessions. I had been struck by the illustrations by Gustave Doré and especially by those of Bruce Connor. I felt myself to be a little like Geryon, like a double being, offering to the world a face—a mask—smiling while the tentacles of greedy desires that inhabited my body closed in on their prey. I was conscious of this duality in each of us and I found in it a certain beauty. I did not feel it as negative, but as the source of our actions. It is why I made Geryon a saint, and I wrote this first long poem in projective verse, this suite of stanzas which all return to this duality.[2]

RH: This fascination for Geryon, is it not indicative of your taste for violence which seems to me a constant in your work?

MM: Not exactly. At that time, I tried to make the violence of our society felt, but I didn't take pleasure in it. I was—and still am—stunned by people's lack of appetite for life, their inability to sense the dramatic beauty of the reality around them, their reluctance to act. They are so alienated by the repressive structures of society that they have lost the power to wonder. They are moved only by cruelty and horror, winded ogres stuffing themselves with strawberries and masturbating in the cinema where they watch drug addicts wrestling on the edge of a cliff and cowboys slaughtering each other with silver chains. But fundamentally what I tried to do, it is to render sensible the stupefying beauty of every bit of reality, of each mode of perception, and the kind of luminous flash that occurs when two objects meet and interact. To show more, more intensely, is a liberation, one of the powers of alchemy.

RH: The word "explosion" returns very often in your work. Why?

MM: Jeff Nuttall, an English writer, explains it very well in his book *Bomb Culture* (New York: Delacorte Press, 1968). I belong to a generation whose childhood was marked by the atomic bomb. In high school, one imagined that the end of the world would come in an immense explosion which lasted fifteen seconds. It could still happen by the way if one of those mongrel politicians goes completely crazy. But in another sense, this explosion has already happened. But instead of lasting fifteen seconds, it would possibly last twenty-five years. This explosion is that of the consumption, of the dissipation of natural energy which continues to accelerate. More and more manufactured objects, more and more concrete and at the same time less and less natural soil, trees, and animals. As one of my friends who is a botanist remarked to me, the representation in three dimensions of this mad belief takes the form of an atomic mushroom. But if we managed to control this growth, the loop would close upwards and take the form of a tree with abundant foliage. It's a very beautiful image for me and that's what it is necessary to work for.

Jean Harlow and Billy the Kid, Mammals

RH: Could you tell us now how you began this attraction for Jean Harlow and Billy the Kid?
MM: I was in a plane and I was going to Los Angeles. This was in 1965. I looked at a boxing magazine and suddenly in a flash—in place of the boxers on the page announcing a coming match—I saw the portraits of Billy the Kid and Jean Harlow, in place of the names of the boxers, I read a short text in Beast Language. When I returned to San Francisco, the taxi which took me from the airport, I saw the poster in the window of a café. I stopped, I copied the name of the printer—Telegraph Press—and the next day I telephoned him to find out if he would agree to make a poster for a "poem." He first understood "polo" then assured me that he would also make a poster for my kind of sport. When I showed him what I wanted, he said to me: "I don't want to do that." The reason was that he found the portrait of Jean Harlow unjust to her. I looked again for another photo and two days later he accepted. I went to see the proof and the printer insisted on having me reread all the words of Beast Language: "Gahr, with one r? Grooor, four o? Grayohh, two h?" The poster was printed in red and blue and I posted it in cafes. I even distributed free tickets for the match.

These two characters obsessed me. After the poster, I wrote ninety-nine poems in Beast Language; then there was *The Beard* and the poems in *Star*.

RH: What are they for you?

MM: Billy is for me a "visionary," a "mystic," the Jacob Boehme of assassins. Jean is femininity, sweet, sensual. Gary Snyder saw this very well. He said that *The Beard* is the first American "tantra," the dialogue of the two spiritual forces of life, yin and yang. And these two forces are universal but they are hidden in daily life. When a man says to a woman: "Where did you stuff the laundry receipts?" and the woman answers: "I always lose the receipts," they are not really speaking about the laundry. They say in fact:

> HARLOW: Before you can pry any secrets from me, you must find the real me! Which one will you pursue?
> THE KID: What makes you think I want to pry any secrets from you?
> HARLOW: Because I'm so beautiful.
> THE KID: So what!

The Beard strips the language of everyday life, gives a concrete dimension to our desires which are so often sexual, which concern the will to power, to occupy territory.

RH: Is that not still a profoundly American dimension?

MM: Not really. The play worked very well in Germany and in Japan. In France, it was necessary to transpose Jean and the Kid to Shakti and Shiva, to present them on stage not with a beard but with four or six arms and find the exact slang equivalent of the language in French. The French translation of Roland Dubillard has not been published.

RH: You seem to be fascinated by stars: Jean Harlow, Jayne Mansfield, and Marilyn Monroe. Why?

MM: First, the Kid is also a "star." About sixty books have been published about him after his death. A "star" is someone who by his physical appearance exerts an extraordinary stimulation on our dreams, gives man the stature of God. Or as Blake said: "The body is the descent of soul into matter."

RH: I read *Meat Science Essays* and *September Blackberries* and I would like you to explain the meaning of the word "meat."

MM: It is exactly what Blake implies: "The body is the descent of soul into matter." A few days ago I had a dream in which I killed our tamed rabbit with an iron bar. I woke up and in my notebook I wrote down, "It is the irrepressible urge to kill that makes us real." We live in a contradiction. Too often we pretend not to have bodies, desires. But we are not immaterial beings. We only live in our bodies and through our bodies. I chose to use the word "meat" instead of flesh, so that people would accept this truth, stop believing in the Cartesian dualism of spirit and matter. It is for the same reason that I use the word mammals and that I gave this title to my last book: *The Mammals*.

RH: *Is* there a morbid value in the world "meat"? Meat is first of all dead flesh.

MM: No, simply to the desire to shock. Meat is to flesh what fucking is to making love. Nothing morbid there.

Theatrical Confusion

RH: What role does obscenity have for you in your theater?

MM: I don't employ obscenity systematically. In *The Beard*, it was one effective way to make people aware of hypocrisy. In *The Pussy*, the employment of dirty words contributed to create a more naturalistic climate. It was also a way to allow the actors to take possession of the scene, as indeed in *The Button*.

RH: The play that shows adults playing the role of children having fun imitating the sexual behavior of their parents.

MM: Yes. I saw this play recently at Merritt College and it had a greater success than at the Magic Theatre. First, the stage was bigger and the actors could use this space like real children. The bed was no bigger than a normal adult bed. The slow-motion acting of the actors added an erotic element.

RH: Did you look for it?

MM: No, I mostly wanted to add confusion for the viewers. In another staging in Los Angeles, one of the actresses will wear a Girl Scout costume and the beds will be sleeper beds. This should work even better.

RH: Could you tell us about the play which the Company Theatre in Los Angeles presented?

MM: It will be very delirious: walls with hands wielding water guns, projections of soap bubbles, a table with wings, the floor covered with feathers. Basically, we will see four virulent and titanic fairies—in principle completely naked—with tails and wings—playing cards. One wins and one of the three losers disputes the result. A ritual fight takes place between the two players who exchange obscenities and childish insults that get bigger and bigger. The table and the two other players are more and more terrified, small creatures cross the stage in a panic, and four musicians in hats and evening dresses play the harmonica. A ritual fight takes place between the two players who exchange obscenities and childish insults that get bigger and bigger. The table and the two other players are more and more terrified, little creatures cross the stage in a panic, and four musicians in top hats and evening dresses play the harmonica. At the most violent moment an apparition takes place: a bizarre being, uttering grunts, rumblings, comes crashing down against the wall. After several songs, they understand that the ogres are torturing a fairy and they prepare to rescue her when they realize that the apparition is hidden in the wall and that they are now talking to her asshole. They sing other incantations and the wall peels off and finally they leave the stage to go and defend their sister. Everything goes black. In a lighted corner, on a haystack, we see three soldiers wearing chrome chains. Two are asleep. The third launches into a skeptical monologue on the existence of fairies. And the play ends when we hear the fairies crossing space.

RH: Wouldn't such a show be more cinematic than theatrical? Are you tempted by the cinema?

MM: Of course, I would very much like to make films, write a script for a director or an actor I know, make a musical or a war film whose starting point would be *The Pussy*. So far, I haven't found sufficient motivation. The cinema is for me one of the most ritual forms, the least liberated. Cocteau at the beginning of his career, Bunuel, Godard, Andy Warhol, and Stan Brakhage, are among the only ones who have advanced the cinema. And then, I find that the theater is a magnificent meat machine, an extraordinary cell. I love the actors, the rehearsals. I experience great joy in working for the stage.

Adepts and Hells Angels

RH: How did you come to the novel? What does this form represent for you?

MM: I tried to fix a certain number of memories of adolescence that I feared to forget. I used a technique close to that of William Burroughs: I took as they came to my mind the different scenes that I wanted to describe. When I was done I made some grammatical corrections on the typescript but didn't retype it. Then I categorized these different scenes at random and published this book *The Mad Cub* in 1965. The book was a success—not a truly commercial success, but I sold between 60,000 and 80,000 copies— which is marvelous for a poet. This novel is now published in paperback. Then I went to New York. At the time, I had just acted in a Norman Mailer film, *Beyond the Law*, and I was very busy presenting *The Beard* in New

York. One evening, I asked Norman what advice he could give me for writing a novel. He replied: "Each sentence should be like a snake swallowing its own tail." This image of the snake biting its tail struck me. A poet has a fragile, vulnerable "ego," which he must protect. I was tempted to use my "ego" and also my intelligence in another way. For a poet, writing a novel is easy and I got into *The Adept*. It took me six months to write the book, writing a chapter in one place, another somewhere else, not always having time to reread what preceded. In fact, it took me really six weeks to write this novel with long cuts where I was doing all kinds of things. The hero, Nick, looks a bit like Bremer (Arthur Bremer, *An Assassin's Diary*). Without being a genius, Nick is still more astute than Bremer. Bremer is America: Hershey bars, Kentucky Fried Chicken, McDonald's, Winchester rifles, massage parlors, etc. He tries to make reality more interesting by projecting his imagination onto it, for example, when he walks around New York and the bushes come up to his nose and he thinks he is in the jungle.

RH: How did you find the idea for *The Adept*?

MM: Probably in my head when I was driving my motorcycle at ninety miles an hour under the influence of cocaine.

RH: It seems that the division of the novel lends itself easily to a cinematographic transposition.

MM: Actually, Jim Morrison and I wrote a script, but the producer killed our project. Other filmmakers have taken an option on this book. I was even told that Paul Morrissey was interested. Personally, I would really like Godard to make a film of it, because Nick is very literary, very philosophical, but I don't think he would be interested.

RH: Have you reworked *The Adept*?

MM: No. Now I think I would rewrite to give it a bit more richness. The difficulty is finding a way to add 20 percent. If I rewrote it, I would add 200 percent: it would be another novel. A real novelist is someone who, having found a style, is able to integrate 20 percent more into his initial project.

RH: What exactly is an "adept"?

MM: He's someone who can turn ordinary metal into gold but doesn't yet have creative power with the philosopher's stone.

RH: How did you come to write the autobiography of a Hells Angel?

MM: I met Freewheelin Frank at a Bob Dylan and Joan Baez concert. We smoked marijuana together. We saw each other several times in San Francisco and I was struck by his excellent sense of language and I proposed to him to write his autobiography.

RH: What is the exact title?

MM: *Freewheelin Frank, Secretary of the Hells Angels, as Told to Michael McClure.*
RH: How did you work with him?
MM: It was very easy. I told him to come to my place every day and to be very exact, if not I would refuse to continue. Frank was exactitude itself. In fact, he arrived in the evening having done nothing all day and bursting with energy. Me, I had taught and I came home dead. And he came back like that for more than four months taking all my bloody evenings. We would go to my studio and I would type his story. Sometimes we yelled at each other when I thought he was lying or that he didn't speak concretely and launched into long-winded and philosophical explanations, especially when he started reading the Bible or *The Divine Comedy* (!). To relax, we made music together: Frank played the harmonica, I played the autoharp and some other guys played with us.
RH: What do you think of this book now?
MM: I didn't want to do a Hells Angels book. I wanted to write the autobiography of Frank who had a hillbilly childhood in Missouri. But he did not want to go into detail about his childhood. As it is, this book is a piece of an anthology for understanding America. It is as if we had the testimony of a practitioner of the cult of the jaguar among the Aztecs.
RH: Did you reread the typed text with Frank?
MM: Not really. I gave the text to Don Allen who was "editor" at Grove Press because I trusted him. He cut all the repetitions in order to make the book more readable even if we thus lost a certain flavor that came from its repetitions.
RH: What was the reaction of the critics?
MM: There wasn't a single favorable review. No one appreciated Frank's honesty and sense of language. He was called a "vulgar debauched pig." The book was said to be a huge pile of shit. I didn't show the reviews to Frank. I have everything stuffed in my mail archive!
RH: What part of the book is Frank? What part Michael McClure?
MM: There is absolutely nothing of me. I simply changed the proper names so that they couldn't put Frank in prison.
RH: Are you tempted to write other novels?
MM: Yes. It's a kind of new pleasure to be able to express yourself with fewer constraints than in a poem, to be able to release these images that we carry within us, to make yourself branch off into different characters.
RH: I would like you to specify, to conclude, what you perceive as a new interest in surrealism in the United States.

MM: First, there is a new interest in orthodox surrealism among poets like Stephen Schwartz and Philip Lamantia. In Los Angeles, Ed Germain is preparing a new surrealist anthology for Penguin. I am sure that this book will be very important. Then, if we go back, we see that many French writers and painters stayed in New York during the Second World War. They had a decisive influence on abstract expressionists such as Pollock, de Kooning, Motherwell, etc. From painting, this influence spread to literature, then to cinema and theater and again now to art: minimal art and conceptual art. In a broad sense, we are in the middle of a surrealist period. The Vietnam War is certainly a surreal act. Overpopulation—the French word is much better than the word "overpopulation"—joins the word surrealism in my head.

RH: Do you consider yourself a surrealist?

MM: The best definition of what I'm trying to do is Gary Snyder who gave it in a letter that I'm going to have framed. After reading *September Blackberries*, he wrote to me that I was a Bioclassic, and for me surrealism is a minor part of Bioclassicism!

Notes

1. Director of the Magic Theatre troupe in Berkeley.
2. Expression of Charles Olson designating a poetic form founded on the energy of the body and the breath of the poet.
3. Bremer is the man who tried to assassinate Governor Wallace.

Michael McClure Interview

David Rollison / 1976

From the Bay Area Writers series at Indian Valley Colleges, April 7, 1976, https://www.youtube.com/watch?v=7Bvft6QnbdM&list=PLdfZ691RCfJr2_nL962NxEDheHwgIyZTS&index=16. Reprinted by permission.

David Rollison: What sparked the writing of *The Beard*?"
Michael McClure: OK. That's a very intriguing question because the answer to it's so long that we could spend most of the time just answering that one. Does everybody know what *The Beard* is? Did you talk about it in class? *The Beard* is a play, in which there are two characters, Billy the Kid and Jean Harlow and the setting is Eternity, and it's all blue velvet, and the only stage set is a table and two chairs and the table and two chairs are covered with fur and Billy the Kid is dressed in costume from 1880, Western, and Jean Harlow is wearing a blue dress and has a purse. The stage is in blackness, and then an orange light comes on Harlow and the Kid, who are sitting at the table, and Harlow looks up and she sees the Kid (she's never seen him before, obviously, they're from two different times and spaces), and she says, "Before you can pry any secrets from me, you must first find the real me. Which one will you pursue?" And the Kid says, "What makes you think I want to pry any secrets out of you?" And she says, "Oh, because I'm so beautiful." The Kid says, "Yeah?" You know, so it starts like that, and that little opening passage becomes a refrain that's repeated several times there at the beginning, which, it's like, brings this impossible vibration of these two people, together, into a more and more solid state. The only other thing in the costume I didn't tell you about—they're wearing little beards made out of torn white tissue-paper, just two little beards. And the question was how I came . . . ?

DR: What sparked . . . ?
MM: . . . what sparked the writing of it. I was in an airplane on the way to Los Angeles and I was looking at a copy of *Ring* magazine, which was a

boxing magazine in those days and I looked at a poster reproduced in the magazine, a sort of classical fifties and sixties American boxing poster, and that boxing poster showed the two opponents, a photograph of each of the opponent on each side of the poster and it would say, like—"Ali versus Frazier—Big Fight—Madison Square Garden," so on and so on—a very large poster like that, and, while I was looking at that poster on the airplane, I saw Billy the Kid and Jean Harlow on the poster, and I saw a whole new poster with Billy the Kid and Jean Harlow on it, and I saw the text of the poster in Beast Language, or a language that I called Beast Language, which was an invented language for writing sound poetry, which has sounds like "GAAHR GRAAHR" in it and combinations of that language and a kind of imagistic language.

So it could say "ROSE." So, instead of saying "Big Fight—Madison Square Garden," it would say, like "GRAAH SILVER SIILVER GRAAH." When I flew back from Los Angeles, I still had that poster in my mind, and I was taking a cab back from the airport, and I saw a boxing poster, and it said "Telegraph Press." So the next morning, I phoned (that was at night), the next morning I phoned, first thing in the morning, I phoned Telegraph Press and I said, "I want you to make a poster for me." And they said, "What kind of a poster?" And I said, "A poem poster." And this voice on the other end said, "Oh yeah, polo posters, we make polo posters, bring it down." So I made a mock-up of the poster (apparently in the discussion he told me to make a mock-up), so I had the measurements of the poster and the size that the boxing poster would be, and I blocked in all the letters the right sizes (it has numerous type sizes on it) and I took out a picture of Billy the Kid and a picture of Jean Harlow that I wanted reproduced on the poster, and I took it down to him, and I handed it to him, and it was a pretty bizarre looking item, and the only posters that they made were boxing posters, by the way, except for one other poster, which was a bumper sticker for the Rolling Stones, which was surprising. And I handed this to him, and the guy looked at it for a long time. His name was Les Jelinski—he looked at it for a long time and he said, "I'm not going to do it." And I said, "Why?" (this is 1965), I said, "Why?" and he said, "Ah" (he was a pretty old guy), and he said, "All you young guys think you know what Jean Harlow looked like, but you don't really know, look at that crummy photograph of her, it makes her neck look ugly. I'm not going to do the poster." I said, "I'll get another picture of Jean Harlow, you're right."

So I went out and I spent about three days getting another picture of Jean Harlow (one that would go with the Kid because there's only two extant photos of the Kid that are in public domain, even today). So I had the photo of the Kid I wanted, lots of photos of Harlow. I found the photo of Harlow I wanted to use; I took it back down, and he said, "Okay, I'll call you in a few days." These posters are very interesting because they use old wooden-block types that are almost like circus-types and almost all of this type was a variation of Cooper typeface so you had Cooper typeface running from this size down to little tiny letters like that, and the lead on this said "LOVE LION, comma LIONESS"—like big battle between "Love Lion" and "Love Lioness" would be the way you would read this if this was a poster. That was one of the few parts of the text in English. And his assistant phoned me about three days later and said, "Come on down. Check the poster before we run it." I went down and checked it. It was beautiful. I said, "Run it. It's fantastic." And we checked out where the red was . . . (it's a two-color poster, red on white, red and blue letters on white), and I said, "Perfect." We checked out where the red was going to be, where the blue was going to be. "Perfect, just, I'll come down tomorrow and get it. We'll. . . ." I think I asked him to run about two hundred, maybe three hundred . . . and I went home, and about an hour later, Jelinski called me again, and he said, "You've got to come down here"—I said, "I was just down there, I'm very busy, I love it, it's great, would you just run it, it's perfect" He said, "No, you've got to come down. I won't run it if you don't come down and ok it while I'm here."

So I went down, and he started reading it out loud to me. He said: "LOVE LION, comma, LIONESS," right?" I said, "Right." He says: "GRAHHHH GAHOO GRAHEER? "Right?"—"Right."—"RUUR?" "Right." "GRAHHHH with four H's right?" "Right." And he read this thing all the way through and there are lots of H's and letters, and at one point he was reading the word "GRAHHHH," which had about four H's in it, and he says: "Grahhhh-h-h-h, right?" and I said, "Yeah." And he turned to me and he said, "What is this shit anyway?" Then I explained to him that it was a language I'd invented to write poetry in, it was a kind of . . . there wasn't any conceptual art at this time, but I described it. I said it was a poster for an event that takes place in eternity. There isn't really any event, because it's happening in eternity, so the poster is kind of the event. And the text is a poem in an invented language. And he said, "I have a friend in the WPA who wrote poetry and I. . . ." He said, "I can really understand it now." Actually, we got to be very good friends too. Over a period of time he did a lot of work for me, and we talked more about his friend who wrote poetry, and over a period of time I brought in other poems of mine in Beast Language, and he used to keep them on his desk as a conversation piece, when people would come in that . . . I think, when he wanted to toy with their minds, he'd throw my book out, you know, very straight, working-class people, he'd show them this and say: "I'm doing some work for this guy," and watch them go through the changes (at least that's what I suspect). So he ran the poster, and I picked up the poster, and then I took it to the liquor store where I'd seen the original poster, and I said, "May I . . . can I put this in your window?" And the guy just looked up and said, "No." I said, "Why not?" He said, "I should get some comps if I'm going to put this in the window." I said, "Okay." So I went back down to Jalinski and I said, "Show me a boxing ticket will you" (and he prints boxing tickets down there too). So he gave me a boxing ticket (or else, maybe I had a boxing ticket at home—yeah, I did—I had a boxing ticket at home), and I wrote a boxing ticket in Beast Language, then I had Jalinski print two comps to go with every poster that was printed and I went back and I said, "Here's your two tickets. Can I put this in the window now?" And the guy said, "Yeah."

So, you know actually that stayed in that window longer than any of the other posters I put up. That poster stayed there for months. That was at the corner of Haight and Masonic, as a matter of fact. I used to stand across the street and watch people go by and go back and stop and look at the poster, go by and not look at the poster, and various people's reactions to that poster. It was an interesting place to have it because there was so much traffic there. Then I went around and I put the. . . . I remember I stapled one over Kenneth Rexroth's front door, and I tacked another one to Kenneth Anger's front door and then I put up a bunch of them at Third and Mission, and put up a lot of them in the Western Addition, and I folded them in half and stapled tickets to them, wrote friends' addresses on them and mailed a lot of them out. And I put one on my wall. At that time my typewriter was, I sat at my typewriter in such a way that I faced west into the sun when it was setting. So on the east wall, behind my head, I put up one of the "LOVE LION LIONESS" posters, and I'd sit there typing. And as I was typing one day, I discovered that Billy the Kid and Jean Harlow . . . maybe the reflection, maybe the setting sun had reflected in their photos, and then it focused into my consciousness, because I had Billy the Kid and Jean Harlow in my head, in three dimensions, beginning to act out this rite. And so I became the typist for their rite. And I guess that's what sparked it. It was a good spark.

DR: What was the beard?

MM: Well, I, at the time, well, the beard would be like the wings of an angel, something to set you off. I mean, even in eternity, I guess.

DR: Something to set you off as immortal?

MM: Something to set you off as even further immortal. And then one day, Robert Duncan another Bay Area wrier called my attention to the fact that lady pharaohs wore false beards in Egypt, as a divine attribute, I suppose, or to show their divinity, and I wasn't aware of that at the time. But perhaps unconsciously, or from some other direction, that was a part of it.

DR: Interesting.

MM: Thank you.

Student: It took me a heck of a long time to understand it. Finally, I'm getting through it inch by inch.

MM: My daughter just told me that they're doing it in an acting class at San Francisco State right now and that a brother of one of her girlfriends is playing Billy the Kid, and I believe it's being done in New York now at the New York Theatre Ensemble, at least it was a few weeks ago.

S: Is it precisely the same as the original production?

MM: I don't know.

S: Well, it was a little different from what you're describing....

MM: There's a lot of variation. There's a lot of individuality and a lot of sets. I've seen it done everywhere from just two chairs and a table to pretty elaborate sets, where people got involved in it. Then another time it was done in a boxing ring, which I thought was nice.

S: Was it open-air?

MM: I don't think so.

S: Did you see it when it was up at San Francisco State?

MM: No, I didn't. My wife and daughter went up to see it.

S: Were they pleased with the production?

MM: They told me it was good. They told me they liked it. I was out of town.

S: I remember seeing it originally....

MM: Where? At downtown? At the Encore, or down at the Wharf or in California Hall on Polk Street? And you know, we also did it in the Fillmore Auditorium.

DR: Oh, did you now.

MM: Yeah—with a light show. It was very beautiful. He used hand-held microphones and the entire sound system. And, of course, the play was considered pretty obscene, verbally, in those days, to say the least. And here the . . . like . . . all the kind of divine scatology coming out of the Fillmore sound-system was great, and Tony Martin did a light show, that must have been about thirty by seventy feet, behind it, incorporating films in the light show (that was the first time I'd seen that done). That was a great performance too.

DR: I think it would have been 1966. I've been trying to remember.

MM: Well, probably, it was '66. We first did it, I think, in December 19, 1965, or December 21, 1965, and then we did it until we were arrested. And then the ACLU protected us, and they advised us not to perform it for a while (I guess that was after we'd been arrested a couple of times, they advised us not to perform it for a while). So probably you did see it in 1966. . . .

DR: When did you first write in Beast Language?

MM: Well, I first wrote a play in Beast Language. Before I wrote any poems in Beast Language, I wrote a play for thirteen characters, seated at a long table, with the character in the middle having lion's paws, sort of like . . . it looked like *The Last Supper*. All of them were bearded also. As a matter of fact, in performance, it was performed, I think, in 1959 or 1960, and (must have been 1961), and all of the characters in it made themselves big beards out of torn white tissue paper because we didn't have any budget. So that was the first torn white tissue-paper beards. They were supposed to be dressed in golden or cerulean robes, so we all rounded up Indian blankets, and they were all supposed to be bearded so everybody tore different beard shapes, their own style of beard. And on the ends of the thirteen, the first and thirteenth person were bearded women and the second and twelfth persons were Negro titans (and we didn't know any Black actors at the time, and that was before the big Black theater movement, so a couple of my friends did that in blackface). And so here we were, like, bearded women in tissue-paper beards and guys in blackface, and the guy with lion's paws in the middle. It's quite a beautiful play. It was very successful. "Very successful!" [*laughs*]. We invited about a hundred people we knew who were our friends to come see us and we thought we were great. That's what I mean by "very successful."

Then in 1962 I began to hear those same sounds, that were more of less born in the play, in a ball of silence within myself. It's as if poem Beast Language sounds were inhabiting this ball of silence. And I intuited that I was going to write a hundred poems in that language, and that probably I wouldn't make any changes in the poems as I wrote them, that they would be spontaneous, and that as in *The Beard* I would be recording (although I hadn't written *The Beard* yet), I would be recording sounds that were there.

And, again, with the Beast Language, there's an interesting organic sidelight for me I . . . (This can't be very interesting to you if you don't have the book to look at) but the first . . . there are ninety-nine, actually one hundred, of these Beast Language poems and the first ones start out like baby-talk.

They start out like "GRI-GRA-GEE-GEER GWEE GWEE. That type of like baby-talk Beast Language sounds. And the language matures as it develops, and develops as an organism might develop into maturity, and into a kind of blossoming, the language in the long series of poems develops as an organism would develop and reaches a maturity and then blossoms. So that around the middle.... And also the English goes in and out of these poems. For instance, like, the fifty-first poem starts in English, probably has more English in it than any of the other Beast Language poems. I can think of one right in the middle, in the kind of, like, full maturity of this language, English comes back in briefly and it's a kind of a night poem. It goes something like: "I LOVE TO THINK OF THE RED PURPLE ROSE / IN THE DARKNESS COOLED BY THE NIGHT / We are served by machines making satins / of sounds/Each blot of sound is a bud or a stahr / Body eats bouquets of the ear's vista / Gahhhrrr boody eyes ears nose / deem thou / NOH, NAH-OHH / Hroooor. VOOOR-NAH! GAHROOOOO ME / Nah drooooooh seerch. NAH THEE! / The machines are too dull when we / are lion-poems that move & breathe / WHAN WE GROOOOOOOOOOOOOR / hann dree myketoth sharoo sreee thah noh deeeeemed ez / Whan eecethoooooze hrohh." And, you know, it's not impossibly far from "Whan that Aprille with his shoures soote, / The droughte of March has perced to the roote, / And bathed every veyne in swich licour / Of which vertu engendred is the flour; / Whan Zephirus eek with his swete breeth / Inspired hath in every holt and heeth / The tendre croppes, and the yonge sonne / Hath in the Ram his halfe cours y-ronne." You know that? That was written about 1380? That's part of the prologue to *The Canterbury Tales*. So that's Middle English, which sounds exotic to us nowadays: of course, it's got a nice rhyme-scheme.

DR: There's a lot of language coming into the beast poems, like Anglo-Saxon and Middle English, and all that.

MM: Yeah.

DR: Were you . . . were you . . . was that going on with you . . . or . . . ?

MM: Not consciously. I wasn't exerting conscious control. It's a kind of tantric language, and I think that anything that . . . anything that would create the tantras flew right into its being. And then, when many people . . . somebody would pick them up and read them as if they were . . . some very Caucasian-looking individual will pick up *Ghost Tantras*, the beast-language poems, and read them and they sound like they're Japanese (and it's like some Japanese sub-being of theirs suddenly decided to speak to them), or perhaps somebody will be Dutch and pick them up and they will sound Dutch. They are interesting to read. If you see a copy of it, try reading them out loud yourself and see what they . . . see what your voice sounds like when you read them. . . .

When I first wrote them, before they were even published in a book, we used to take them out at dinner time and pass the manuscript around, after dinner and everybody would take turns reading them. It got to be kind of a party game. See, you know, which ones you'd open to spontaneously, and if you sounded like a Dutchman, or if you sounded Japanese, or if you sounded like an elf, or . . .

DR: You have a lot of lions and lion themes in your poems.

MM: I did then. I did indeed then.

DR: Does it have any more an attraction? What's your relationship to lions these days?

MM: I think I had some then, I was interested in that time in the way I saw lions looking at things. I felt that there was a particular consciousness there. I think what I was seeing was the consciousness in a completed carnivore. I saw several times in lions a kind of lucidity of consciousness that up until that time I'd not seen in any other being.

DR: Can you talk a little about *Meat Science*?

MM: No, that's so long ago, David. No. Do you mean the book of essays?

DR: No, I mean the theory, the idea.

MM: Oh, I don't know that there was a theory. "Meat Science" is a name that I gave to a book of essays, and it's a . . . it's the way I'll appreciate something—I'll say something is an act of meat science if I like it, if I feel that the totality of the person is in the act of the gesture that he's making. I mean, if you fulfill the whole sweep from what we call mind to what we call body and do it with the wholeness, so the whole mind-body is in it, then I see that kind of thing as being an act of meat science. If enough of the potentialities of a person are fulfilled within the possible potentialities of a series of actions, then I really think that looks like an act of meat science to me.

So, everything between Kwan Yin and Shiva. It's everything between the Goddess of Mercy and the God of Destruction, I guess, within ourselves, and including those as the two ends? That sounds obscure doesn't it?

S: It covers a lot of territory.

MM: Yeah.

DR: I get it, it's like in some ways, it's the spirit *in* the body.

MM: I think so.

DR: Is that more accurate?

MM: Yeah. Yeah.

DR: That's kind of what I wanted to hear you talk about today. That sense of the body, I think you . . .

MM: Bob Creeley's book *Pieces* is, I think, a really great act of meat science. You know, Bob who . . . a lot of Bob's early poetry is really thought poetry. Then he, Bob, just inhabits his body for that time that he wrote *Pieces*, and those are like, very great and beautiful organic pieces of a great poem (it seems very natural to me), Then, in another way, I think Francis Crick discovering the molecular, or the atomic structure of the DNA molecule is a great act of meat science (or a great elucidation of another aspect of it). . . .

[*McClure reads "EL CERRO ES NUESTRO!" and "A BREATH" from his book,* Jaguar Skies.]

Here's a sort of medium-long-ish poem. This is six stanzas of six lines, and . . . it's a Medieval French form called a sestina. It was invented by a troubadour poet named Bertrand de Born at the time of the Crusades, and probably the formula for the repetition of end-words . . . (you'll hear that it doesn't rhyme, but there's a repetition of end-words, and a pattern), and the formula for that pattern may have its origin in Mohammedan mysticism, the numerical formula for that. Remember the knights from Europe were confronting the knights of the Moslem, or Mohammedan knights, in North Africa and the Middle East and there was a lot of communication back and forth. So this form of poetry was originally invented by a Duke of Southern France who was also a troubadour, but the word-repetition at the end, may be influenced by Mohammedan mysticism.

Well, there's a story about this too. I'll tell you what sparked this! I'd always wanted to write a sestina (this kind of poem is called a sestina), and I was with Allen Ginsberg at John Ashbery's reading at the San Francisco Museum of Art—(John is a New York poet), and I'd just finished reading a book of John's poetry, and he read one of the poems ["Farm Implements and Rutabagas in a Landscape"), and it's a sestina about Popeye and Olive Oyl, and . . . what was the (next)?—the Sea-Witch [Sea Hag] and the Goon [Alice the Goon] (remember all those characters from *Popeye*?). It was a sestina about *Popeye* characters. And I was sitting next to Allen and I said, "Allen, that's a sestina!" And by the time Ashbery had finished reading his sestina, Allen had started *his* sestina! And I wanted to write one very badly after that myself. Ashbery had read one, Allen had written one, on the spot; I'd been meaning to write a sestina for years, but I'd been trying to write it kind of formally, in some kind of measured line, and I said, "Oh, I just want to do this. I'm not going to use a measured line." So I just used a cadenced line and wrote this (and since I sort of assigned myself the subject of a sestina, at the time I had a chronic headache, and the headache became the subject of the sestina). So, it's a headache sestina. But I was trying also almost to use it as if it was a tool. I wanted to know what caused that headache, I wanted to experience that headache in any way I could. I thought that maybe in some way this would help me find out about the headache. So, I used the sestina that way—for exploration.

S: Did you find out about your headache?

MM: Not through that sestina! Maybe a little bit, maybe it put me on the right track.

"The lines of flame." No, "The beautiful lines of flames." That's it. You ever feel those lines of flame inside of your head when you have a headache? [*Reads poem.*]

I don't know if you could hear the repetitions in there or not, but the interweavings of word repetitions at the end of lines.

[*McClure now reads "EACH/MAMMAL."*]

It's that area that Bob has so perfectly, you know—of an area of grace that we move through, a kind of dimension.

DR: Is that dedicated to Bob?

MM: Yeah, that's called "For Robert Creeley." There's a lot of poems in here for people. Let's see. . . . Here's poem for a friend of mine's wife who makes stained-glass windows, incredibly beautiful naturalistic representations of things in nature, of little waters, of little streams with a snake swimming across then, or seals floating through the water. This one was the chrysalis of an oak moth, actually the cocoon of an oak moth which, you know is only *this* big, but she made a stained-glass window of it in which it was *this* big. It was this enormous representation of an oak moth cocoon in all of its beauty with, like, the sky behind it, and the twig that it hangs from is the size of a branch. And I saw (I already had two or three of her pieces), and I had to have it, so I bought that one from her too, and then couldn't stop there, even had to write a poem about it, for her, which is kind of an occasional poem.

[*Reads "Stained Glass Window Portraying and Oak Moth Cocoon: For Kathie."*]

I guess it's the challenge in something like that to change, to open up like a. . . .

Here's some more poems that I wrote in Peru. The first one I wrote was about—the first one I read you—"the flame is ours we are the candle that holds itself aloft"—that was written in that pass. . . . This was written in a little

Indian town way up in the mountains, called the town of Huancayo, written the next day.

[Reads "Revolucion."]

This was written after coming back up out of a few days in the Amazon jungle and coming into Bogota, and the difference of like being back in a modern city and looking back on what we'd seen. And I found a physics text, a Russian physics text translated into English full of quotes by Lenin, and I used a couple of lines, I used a line of Lenin to start this poem ("The world consists of nothing but moving matter").

[Reads "MODELS OF COMPLEXITY."]

I was looking back remembering places like Machu Picchu and the jungle and the animals that we'd seen—written in Bogota the next day (or the same day, I guess, I can't remember) I went into a restaurant and had that feeling of . . . what. . . . Remember when you were in high school? When you had to walk across the cafeteria and "oh god, everybody's looking at me?" I had like a total self-involvement with self-consciousness in this perfectly wonderful restaurant. It was a great place to eat, and I just felt thrown back to that high school cafeteria, that whole experience again. A grown man, in control of my own ship of destiny, back up out of a long, exciting trip, and then suddenly back into the high school cafeteria again! Why?

[Reads "Bare as a Star."]

Yeah, these are very recent poems. It must be difficult to. Usually . . . (I didn't know I was going to give a poetry reading, I thought it was a discussion.) Usually, when I give a poetry reading, I try and make myself more three-dimensional for the people I'm reading to by reading poems from different eras in my life, so that somebody can look at what I'm telling them and understand the direction that I'm coming from. It would make me. . . . My work would be much more three-dimensional for you if you could get some sense that, for instance, here's a poem that I wrote when I was seventeen, back in the Middle Ages. Before this I'd written free verse too. This is when I discovered William Blake and I discovered metrics, and I wanted to write in meter. I wanted to write poems like Blake's little youthful visionary song lyric poems and, although I'd already written free verse, I wrote "My mother said to me tonight." [Reads poem.]

I recollect another one I wrote right about that time, only I'd been reading a little Baudelaire too. I wrote another little set of quatrains. [Reads "What strange odors in this room."]

DR: And what age were you were you on that one?

MM: About seventeen. But just a few years later, my awarenesses in poetry were directing themselves many different ways, multiple ways, and biology, interest in organisms, was making itself very strongly apparent to me, and interest in what was being done by the abstract expressionist painters—Jackson Pollock or Clyfford Still or Franz Kline, the work of these men, and it was pretty new in those days, was of a great deal of interest to me and I wanted something like that in poetry. And a little while later I discovered a man named Charles Olson, who had invented a kind of projective verse, which was close to what they were doing, but already, I was experimenting in the direction of those painters, that I considered to be artistic ideals in many ways, were endeavoring in, and I was writing poems like. . . . This, you'd really need to hear a couple of times. In fact, let me see if I do know it. In fact, this would sound almost like an abstract poem, but if you look at it on the page (or maybe hear it again, in a couple of days) I think it would be a reasonably clear poem to you. [*Reads "Linked part to part, to knee, eye to thumb."*]

Gives you something to think about, doesn't it—I think that was the first time I'd seen the word "rishi" used in a poem, as a matter of fact. Now we use the word Roshi, a Buddhist abbot, or a Buddhist teacher, or a Buddhist wise man is what we now call a roshi. The word I knew in those days for that was "rishi" and some of the various elements in that poem are biology, the fire-sermon of Buddha, they're all submerged within the context, the things that I had in mind when I was writing it. That was probably written 1954. So these poems that I'm writing are coming out of a development. David was saying it would be nice you know, to say where your sense of being comes from. That's where it comes from.

Here's a poem I'd like to see as a song for Joan Baez. But I think the first line would be wrong for her because the first line would sound mechanical in the context of the kind of songs that she sings, where it isn't meant that way at all. [*Reads "Up Beat."*]

Then I was in I. Magnin's, and I've been writing nature poems and I wondered "Could someone write nature poem in I. Magnin's? Is I. Magnin's nature?" Somebody once asked Nietzsche about what was natural and what was unnatural, or what was nature and what wasn't nature, and Nietzsche's reply was something to the effect that, "it if exists it must be." So I found myself standing in I. Magnin's and I thought "Could I write a nature poem about this, you now from the viewpoint one would write a nature poem," not to go in and say, "Oh, well, this is bad because it represents the military industrial society or this is foppery because it's fashionable clothing," but just like, "OK, this is nature. I'm going to look at it the way I look at a cliff or something." And I don't know how well I succeeded but this is an attempt to stand in I. Magnin's as if you were standing by a waterfall. [*Reads "Nature Poem Written in I. Magnin."*]

I think I'll read one last poem, and then, if anybody has any questions that occur to them, I can answer a couple of questions. Then it's up to David. It's going to go back to your hands. This is a poem about Thornton Beach, a place that we like to go and body surf, a mile or so south of San Francisco. [*Reads "Thornton Beach."*]

This is just a little poem of appreciation of something that happens in my life, of a place where I can body surf and you know, the beauty of the place where Indian paintbrush and lupin actually hang out over the cliff, over the surf. You can body-surf there and when you come in, roll over in the wave and look up and there's lupin almost over your head. Lupin, it's that little blue flower that looks like a wild pea blossom, and you know what Indian paintbrush looks like. . . . Arthropods are those little . . . you call them sand fleas, only I don't know what you call the big variety.

S: Big sand fleas!

MM: Big sand fleas. Gotcha!

An Interview with Michael McClure

Stephen Vincent / 1977

From the *San Francisco Review of Books* 3, no. 8 (December 1977): 10–16. Reprinted by permission.

In 1955, the late Six Gallery, then located at Fillmore and Union in San Francisco, staged an event which, if we can take Kerouac's word for it, marked the birth of the San Francisco Poetry Renaissance. The event was a poetry reading, not a particularly common occurrence in those days, and everybody, as they say, was there. Kenneth Rexroth introduced poets— Philip Lamantia, Philip Whalen, Gary Snyder. Allen Ginsberg read a new poem. It was called "Howl." And a young poet presented his work to his first public audience. His name was Michael McClure. Now, twenty-two years later, the poet and playwright McClure is still in the forefront of the continuing San Francisco artistic renaissance.

McClure's early poetry aligned itself with the Beat Generation. Two fledgling fine presses, Jonathan Williams's Jargon Press and Dave Haselwood's Auerhahn Press, began publishing the poet McClure's work, as did Lawrence Ferlinghetti's City Lights. The playwright McClure began working with the Magic Theatre, and his long and vital association with poetry and theater was launched.

McClure has had two collections of poetry, *Jaguar Skies* and *September Blackberries*, as well as his musical comedy *Gorf*, published by New Directions. This spring they will issue *Antechamber*, a new collection of poems. His play *General Gorgeous* has been performed by ACT, where McClure was playwright-in-residence for a year. And his work *The Beard*, the "scandal that became a contemporary classic," has won two Obie awards; it is now being performed in Paris.

Stephen Vincent: Since you came to San Francisco in the early fifties you've had a close relationship with a number of printers in the area, and this issue of the SFRB is in part devoted to an exploration of the book arts including a number of the fine presses in the area. I believe your first book was published by Dave Haselwood at Auerhahn Press. Correct me if I'm wrong.

Michael McClure: My first book was a Jargon Press book titled *Passage*, published in 1956. Jonathan Williams visited San Francisco in 1954 and 1955 and, as I see it, Jargon Press, because of Jonathan's early journeys into San Francisco, fits in as one of the many sources for Bay Area printing. My picture of printing in the Bay Area begins with the arrival in San Francisco of the anarchists from the conscientious objector camps in Oregon. Adrian Wilson came here at the end of WWII, about the same time as William Everson. Before that there'd been a background of magazines from Berkeley. Then there's the famous *Ark* magazine, an anarchist literary magazine that came out right after WWII.

SV: I remember *Circle* magazine from Berkeley.

MM: That's right. Wesley Tanner tells me that Jack Stauffacher of Greenwood Press was the printer of *Circle*.

SV: I read *Circle* magazine, and there's a real connection between what was happening among painters and writers. There was an attempt to make some kind of cohesion between painters and printers.

MM: Jonathan Williams came into the area with Jargon Books, bringing early publications of Robert Creeley and Charles Olson. Soon after he published Robert Duncan's *Letters*. In the meantime Dave Hasselwood, whom I'd known in high school and had gone to the first year of college with, joined the army in despair, feeling that he had written his last poem and was trapped in Kansas. Dave became interested in fine printing while he was stationed in Germany. I was corresponding with him from San Francisco and he decided to design and publish my *Hymns to St. Geryon* poems in Europe.

SV: What year was this?

MM: It was around 1956 or 1957. Because of the loss of the manuscripts in the mail Dave was not able to publish the *Hymns to St. Geryon*. After his discharge he moved to San Francisco. He met John Wieners and Philip Lamantia and Philip Whalen and became enthusiastic about all of our writing and decided to publish us. In the meantime, I determined to expand *Hymns to St. Geryon* and the book began to grow. While waiting for *Hymns*, Haselwood settled on publishing John Wiener's *Hotel Wentley Poems*. When he had the book printed for him it did not live up to his expectations. Dave had both a poet's and a craftsman's eye. He bought a turn-of-the-century press from Adrian Wilson, purchased typefaces, set up a shop, and began as a publisher. He became a self-taught craftsman. His next book was *Extasis*, a visionary surrealist book, by Philip Lamantia. A number of years earlier Bern Porter had published *Erotic Poems*—Lamantia's first book. Porter published a number of books, including Kenneth Patchen's *Panels for the Walls of Heaven*. There was a rich background here and Jonathan Williams was acting as an artistic enzyme, moving through and bringing books that he'd designed and others of the Black Mountain style—I mean publications brought out by Creeley and by Origin Press, and so forth. Those books had various degrees of quality of design and a lot of interest in the interaction between poem and page—with the page acting as a field for the poem. Haselwood's third book was my *Hymns to St. Geryon and Other Poems*.

SV: Let's go back to Johnathan Williams for a minute. Who was his contact point here? Was it Rexroth?

MM: Jonathan came here to see Rexroth and Patchen and to see Duncan. Duncan was in correspondence with Olson and Robert Creeley.

SV: Of course Patchen was also a typesetter. I don't know if you know that. But he typeset a number of his books.

MM: That's right. Another facet is that quite often in those days poets and magazine publishers had to take on the function of design because so many of our magazines of that period, and privately printed books, were being done through Villiers Press in London. If one edited a magazine his next step, as editor, was to design it. You could partially turn the design over to Villiers Press but you had to have a keen eye yourself if it was to have a unique and balanced appearance. That was a challenging entry into design.

SV: Go back a step for a minute, Michael.

MM: All right. Jonathan Williams published my first book in 1956, as *Jargon 20*, the twentieth book in the series. It was titled *Passage*. It was fine printing and limited to two hundred copies. It was done in two colors and hand-sewn by the Wind Hover Press in New Jersey. It was six poems. For sentimental reasons *Passage* was "published" in Big Sur. Jonathan, Joanna, and I had spent time in Big Sur with Ephraim and Rosa Doner. Doner had me to dinner with Henry Miller and Jonathan introduced me to Jeffers in passing.

SV: So the spirit of the place marked the publication. On one hand you're suggesting that printers and poets were drawn together to design books, partly out of the relationship of Villiers Press in London, because I assume it was cheaper to get things printed there; then on the other hand there's the fine press tradition in SF that people were able to take advantage of as well. I'm curious about your own work—

MM: Another factor is the independence of action engendered by the radical movement here. One would take his publication into his own hands. A fine, old tradition going back to the Romantics. Back to Shelley's private publications.

SV: A part of the spirit of what was going on was to take control of the printing and publishing process.

MM: To take control of the means of production.

SV: But in that process, it seems that a number of your own books were very attractively produced. It's not just a question of getting things done cheaply and controlling the method of production. There's a real esthetic that's involved. I mean, one has a choice between doing typeset, offset work that's just kind of ordinary, or wanting to explore fine press tradition where you make use of types and a whole tradition of printing. That's certainly not true of most books published in New York.

MM: That is one of the things people aren't aware of nowadays. They look back to the Beat movement and see that the people associated with the Beat movement and the SF Renaissance were in a ferment of action and were focused on the breakthrough—what we call the breakthrough poem. But before that, leading to that stage, in that period from 1954, the time I first came to SF, to 1957 or 1958, there's a period of three or four years in which many of us were intensely focused in on our craft. I was intent on my craft, not that I've ever let up, and I remember Philip Whalen's intent on his and Allen Ginsberg was focused on his craft, and Gary Snyder was hewing his craft. There was the continuing example of Robert Duncan's development of his skill. We were intensely involved in the structure and shaping of our poetry. We desired the same style in the presentation of it that we were putting into creating it. The two things go side by side. Then we became interested in a breakthrough. Allen broke through with "Howl." Then later he broke through again with *Kaddish*. I broke through with *Hymns to St. Geryon* and later again in my revolutionary poem *Dark Brown*—both published by Auerhahn. Along with new intensity of expression is a fascination with structure, shape, and form of poetry, and it required, in part, a new kind of book to express itself. A well-thought-out book to express a poem sculptured by the mindbody.

SV: So you really were interested in the appearance of the book, how the language was placed on the page.

MM: One of the first things I remember Kenneth Rexroth speaking about was the designer Mardersteig. In the same way that Rexroth was interested in Oriental culture, Eskimo songs, and T'ang Dynasty philosophy, he had an interest in book design. It was in the air.

SV: Dave Haselwood did finally publish *Hymns to St. Geryon*. What happened to Dave Haselwood? What happened to the Auerhahn Press?

MM: It was very alive in the form of Dave Haselwood Books until about 1965 or 1966.

SV: Did it just speak for a point in historical time, and then it was time to close down or what?

MM: Haselwood published forty pieces, including the books I've mentioned and books by William Burroughs, Jack Spicer, Lew Welch, Diane di Prima, and Meltzer, and he finally copublished, with City Lights, Ginsberg's *Indian Journals*. Also he copublished with Four Seasons Press my *Sermons of Jean Harlow and Curses of Billy the Kid*. Andrew Hoyem, when he was associated with the Auerhahn, produced Olson's essays *The Human Universe*. Alastair Johnston of Poltroon Press had just finished *A Bibliography of the Auerhahn Press* in which he writes the history of the books and what Dave Haselwood confronted in those days of publishing. You have to remember at the time Dave started in 1958 or '59, there was nothing similar. He was publishing fine print editions of new or unknown poets, and Dave did the printing himself and took on all the problems of distribution and billing that were even worse for the publishers in those days.

SV: No government grants.

MM: That's so.

SV: So are you suggesting that partly just the economics of trying to survive was too heavy?

MM: Well, there's more to it than that. The Auerhahn Press was like an extremely beautiful blossom, and it fully blossomed, and I feel it was a complete success. I think probably it did everything that Dave intended it to do. By the time that Dave retired, folded up the Auerhahn Press, and disappeared into his other interests, there were other presses publishing fine books. It was a more vigorous scene thanks to the Auerhahn. Haselwood's influence continued because he became a source for Wesley Tanner at Arif Press, and he became a source for Clifford Burke at Cranium Press. Also Graham McIntosh worked in conjunction with Dave and took impressions from the Auerhahn in a direct way. The books that Dave did of mine and Philip Whalen's and John Wiener's were of influence on the early paperback book trade. I believe the Auerhahn Press did something to improve the design of early paperbacks. When I walked into the Grove Press office in 1961 and they gave me the first copy of my *The New Book/A Book of Torture*, they told me that they'd be inspired by Auerhahn design and they'd tried to make an especially fine-looking book. You can see that after 1960 there was an improvement in the appearance of Grove Press books. As Kropotkin points out, the best immortality is to see the mirroring of your good actions in others reflecting on through generation after generation. Dave's ideals were spirit, fine design, and personal generosity.

SV: It's called redemption. What's happened to Dave?

MM: Dave's living up north in the state now. When he broke with the press, he became involved in a Gurdjieffian movement and has followed his other inclinations. He married and has a couple of children. He's living on a small farm. The vegetables he was growing were wonderful.

SV: I remember attending a reading at Norse Auditorium in 1968 where he was master of ceremonies. Allen Ginsberg and everybody were up on stage and they had a big overstuffed chair for Haselwood to sit on. He was a master. You've continued to work with people like Wesley, and now you have one book with Clifford Burke's now defunct Cranium Press.

MM: Yes, that book, as a matter of fact, was designed by Haselwood. Now there's an example of continuation. *The Mammals*, which was published by Cranium Press, was designed by Dave Haselwood years earlier.

SV: You mentioned the sense of spirit that pervaded the anarchists and the early printers of the fifties and maybe from there go on to what you sense is occurring today. There was the influence of the anarchists in the late forties and fifties. There was also an atmosphere here which was anti-Eastern in the sense that people weren't going to be determined by corporate lives in New York. There was a sense that you could shape your own life out of what you could provide from your own self and from the people that you worked with.

MM: The feeling here was not anti-Eastern, but there was, and is, a major difference between the West Coast and the East Coast and it was even more pronounced in the fifties. Northern California was in the midst of visible nature and the Eastern urban centers were centered in what was then, as it is today, an industrial sprawl. There was the industrial basket, so to speak, of cinders and concrete and machine construction and old politics and overpopulation on the East Coast, but in San Francisco we find that the city is the center of spokes that lead to many aspects of California nature. From San Francisco you can go to Mount Tamalpais, to Mount Diablo, you can go to the Sierras, you can go to the desert, you can go to the Valley, you can go to the foothills, and you can go to the southern or northern California coast. San Francisco is in proximity to Seattle and to Los Angeles and San Diego, all of which are ports to the Orient. When you came to the West Coast in the fifties you were, if anything, more sharply aware of the proximity of the

Orient than you are today when the Orient has made some impression on the East Coast also. When you came to San Francisco in those days you were aware of the Pacific Ocean, and the Pacific Rim, and the way it was edged with chaparral and redwoods. With nature visible there is an entirely different concept of self. The concept of self in a city of nine million is very different from one's self-image in a city of 500,000 with immediate access to deserts and the sight of deer walking through oceanside meadows.

SV: Along with that there was also the requirement of creating a vocabulary, a new language that would work here. There were the precedents of people like Rexroth, all the way back to Joaquin Miller but at the same time you had to seek out a definition that would work in this new space. Was that part of the angst that was present? There was a kind of romantic pleasure in coming to the West and having all of these—Mount Tam, the Sierras—at the same time. Didn't it present some kind of terror combined with the excitement?

MM: A terror? No. But there were fierce, wild, alien places. And we were all aware of them.

SV: For example, I heard descriptions by easterners of the first trip they take down the coast of Big Sur.

MM: I wasn't an easterner. I was born in Kansas. You were born in Port Richmond, Steve, so you're a westerner. Gary Snyder was born in San Francisco, Robert Duncan was born in Oakland. I didn't feel terror of nature. I was with Jack Kerouac when he spent some time in Lawrence Ferlinghetti's cabin in Big Sur. Jack was in a state of terror sometimes but it was not from nature as much as from a dark night of the soul abetted by the horrors of drinking.

SV: Maybe terror's the wrong word.

MM: Not entirely.

SV: In truth, you worked closely with a number of biologists, people in the life sciences.

MM: Yes, many of my friends of this period were people in the sciences. Sterling Bunnell, a visionary biologist, has had a lasting influence on my thinking.

SV: It's not very often that someone's able to get attention as both a poet and a playwright. I'm curious—do you see them, not as simultaneous, but as connected events, or did you move from poetry into plays because you felt poems weren't working on a certain level that you thought a play could. How do you see the connection?

MM: I find that writing poetry and writing theater are complementary. They don't compete with each other. They use separate parts of the ego. The parts of the ego that creates poetry is a sensitive organ that almost wishes to protect itself through the creation of art. And the part of the self that writes theater is a probe that likes to deal with projections of reality. So I find that the two are complementary, and as I write theater, I write more poetry and as I write more poetry, I write theater.

They mutually reinforce each other without feeding on the same interface of creativity. Lately I've been called a poet/playwright so often I've begun to accept the tag, but I think of myself as a poet.

SV: You suggest there are differences in what can happen to language on the page, language spoken, and language as theater.

MM: Yes, I don't think theater is meant to be read. We read plays because a play that we want to see is not being performed. But one of the things poets often ask me, when they write their first play, is where they can get it published. I say, don't get it published, get it performed. It doesn't matter on the page. It doesn't really live on the page. The page is like the DNA. You pass it around to theaters and you hope it turns into RNA and you can have an organism—a live play.

SV: How do you want the poem to work on the page? I hesitate to use the word "work" because of several connotations.

MM: How do you want it to play on the page?

SV: Dance on the page. These are all physical images and it seems that somehow just the fact of the page, the print on the page, betrays the physical intentions of what is often being indicated in the poems. I think perhaps in the theater there is a greater field of expression possible. One of the excitements, or one of the advantages of working with local publishing people, especially people who have access to various types and have a good design imagination, is that you can get a poem out on the page in a way that amplifies the spirit with which it was originally spoken. You can give the words their play.

MM: Let me clarify a point. Theater is not a matter of words. When I say that a play of mine is a poem, I don't mean that the words make up a poem. If you look at the words in a play of mine done here last year, *The Grabbing of the Fairy* (I consider it one of my finest poems), the words on the page are silly. The play is three naked girls with long, furry tails discussing the nature of reality in ritualized combats with one another while an apparition in the form of a giant caterpillar busts through the wall. The reason that the words of the play are not a poem is that in theater it is the-organism-in-action of the play that is a poem. The theater poem is the bodies in action, the movement of the characters, their rites, their speeches, their songs, their conflicts are the poem. Not the words. The words are a part of it. My play

The Beard is a poem because Billy the Kid and Jean Harlow are in conflict about the nature of what is divine. The words they use join with the shape of the actions.

SV: Then we see words in relationship to your body in the process of creation as a. . . .

MM: I see my poems as extensions of my physical body. That's the doctrine that I learned from the abstract expressionist painters. Jackson Pollock and Clyfford Still are painting spiritual, autobiographical extensions. My poems, although they're far from abstract, expressionist poems (are very concrete poems generally) are extensions of my body. In theater you have an entirely different situation. The poem in the theater is the play that's presenting itself in its enaction—as it happens on stage. The director is the RNA and the actors are the proteins; the designers are the Golgi bodies; the tech people are the mitochondria—however you want to see it in a biological metaphor. A play is a real physical body that exists for an hour or two in real time and space. It comes together each night that it's performed, and it exists and dances and sings in the symbiotic body that it is. It's a real and true spiritual occasion. Afterwards it's collapsed, folded up, and the scenes are put away and it never quite exists the same again, and yet somebody, sooner or later, takes out the pattern that the poet/playwright made and they revive the play.

SV: Let me go back a second to the poem on the page. When you place the poem on the page, how do you want it to be heard? What do you want to occur? How do you want me to experience it?

MM: Twenty-five years ago, there was little chance of the reader of the poem ever hearing the poet. Nowadays there's a good chance that you have either heard the poet reading or have seen a videotape or heard a recording of the poet.

SV: I've been reading your poems for the last few days and because I've heard you read a lot, I do hear your voice as I read. It's a larger event than if I'd only experienced it on the page.

MM: I like it most when I've read a poet's poems and then hear the poet. I love the experience of reading the poems and then having the sound corrected, tuned in to the poet's voice.

SV: How much was Dylan Thomas an influence?

MM: Thomas was a potent influence on people of my generation. Many people were introduced to poetry by Thomas's recordings. Thomas's readings are more beautiful than the poems themselves. The style of Thomas as a singer enhances the limitations of the poems themselves.

SV: I get the feeling that Thomas's readings in this country in the fifties were a really large influence on the whole.

MM: They were. Bob Zimmerman changed his name to Bob Dylan—a very clear statement.

SV: I want to go back to the question of the poem on the page—of how you write the poem, of how it initially occurs, and of how you choose the structures that you use. I've noticed that in your poems there's a symmetry involved.

MM: Yes, the poems are on a center axis so they look like a little whirlwind or a gyre. They have the bilateral symmetry of an organism. I write the poems that way. I just wrote a play in verse and the entire play is accurately centered in the manuscript. It happens that way in both handwriting and typewriter composition. The style answers a need. There are numerous reasons why I break a line, and the centered poem has answered the root requirements. I've come to intuitively thin in terms of the centered line. We are centered organisms, in the sense that we're bilaterally symmetrical, so poems come out that way with ease and naturalness. Since writing my long poem *Antechamber*, which will be published this spring by New Directions my poems have begun a dance on the page. They dance away from the center axis. And as I write poems now that are dancing around the center axis, I find they are a biological extension of my new body condition. As I write them they appear as a dance in the manuscript. That does not mean that I do not learn from other people. In the case of *Antechamber*, which whirls around the center axis but is not fixed on the center axis, I was helped by Maria Epes. When she published it in limited edition as a Poythress Press book, she set up some changes allowing more than the several axes that I was suing. I was immediately taken with the beautiful placement on the page. It increased the dance of the words and I accepted the grace of her sensibility. It opened me to new poems that are whirling or dancing about the center axis. Originally, in the fifties, my poems were only roughly centered and swayed back and forth on the page. In the Auerhahn publication of *Hymns to St. Geryon and Other Poems*, you'll find that they're not strictly centered on the page, but they're swirling, as they go down the page, from side to side. It's as if they're drunk, mad, impetuous creatures. I realized after we began to be anthologized and appear in commercial books, that I could never get the patience that I'd had from Auerhahn Press. I decided to suspend poems on the center axis or else the future would do bizarre things to the poems in trying to approximate their swirl and the poems would be bastardized. I went to a firm center axis and within a few years I was thinking on a centered axis. Finally, whole verse dramas come out precisely on the center. I find that the poem is so much where I am at because the best of my thinking is done through poetry. I don't write a poem and then center it. It comes out centered and if it doesn't come out centered I'll publish it uncentered. That doesn't mean that I don't make changes, corrections, or variations.

SV: So when you're writing you're actively responding to this sense of the axes?

MM: Yes, it's a physical response, a very pleasurable response. It enables me to feel even more strongly the awareness that I think—as Einstein said that we all do—with our bodies, not merely with our brains.

In *Antechamber* I was using numerous axes. She opened some additional axes that I hadn't seen before. She gave her intuitive understanding of the steps of the dance on the page. As the inventor of the dance, I was restricted by past concepts. I had held myself back. Wesley Tanner has been a great help to me as a friend and as a gifted designer. Many times I've had a typographical problem and gone to Tanner for advice. *How will I deal with this use of capitals? With this line of noncapitals? Or, How far can a line go before I must break it in its publication?* Often I've gone to printers and many times seen printers do very beautiful things for me. Graham McIntosh took my poem *The Surge* and separated out its stanzaic patterns and published it as a small book for Frontier Press. It's not a way that I'll continue to publish *The Surge*, but it's a way that I've enjoyed.

SV: You once suggested that I look at that Dover Press art book publication of Ernst Haeckel's *Art Forms in Nature*. It's mainly sea creatures.

MM: Yes. Haeckel's primary study was of free-swimming jellyfish which are known as medusas. His general field was evolution and phylogeny. He was a popularizer of Evolution.

SV: The symmetry of the creature he portrays in his drawings is wonderful.

MM: Haeckel is a visionary like William Blake. They are at opposite ends of the nineteenth century. Haeckel is at the *fin de siècle* and at the other end there is Blake dying in 1827. Blake did drawings of real angels of the imagination and Haeckel did angelic drawings of real living beings. Haeckel's were jellyfish resembling protoplasm temples and Blake's were spirits of his own perceptions.

SV: That's what you do in your work—connect with both the angels of the imagination and a radiant sense of the actual.

MM: That's a beautiful way to say it.

SV: I'm struck going through your plays with the way they seem to come from a very futuristic place.

MM: My plays are in some cases more understandably complete organisms than my poems. That does not mean any dissatisfaction with the poems, but I want the poems to be living creatures like medusas broken away from a colony and swimming away in the waves—as if I was the colony and the poem was one of my heads, moving to find a new life of its own—to give pleasure, or awareness, or perception to another consciousness out there in that sea of the universe. Sometimes when I see a little play, like *The Grabbing of the Fairy*, on the stage, I say, "There! Now everyone can see that's an organism!" It's on a shelf which we call a stage, and it's moving around in the light and it's dancing and singing. Surely no one can deny that is an organism—except, of course, the drama critics who will not only deny that it's an organism but give me a moral lecture.

SV: Why do they deny that it's an actual organism?

MM: They begin by denying it is a play because it's not like Clifford Odets or Eugene O'Neill, which is the last thing I want it to be like. The dramas that I value are poetry. I don't enjoy "traditional" recent theater. I have a strong feeling for the theater of Aristophanes, the Greek comic poet, the theater of John Ford, John Webster, Shakespeare, Federico García Lorca, Artaud, Genet, or Samuel Beckett and others such as the Japanese Zeami, Yeats, or Sophocles. There are wide snowy continents between Arthur Miller and Aristophanes.

SV: Let's go back again to Blake and Haeckel. It seems to me that your poetry, not always but sometimes, is in contact with the immediate universe. If you're in a situation you respond to it.

MM: I'm an atheist but I have the highest respect for the religious experience. I've come to realize that the entire universe itself, and all the universes and all the dimensions of the universe that any of us can conceive of or that may exist or may not exist—all of it, as Whitehead saw it, is the Messiah, and that we only have our redemption, our freedom, our continuation, and our death in contacting, in touching, rubbing against, brushing against, being part of, and expressing ourselves in, and of, the universe. It is all what is called the *Tathagata*. All the *dharmadhatu* is the Messiah. Our contact with it both creates it and expresses it. Or, as Whitehead suggests: we're all moments of novelty in the universe. At any given point we are the universe's awareness of itself. The universe is the absolute nothingness of real Buddha stuff—that's what I believe.

SV: So your poems are moments of novelty.

MM: They're proportionless bagatelles of experience. I'm looking at a buttercup or by holding a rock in my hand, or in going for a run on the beach, or in walking on Mount Tam and feeling the sun on my back, and in looking at the deer who no longer even bothers to run—I feel myself. That's what I write about.

SV: Well, when people go to your plays, like *The Grabbing of the Fairy*, and say, I've never seen anything like this, give me back my Eugene O'Neill or my Arthur Miller, what are the consequences of the organism that you've filled up on stage? You speak of it as though it's real. It is real and at the same time there are always people out here who will ignore, or give you lectures, saying that it isn't real. . . .

MM: There are some people who love it.

SV: Do you see yourself as a visionary in the sense that the images that you're generating will be, twenty years from now, as current as some images that were created in the twenties by the Dadaists and were considered totally bizarre?

MM: That's possible. The most beautiful compliment I've had was on some of my *Gargoyle Cartoon* plays. Someone came to me and said that they felt when they were seeing the *Cartoons* that they were enjoying classics of the future. I was enormously touched. I've had good luck with directors. They must be seers. My work with John Lion has been one of the best experiences. Having my *General Gorgeous* done at ACT with Ed Hastings as director is a stroke of luck. If you wrote a play and saw it produced, you'd understand why the theater was sacred to Dionysus. It is like the joy of drunkenness to not only create your hallucinations but to turn them into living organisms dancing and prancing and laughing and singing upon the stage. You sit in the audience with other people watching with wonder and delight, shock and horror going through your nervous system. It's a rare and beautiful gift and it is like being the universe. You and I, as organisms, are expressions of the substrate that we walk upon, and the substrate is enormously more complex than we can conceive of because we only think in terms of matter, and not-matter, and time, and space, and light, and dark. It's much, much more complicated than that. That's only the surface of it—as we come out into being as organisms expressing the substrate. On having a play, that's a poem, come out of yourself, you kid yourself, you say you're expressing yourself and there it is, that you're watching it, and that you're privileged to sit in the audience and watch your hallucinations. But *in fact* it comes from much further back, deeper than that. The universe reached through itself to present you as a "moment of novelty." And then the universe, in all of its reason and unreason, has reached through you—and through those other people—and plunked down a living organism on stage. You're there laughing at it, and singing with it, and enchanted with it, thinking that it's yours—but, on the other hand you know that the universe's hand reached through you, far, far, far, farther back than you ever dreamed, and the manifestation of the play in terms of your hallucinations and authorship was merely a convenience that the universe bothered with.

SV: So you don't believe in the Messiah?

MM: I believe it's the universe, which by the way, is Haeckel's view. He called it Monism. It's a lot like Hua-Yen Buddhism.

SV: Well, tell us what the hand is going to bring us after the turn of the year.

MM: The hand is going to lay out on the stage of the Julian Theatre a play called *Goethe: Ein Fragment*. It is about an imaginary life of Goethe, in which Goethe is approached by Mephistopheles with the proposition that he write a play on a Faust theme.

SV: Is there a printer in the play?

MM: There are two guillotine makers in the play, and they operate a piece of their machinery.

A Conversation with Michael McClure

Kevin Power / 1978

From *Spanner* 16 (December 1978): 122–37. Subsequently appeared in *Where You're At: Poetics and Visual Art* by Kevin Power (Berkeley: Poltroon Press, 2011), 47–67. Published here courtesy of Poltroon Press.

Kevin Power: Could you begin by talking about the nature of the exchanges between poet and painter in San Francisco in the fifties and sixties?

Michael McClure: Well, around 1954 Joanne and I moved up to Telegraph Hill. We lived in Genoa Platz, an alley on the slopes of the hill; a half a block below was Grant Avenue, and right around the corner was a bar called *The Place*. It's a bar that doesn't exist now, but it was famous for us as a "beat" bar before the word "beat" had come around. We used to go down there at night and have a glass of wine, or a schooner of beer, or whatever, and sit there and admire the shows of paintings that they had. Knut Stiles must have been the bartender at that time, or else he was setting up the shows. One of the first shows I remember was Jay de Feo's incredible postexistentialist, post–abstract expressionist gouaches. They were just beautifully rich black poster paint squiggled onto a luscious background of grey with maybe a dot of red on it, and they'd just be thumbtacked onto the wall with maybe a piece of plastic over them.

KP: These were rotating shows that gave local artists a chance to show their work?

MM: Yeah, I remember a show of Bob La Vigne, another show of gouaches. They were flower paintings, and he'd called it *Torture Garden* or something like that. Each one was a gouache on brown paper with a type of flower on it and a beautiful poem by Allen Ginsberg in his pre-"Howl" style. In those days many people seemed to be working on brown paper.

KP: Was that a result of economics like the use of commercial paints by Pollock, Kline, etc.?

MM: It's economics and style.

KP: So, *The Place* was a meeting place for poets and painters. Who did you meet there?

MM: Well, I didn't know many people at that time in 1959. I'd just met Robert Duncan. I was in his class at State; I also knew Paul Cox.

KP: This was just after you'd come to take those classes from Rothko and Still?

MM: Yeah, and they weren't there. Actually, I'd come because Joanna had just moved out here. She'd left her husband and I was pursuing her, and I used the classes with Rothko and Still as some kind of justification. I'd seen the catalogues of their work in the preceding year when they were still here, so I thought I'd be able to take classes from them and immerse myself in the philosophy of abstract expressionism.

KP: What other connections were there at that time?

MM: Well, around 1957 we moved into Harry Jacobs's place on Sacramento Street. He'd gone off to Mallorca. I can't recall if he went with Robert and Jess. So we had paintings by Jess that he'd given us and paintings by Harry Jacobs and Ralph Ducasse hanging all over the walls. We then moved to what today would be called a commune with Ronnie Bladen, one of the original contributors of *Ark* magazine. We each had a floor or a suite in a very large house. From there we moved to a building on Fillmore Street. It was again a painter's house where I was the only writer. There was a pet shop below us and the two enormous upper floors on both sides of the building were studios. Sonia Gechtoff, who was a really well-known abstract expressionist at that time, and her husband James Kelly lived in one of the flats. This flat was later to be taken over by Joan and Phil Brown. Above them lived Ed Moses and Craig Kauffman and below them lived Jay de Feo and Wally Hedrick. While I'm talking about this period let me also take a step back a couple of years to the time of the Six Gallery for another instance of the connections between the poets and the painters. During the readings at the Six Gallery there were works of Fred Martin on stage. If you ever hear a tape of that you'll catch Rexroth saying, "It looks like furniture for a Japanese dwarf," and he's referring to those sculptures of Fred Martin's that were made out of orange or apple crates that had been altered and covered in bunting and then dipped in plaster of Paris. I thought they were extraordinarily interesting pieces. Some of the others also connected with the Six Gallery were Jay de Feo, Wally Hedrick, and James Weeks, who was one of the earliest figurative painters but still had abstract expressionist drips on his figures. The Six Gallery had previously been known as the Ubu Gallery and Robert Duncan had been the manager. The last poetry reading given there before our reading of the Six Poets of the Six Gallery when Allen read "Howl" for the first time was a truly beautiful reading by Robert of *Faust Foutu*. I'd been a participant in that reading and Wally Hedrick wanted to arrange another one. He stopped me in the street and asked me if I could organize it. I met Allen Ginsberg at a party for W. H. Auden and he asked me what I was up to. I told him I was very busy and asked him if he could set up the reading. So there was a real swirl of interaction at that time.

KP: What were the ideas that initially so attracted you to the painters? Were they saying things in advance of the poets at that time?

MM: I'd always been attracted by painting, especially at that time by surrealist and Dada work. I think it's the evident power of the action and iconography that attracted me, the fact they're blended together. This was something that was very close to me in the writing of poetry, although I was attracted to painting even before I knew I was writing poetry. As a matter of fact I was reciting poetry in the form of word games but I hadn't realized it was poetry and if someone had asked me I would have said "no." I was, however, very immersed in looking at painting and studying it. I was fascinated by Dada and surrealism and particularly with contemporary painting that was directly related to an interest in natural history, through anthropology or archeology. In other words from natural history into man as animal, into man as an animal actor, in a definite way, because that's a basic, primitive, direct, primeval, vital way of acting, as a typewriter is too, or a pen, or chipping a flint or scratching periods of lunar progression on a bone—it's all the same.

KP: And the actual processes that some of the painters were using had that direct link back into the primitive, as in Gottlieb's pictographs or into the biological as with Stamos.

MM: Yes that's particularly the case with the abstract expressionists. They take you back into the mammalian again, into the kind of thing that very early man was doing. With them you're grasping, in one of the most blunt, acute, and Faustian ways, for the very rites of magic or science of alchemy or chemistry. You're at that fundament again. But let me go back to my first year at College at Wichita in 1950. I was, then, paying a lot of attention to surrealism and wanting to see it. Bruce Conner was a friend of mine and he took me to see the work of the intrasubjectivists at the Kootz Gallery. He was included in that group which consisted of Motherwell, Tomlin, Baziotes, Kline, and Gottlieb.

KP: The biomorphics, in fact.

MM: Yeah. Well, Bruce got me off into that and it was very easy to go straight from there to Pollock. I also got very involved in watching Bruce paint since he was going from doing the most incredibly beautiful "modern" art to looser abstract forms. He was doing jewellike canvases of great splendor and beauty, like Chagall, Modigliani, or Klee.

KP: Were you also reading a lot of surrealist literature at this time?

MM: I don't know. I was certainly reading a lot of Sartre at that time. I remember reading *Nausea* but I was also just as involved in the jazz world. Bebop had been driven out of Kansas City by the police and had moved into the area where we were. So I was also listening to a lot of Parker, Monk, and Powell. Anyway, I planned this trip with Bruce Conner to New York in the summer before I left Wichita to go to the University of Arizona. We wanted to go up and look at the paintings, but we hadn't realized that most of the galleries are closed in the summer. On top of that most people we wanted to see weren't being collected in the museums. We were both particularly interested in Motherwell, who really operates with the unconscious processes and has the deliberate French quality that we liked so much.

KP: I noticed that Creeley picked out for particular mention your "intellective kinship" with Motherwell.

MM: Yes, I liked that beautiful series he did called *Poets* and that superb series of pieces on Lorca. And I still like it. I've recently seen a show of his sumi work that greatly impressed me.

KP: I guess you'd read his *Dada Painters and Poets* by then? And also such magazines as *Tiger's Eye* and *It is*?

MM: Well, I'd read all the books that Motherwell had edited in the Museum of Modern Art series, as well as the *Tiger's Eye* magazine in particular. I bought a lot of those that I didn't have on that trip. I'd gone from reading Sartre to reading Celine, but I was reading everything that came my way.

KP: Were there any qualities in Motherwell's work that particularly impressed you and seemed relevant to your own writing needs?

MM: I think maybe the ebullience and the swiftness, and also that kind of willingness to do it and be damned, to throw it away if it wasn't right and love it if it was. To go back again to this trip to New York, what happened as far as Motherwell was concerned was that I looked in the phone book, found his name, and phoned him. I told him that I was with a friend of mine from Wichita and that we'd come to New York to see his work, and he said, "Well, come right over." I went back and told Bruce and his eyes opened very wide since it was a case of out and out hero worship on our part. We thought Motherwell was really *it* and he was. I'll never forget it because we went over there and he had opened a good bottle of wine and took us on a tour of his work and of his collection. He had little miniature paintings by Yves Tanguy that were like an inch high and two inches long and full of astonishing detail. I still cherish that memory. Then there's another story from those days. When we were living on Filmore over Jay de Feo and Wally Hedrick, the house was always full of parties and endless numbers of people from de Kooning to Bischoff. I came upstairs one day and found a drunken man lying halfway up the steps. I took him up to my apartment to sober him up a little. He was a very distinguished looking man. I didn't know who he was, but he appeared so sadly drunk. He liked my daughter a lot, apparently he had a daughter the same age. He was showing her how to make clay animals, they had all these pieces of sculpture all over the place. I went in and it all looked fine. He was sobering up so we gave him some coffee. He left soon after and later on Jay de Feo came in and asked me if I'd seen "Bill." I said, "Yes," and she answered, "Well, that was Bill de Kooning." I looked down and all the clay animals had been put back into the ball of clay.

KP: Had Herms or Berman arrived in San Francisco by then?

MM: Yeah, they'd already moved up, and Bruce some time before that around 1956, I guess. Bruce had thought up an idea of starting a pre-Raphaelite Brotherhood movement again and of getting a bunch of people to sign P.R.B. at the bottom of their paintings, but instead of that he set up the Rat Bastards Protective Association and as a fait accompli announced to everybody that they'd just become members of it. The members as far as I can remember were Jay, Wally Hedrick, myself, the Browns, Manuel Neri, Bruce, and some others I no longer recall.

KP: A kind of surreal get together?

MM: Right. I believe that we had a show at the Spatsa Eye Gallery, run by Dimitri Grachis, and later I had a one-man show down there of things I was doing. Then in 1958-59 Billy Jahrmarkt opened up the Batman Gallery where we had the Gang Bang Show that had all of us in it.

KP: He also did the cover for *Rare Angel*.

MM: Yeah, that's right.

KP: How did you get involved in *Semina* and what were the intentions behind that magazine?

MM: One of the issues consisted of my *Peyote Poem*, and you read Crick confirming what I said in that. The God of Foxes in that poem, by the way, is George Herms. I knew it as soon as he walked into the room for the first time. Wally sent me the first *Semina* and I wrote back a letter which he thought was very funny saying: "Dear Mr. Walter Berman, I would like to contribute to your magazine . . ." I thought *Semina* was a neat effort.

KP: Did Berman have any kind of specific program?

MM: Yes, he wanted to make a packet. It's an assemblage idea. He's really making a spiritual bundle. I don't think he ever thought of this but it's very much like an American Indian practice of making a medicine bundle. He wants to get Orson Welles, Hesse, Jean Cocteau, Wally Hedrick, Wallace Berman, Michael McClure, George Herms, David Meltzer, etc., all into one spirit bundle and then put them into a pouch and that's it. It's as if that's the only way you can get the perfect taste of things. One of these issues was completely taken up by a twenty-line poem of mine, it was in the envelope and the cover was done by Wally. It's a poem on the J. F. K. assassination, the shooting of Lee Harvey Oswald in fact. So there again you have the magazine pouch idea. It looks slick on top like Cocteau or surrealism but when you start to think about it, it's very ancient and very mammalian. I don't mean ancient in the sense that it's got lichen growing all over it, but ancient in the sense that it's got muscles and blood.

KP: What was Berman's interest in the poets?

MM: I don't know where his sensitivity to poets came, perhaps through Cocteau. He was also a mentor to David Meltzer.

KP: Yes. Meltzer has acknowledged that Berman put him in touch with a lot of useful texts.

MM: Then there's the same kind of cabbalistic pressures behind them. Herms also came out of the same kind of jazz milieu that both I and Meltzer were into.

KP: What was it that appealed to you about Herms's work? I notice that he did the set for the production of *Blossom* in New York and a poster for it when it was done here.

MM: I first met George in about 1957. I was high on peyote and as I said recognized him as the God of Foxes, and then I also found that he was very much a Lorca figure. I mean in the sense that he juxtaposes images that are clear and lovely with others that have the rich patina of age, so that you find, for example, a toy train side by side with a velvet cushion side by side with a palm leaf. It's not jasmine and aloes in plastic but it's the same vocabulary of sensory perception that you find in Lorca.

KP: I remember that catalogue introduction for a show of his that you did where you mention his creating new spirit constellations by contrasting sensory images and modes, and that the materials he uses have this wealth of associations going right back to their origin.

MM: That again is a Lorcian quality. Whereas I think of Bruce Conner in a different way as coming out of a very American thing, out of Marin and Marsden Hartley and Dove, and at the same time as coming out of the Renaissance. I mean he comes out of Masaccio as much as he does Marsden Hartley. He's really one of the great painters of this century and I think we'll see this in the retrospective he's having next year. He quit painting ten years ago but has started up again recently. Most of his work is in private collections so nothing is really lost.

KP: What was in the Conner's film he did on you?

MM: He did a great portrait of me but it was stolen. In one fell swoop I lost a play dedicated to LeRoi Jones and Bruce's film portrait of me, both prints of it, and several films of Brakhage's. Conner took all my childhood portraits and filmed them. Then he took some footage of me, and finally edited them altogether. It was quite some loss; it was stolen from my office in Haight Ashbury—I hope it'll turn up again some time.

KP: Let me go back again to Herms's set for *Blossom*. What was that like?

MM: I didn't have anything to do with that, aside from applauding the accuracy of it. Diane di Prima and Alan Marlowe were then running the New York Poet's Theater and they got George Herms to go to New York and work as their set designer. George is wonderful in the theater because not only in his work so moody and so rich, but he can work so swiftly that he can put things together in a few days. I didn't ever see the sets, only photos of them, and as a matter of fact only one little piece of the set. At that time we were all so poor that I couldn't have gone to New York to see the play.

KP: You also used his work in *The Beard*, as a kind of extension of the play into the gallery.

MM: Yeah, we did that here in San Francisco, and then in LA. George was able to put together a larger and more dramatic show.

KP: Did that relate to the play in any specific way?

MM: Oh I don't think I saw any great relationship of it to the play. By that time the Assemblage movement was in full swing and I was seeing everything in terms of a spiritual occasion. As far as I was concerned these were not art movements but spiritual occasions, and they opened up your feelings to a whole new area just as abstract expressionism had done. The Assemblage thing meant that you walked down the street and saw garbage cans, pop bottles and a pillow all in a new way. You could begin to see the inner relationship, new constructs, new gestalts. I was seeing things in those terms at that time and George's work was very appropriate.

KP: Was it the confusion of origins in these discarded materials or objects that so appealed to you? The Assemblage movement was opening up the variety of possibilities of meanings?

MM: I think it was more like trying to see it without its origins but now I like to look at things with their origins. At that time it was like a miniature panorama of what it was. I think that then we were trying to get into the *now* and now there's too much *now*. Now "now" is the word of the middle class, "Hey, man, let's live in the now!" It's not Norman Mailer saying it anymore, it's the grocer.

KP: Did you go to Herms's houseboat at all?

MM: Oh yeah, at Larkspur Flats.

KP: And they made that into a kind of environment?

MM: Very much so, and Kirby Doyle lived up the hill, overlooking it from a Redwood grove.

KP: Was there anything that you could take over into your own writing from the Assemblage movement?

MM: *Fleas* are assemblages in one sense. The whole series of 250 are a kind of mammoth Sistine doodle assemblage.

KP: And X's?

MM: I think so, but, by that time, one had been influenced by so many things that it's difficult to say exactly what was an influence. It's you along with a million other things and it's difficult to find the right kind of emphasis. The wonderful thing that happened to all of us, after we'd got together as a result of that Six Gallery reading was that we got to know each other and knock each other's edges off so that we weren't afraid of saying exactly what we thought. And this was at a time when everybody was afraid to acknowledge that anything had influenced them. I mean, just imagine people like Theodore Roethke or Wilbur saying that they were influenced by anyone, not on your life; they were too important to be influenced. They weren't chumps like Goethe or Shelley or Shakespeare who were influenced by everything in sight. Like them, the original creators, the discoverers, we took everything, went on every ride we could go on. We wanted it all.

KP: Were there any other aspects of the Assemblage movement that interested you?

MM: Well, in theater some people distinguish between incident and event. Incident is when somebody is discussing knocking over a martini glass; an event is when a birth, a death, a marriage, a divorce, an apotheosis either takes place or is conversed about. So there's incident and event in life and in painting too. One of the things that Herms and Conners did was to see the event. Bruce would see the event in these naked pin-up girls which you saw in the mags at that time and he'd put them into a context with a mirror and a plum and it would take on all these new aspects. Or George would take a palm leaf which is certainly an incident and not an event, and contrast it with a toy locomotive so that it became an event.

KP: And that's more than just a surreal juxtaposition, there's something else going on there?

MM: Yeah. All those guys were operating with subtle kinds of feedback. La Vigne was doing assemblages of this type as well but on the superhuman scale.

KP: Did they have any impact on your tendency to reduce towards high-energy blocks? I was thinking of *The Beard* where you cut down both thematically and linguistically to hard blocks that push against each other.

MM: I can see what you mean but I don't think I ever talked to anyone about my work in any specific sense. We had a tendency not to talk about work, although I did talk a lot to Bruce.

KP: Could we talk a little about your interest in Pollock. Was your affinity with him in terms of a parallel "spiritual autobiography"?

MM: Is that one of the Rosenberg Greenberg terms? It must be one of them that pointed that out. It's especially evident in Still and Pollock.

KP: That physical involvement with their work seems close to your own concerns?

MM: Let me approach that from a different tack. When I found Olson's "Projective Verse," it took me quite a while to work out what Olson was doing. I got to figure it around 1955–56, and felt that I'd understood his concept of field. Then a couple of years later I realized that the projective verse ideas could be applied to a new verse drama as in *Blossom* and as in *!The Feast!*. I saw that I could make a really athletic use of it, and by that time it had all come together with Pollock who was also physically demonstrating it. Clyfford Still is more of an ideal, a straightforward desire not to present oneself as one isn't. Mind you, I don't know him but I hope to when his show opens here. He's just given twenty-eight paintings to the museum. Then, also, the tragedy of Pollock fascinated me. It's very romantic. Just as he really made it, just as those faces started coming out of the paintings, or the subject matter started to come back in so that you could find hands, arms, legs, the whole body swirling around there again, he suddenly pulled back from it and did a few other pieces. Then bang, the death.

KP: What was the painting you were referring to in your "Ode to Pollock"?

MM: "Guardians of the Secret," it's very much like the She-Wolf, it's from that same period. I just hope the museum has still got that one; they traded an incredible early Rothko from his surreal period for a later color wash!

KP: You could actually see in the big retrospective of Rothko's work, his progression down to that black and grey area, introverted death space.

MM: I met Rothko a few years before his death. I think of *Ghost Tantras* as being a book he could really have appreciated visually on the page.

KP: How do you organize the shape on the page? Do you break the line in favor of overall shape?

MM: No, it's all one thing. I can tell after the poem is done if it's the wrong shape, and if it's the wrong shape it's not a good poem. I don't work visually in any conscious fashion. I don't go through it afterwards and reshape. I thought once that I'd found seven rules for the line that were personal but now there are a great many more. I once made an analysis of their structural feedback.

KP: The poem, then, finds its correct shape or imposes it.

MM: Yeah, in my case that's the way, and in some of Gary Snyder's poems the same process appears to be going on, and of course in Olson and Duncan.

KP: Olson didn't appear to have any particular concern with painting although projective verse is obviously close theoretically to abstract expressionism.

MM: But, of course, at Black Mountain, it was all there. It's hard to say, people deal with an area verbally that's significant for them but at the same time there are often many more areas that are just as significant for them as those being verbalized but one will avert from the verbalization in those areas. Sometimes this may include *the* area of import for the person. I'm not talking about something psychological. I'm saying that it's because it's an area that's linked up with other areas in a specific way, like physiologically, that it never gets verbalized. The fact that it doesn't get verbalized doesn't mean that it isn't important, we live by many things we don't verbalize. So the fact that Charles didn't write about them doesn't really mean much.

KP: He took place in the Happenings and that supports what you're saying. Yet it's strange he wrote nothing direct about painting, especially since he managed so successfully to get the right people in the right place at the right time.

MM: That's for sure!

KP: I wondered if you felt that any of the following concerns of Pollock parallel your own defining of a poetic? I was thinking specifically of such things as technique being the result of need, the emphasis given to organic intensity and energy and motion made visible, or the notion that new needs demand new techniques?

MM: I think you're probably right to draw those parallels, but I find it's so easy to get confused in talking too closely about those areas.

KP: When one looks at the *Book of Torture* and at one of your latest books, *Rare Angel*, there is a remarkable consistency both in your concerns and in the way you've expressed yourself. There's now a greater refinement and a deeper push but the same concentration on bursts of energy. In that sense abstract expressionism has been a continuously formative parallel.

MM: I think you're right. One of the things that might be obvious, although I haven't seen anyone pick up on it, was that the spelling mistakes and weirdnesses of *Book of Torture* were intentionally left in and are like the drips in abstract expressionism. Somehow that seems to have escaped many people. It was like Conner, Rauschenberg, or Pollock. It was like saying, "Well, why not!!" It was just as if I was doing it against the wall, as if my mind was thrown against the wall while I was doing it. My mind was like a plum thrown against a white clapboard wall.

KP: Like Pollock's acceptance of what he did. How were these accidents absorbed into the poem?

MM: Well for example, "Rant Block" was written like a Beethoven String Quartet. I made study after study for that poem, and then I did studies for many of the individual stanzas, four or five variations that I even gave to people as poems. Bit by bit I got the parts right and then I sat down and did the whole poem from beginning to end, referring to the studies, of course, but working right through. Most of the poems in there, however, are written like right out of the typewriter, and those were the errors, as I've mentioned, that I kept in. And to be totally honest, it was out of hands, I was so crazed when I wrote those poems and when they came out that I didn't really have much control over them. To get them between covers, to get them to the publisher and see them come out as a book was about all I could manage.

KP: What about the actual finishing of the poem. Was that similar to abstract expressionist principles? Did you simply know the poem had finished when it came to an end, when you'd followed the process through as it were?

MM: No, finishing a poem is a pretty complicated process, even if you're crazed! The endings and the beginnings are very difficult to say anything about. It's fairly easy to talk about the middle since that has a shape. The beginning of the poem is just whiteness and the end is just whiteness. I find it hard to say much about them. There's got to be the right fire for both of them.

KP: Could you say something about your ideas concerning "revelation"? Does revelation come from allowing a sequence of feelings to speak freely? You've said that emotions push you towards discovery and that afterwards you recognize intellectively what in fact amount to glimpses of physiology?

MM: Yeah, that reminds me of that Olson remark that has been such an inspiration for so many people—one perception leads immediately and directly to another. It's a wonderful formulation and I think it's true on the level of perception and true also in a visionary sense in that every mystery in its moment of revelation has another mystery behind it. I'm not speaking in the gnostic sense of going down through layer after layer of an onion but in the sense of Buddhism or contemporary physics as just going out and out. There's always another mystery behind it, and you really are going *out* and not *in*. You're making reality as you go.

KP: I was wondering if that immense power of movement in your poems, swooping from one area to another, has any affinity with neurological theories concerning different brain centers—what Bly, for example, has termed different image banks.

MM: I don't usually think in those terms. I think of myself as being integrated on a mammalian level. Robert is referring to McLean's theory of emotions where he talks about the animal cortex and the reptile brain. In fact in vertebrates there is a set of several brains developing out of the spinal cord. The third, most recently developed brain has a pair of extensions that we call the cortex. If you spread out the cortex, which is normally compressed within the skull, and look at it as an organ, it resembles a big pair of wings. And in a way that's what it is. We fly through the dimensions with it. The cortex knows we're a mammal. It's a dynamite thing, it's good, it's meat, and it knows it! But the brain is an integrated thing and if you start breaking it down into concepts then it soon becomes very complex rather than simple. For example, if you go back to the reptiles a lot of visual processing is done on the retina, on the spot. So to start talking about the old reptile brain becomes very dubious. The retina of the eye is part of the brain. We are dealing with incredibly beautiful, complex, and luminously brilliant systems that are always shifting with evolution and development. It's a holistic thing. Of course, you can break it down excitingly and interestingly into all of those areas and their needs but your grasp of physiology needs to be good. It's wonderful, really beautiful. A lot of clarification is going on right now in biochemistry and neurophysiology.

The brain is a reasoning chamber—with a lot of incredibly interrelated subchambers. If you let it work it, works right. I mean by that if you let it work with some sense of the fact that it does work—and that the gates are being kept open—it'll bring things back home to you holistically.

KP: What about those key words? They seemed almost gestural identities of a kind, carrying an immense energy charge.

MM: Well, Joanne says I have a lot of buttons that I like to press and like to directly work on people. I think she's probably right. I like words that can be put into arrangements and then alter their meaning.

KP: Animals such as the wolf and the snow leopard clearly held a particular fascination for you?

MM: Yes, both physiologically and symbolically.

KP: Did you want the physiological charge to carry over in some iconographic sense?

MM: In a way, they have a large charge in themselves as animals, and now that we know what that charge is they'll soon be like unicorns and have that new charge in them as well.

I also like words used stochastically. I like to reach people to use the basic, single, sensory or physiologically symbolical word. I've made word decks at various times and I like to teach people how to use them. I have a videotape showing how to make a deck of one hundred words, each student has his own deck with his own words. We then work with them so that if they choose to be honest they can, or if they choose to be concrete and sensory they can, or if they choose to be abstract they can. It liberates the imagination.

KP: *Rose, Blossom, Star, Wolf* would be part of your own deck then?

MM: Absolutely, but you can make a different deck all the time. *Blossom* is perhaps a bit too general but now that you mention it I'd certainly have *star*, *wolf*, etc. These are universal concrete words used for making associations.

KP: Similarly with Billy the Kid or Jean Harlow, they're not so much iconographical pop figures as embodiments of energy in Pollock's sense?

MM: Both.

KP: What lies behind your involvement with Odum's work?

MM: An awful lot of clarity that I've had in the last few years has come from Odum's work. Odum has limitations but the basic information he delivers is how loop systems work and how when a loop system becomes more complex, it becomes more stable and also the fact that it keeps moving all the time. It's the picture of the way energy works, the way it flows through systems. It's so basic, so deliberately at the bottom rung of the ladder that if you can begin to see that, then you can start seeing how so many things work. It really does clarify a great deal, aside from questions like how the sun heats the surface of the planet and then is dissipated in the atmosphere. I mean that basic energy movement that's going on of the earth being hit from both sides and the heat being reflected off the dark side as the movement turns the earth around. However, apart from that kind of question, if you get into any system more complex than straight chemical change, you begin to get something related to a loop and that in turn leads to more and more complex loops.

KP: Is that the idea of a systemless system? It reminds me again of Pollock's paint loops.

MM: Well, I'm able to go an entire step closer, a step that I could not have taken without Odum. Gary and I both found Odum independently and that's quite something. Steve Beckworth gave Gary Odum, and I found Odum reviewed in *Science* magazine. I've just recently returned from a symposium in Florida with Odum, Gary and Allen Ginsberg. At another conference Gary showed up with Margalef's *Perspectives in Ecological Theory* most of which is going to be reprinted in the next *Co-Evolution Quarterly* with a short introduction by me—more of a tribute than an introduction. Some of the best parts have been cut out as being too difficult but they're really fun to follow through. It's Margalef who's right on the edge of explaining things, of explaining the spiritual, mechanical, biological terms of a systemless system. He's right on the verge of conceptualizing it. The spiraling interrelationship of evolution and succession is what he's dealing with. In other cases he's dealing with the complex edge of the ecotone, or rather the ecotone is the edge, so he's dealing with the ecotone of the system. He's also tackling the problems of memory and evolution. It's wonderful, like calligrams.

KP: Was *Organism* dealing in any way with the idea of the division of the brain?

MM: Not intentionally.

KP: What was your intent with the reversal and repetition of the text?

MM: That's a pattern poem, a way of freeing the imagination with a pattern of words. It's a pattern midway between crystal and organism, certain cells and certain crystals have strong affinities biochemically or geochemically. It's stretching a fact, but they do. I'm doing in *Organism* something like what I did in *The Surge*. It's the blowing-up chemical attempt to say I'm going to create a living organism with words. I'm trying to say an organism is like this and with each one I'm hoping to get closer to it, or hoping that this series extended indefinitely would by chance bring one of them to life. But, of course, it only extends to seventeen or so. I didn't explain because I was afraid it would detract from the work but I wish I had now.

KP: But as they come back the other way they are in themselves changing their initial meaning?

MM: Yes, that's true. On an entirely different level they're lessons in the fact that words will ripple through at different speeds like cytoplasm flowing inside of a cell. You read it through one direction and you get one movement, and you say "that's a philosophical statement," "there's a quote," "there's a riff of words." Are they chance or not. But, in any case, you can keep with it and you pick out a series of images and wonder if it's a pattern. Then suddenly they pour and they become waves going in all different directions and furthermore their meaning shifts as you set out in the new direction back up to the beginning again. It's like within an amoeba, the endoplasmic reticulum can be expressed within many different shapes ... this and that pseudopod are extruded and withdrawn and the creature flows in movement. So on this entirely different level I'm showing organisms. The pamphlet—the booklet—is a statement that the pieces of it are organisms.

KP: They retopologize?

MM: Yes, they retopologize as you pour through. Crick didn't like them. I don't want to defend them, but I'd like Francis to see what I was doing. He prefers the poems in *September Blackberries*, *Peyote Poem*, and *Star. Organism* lost him and I'm sorry. They shouldn't be presented as poetry and they're not. I think they're in exactly the right place, they're for Charles and for people who share those interests.

KP: You see the poem as an extension of our inner life. You said that the tendrils of the poem are also tendrils of the selves, and in *We* are you showing this multiplicity of selves taking their language form? Is this related to your idea of bioalchemy?

MM: Well, it's certainly monistic. It's certainly saying that all living organisms that we know of are part of the same molecule. A huge breathing, eating, quaking thing. And in one sense that's a fact, all the trillionic forms of life began on this planet—or drift through space as chemical triggers that develop life ... or there can be complex combinations of hereditary endosymbiosis. But it can be imagined to be one act of expansion, and recombination, and imagination.

I was using the word bioalchemical to say that we're really doing it. What goes on in biochemistry really is alchemy, it truly is. In alchemy the idea was to change substance into gold and while that happened one underwent a spiritual transformation. In other words the individual became spiritualized, or as Jung would say individuated, as an afterthought of the process. The gold was the philosopher's stone and with the philosopher's stone you understood, and the gold and your spiritualization were then inseparable. When you had the philosopher's stone you *were* the philosopher's stone. You did know *everything* and you consequently *were* everything. Therefore, in a sense you *directed* everything, as well as partaking in everything, and that's almost like saying, although I've stated it rather crudely, that all living beings are a part of the same molecule. That's not a realization, that's just a statement, but there is a similarity. In biochemistry now we're really getting out to that edge.

KP: A kind of spiritual evolution?

MM: Yeah. We call it liberation. To have the philosopher's stone is liberation. The Buddhist says to be free of karma is liberation; the political individual says to be free of government is liberation. It's all striving for liberation, which is the point of revolt and the point of *Meat Science Essays*. Liberation whether it's through Buddhism or through bioalchemy is what we're all after. I don't think we want any state permanently but many of us have come recently closer and closer in our lives to a state that is satisfactory from the viewpoint of liberation. I'm sure Schiller felt that some of the time, or Shelley sometimes, and I'm not therefore suggesting that we're suddenly getting there but that simply that it's good to talk about since there are a few people who're really interested.

KP: That's why we're nuevo-alchemists?

MM: Yes, but we can't put it in moldy terms because that wouldn't work. Yet on the other hand we can't be airy since that wouldn't work either.

KP: So that's why man has to get back into a fuller body presence so he can reopen the possibilities he has.

MM: I think so. And a good way of starting is to remember that words are real. Real sounds come out of your mouth, real chemical charges or real electrical charges depending on what media.

KP: Yet with *Ghost Tantras* or *!The Feast!* you used that tantric expression of sound. They could be read directly as pure emotional states, but they carry their own restrictions. The mixing of ordinary language with body language, did that present any kind of dilemma for you?

MM: No, I still try and use all those modes. I strongly disagree with Pound about the poet and the poet being separable. I think that's a division that has crippled a lot of poets' ideas about poetry.

KP: Did your invention of body language spring from a recognition of the limitation of words to carry the emotions apparently implicit in their meanings?

MM: The desire to do that came from the fact that I was working with Kundalini yoga. There's a very strong relationship there. It's quite a physical or physiological type of yoga. Lately I've been working with the Alexander Technique, which I find wonderful. It's a way of lengthening the spine and releasing the head from the habitual domesticated posture that we get into and that we grow up with. It's a relearning of a way of carrying your body so that your spine is much closer to what they call the primary curve, the curve of the embryo. There aren't any curves in the embryo's back. The first thing the baby has to do is to learn too make that curve at the neck so that it can lift its head up. The child stands up and then he develops the lumbar curve in the back. The primary curve is then the one the child is born with, the secondary curves are in the neck and back. Apparently, part of our self-domestication comes in the kinking of those secondary curves to the point where they excruciate us and maybe limit our emotional and physical life by causing us undue stress. That stress shows various symptoms. I don't want to sound like a quack, I'm not saying that Alexandering cures things, but it can help with such stress symptoms as arthritis or chronic headaches. For example, the whole posture we get into with your chest thrown forward and our head thrown back that's so common in educated people who've been trained a lot, spent a long time sitting in classrooms, they often end up with severe pains in the upper area of the body. All the Alexander method does is to provide a nonverbal hands-on untraining technique. They don't make any claims for it.

KP: Does it make you more conscious of energy moving through you?

MM: Maybe I'm just a lot more aware of myself as an animal. I was born into being more aware of myself as an animal. I've always been going in that direction and have always been limited by something and unable to see what it was. Now it's certainly clear that one of the limiting factors was an accumulation of bad postural training. And as there isn't any one big thing that solves it, so to find a little bit that solves part is a large step forward.

KP: Is it also possibly increasing receptivity by releasing tension?

MM: I hadn't ever thought of it in those terms. I went for a specific reason. I had bone spurs growing out of two vertebrae in my neck that were poking a nerve. After two years of chronic headaches somebody finally X-rayed my neck instead of my head and found it. Nikolaas Tinbergen when he received the Nobel Prize wrote his Nobel essay about stress diseases. He wrote it about two separate subjects, about autism and about the Alexander Technique. I looked at the illustrations and read the piece and said, "That's for me." I lost most of my headaches after the first lesson. It's harder to get rid of the last 10 percent because I'm dealing with the fact that there's a physical problem there.

KP: Can I finally ask you about Ed in *The Adept*? Is he a Pollockian hero figure, a kind of pure energy flow?

MM: Yes, it'd be a tremendous role for a film.

KP: I was surprised by the way the murder scene presents itself twice, in two different forms as far as their effect is concerned and without any loss of tension in the repetition. The first time he jumps over the rock it appears as part of some drug induced nightmare, a possible flashback. Whereas in fact it's a flash forward, a premonition that later becomes reality.

MM: He's a real ogre.

KP: He's also meat spirit. Was the killing the only action capable of matching Ed's primal force?

MM: In a way. I just thought that if you saw that as being the ending of the novel and the rest as being a coda that might structurally give greater cohesion to the novel.

KP: I'd read the fragments as kinds of energy bursts in the expressionist sense.

MM: That's what they were. I wrote it before I'd seen the Godard movie. I don't know how I'd kept away from them since if I'd seen them I probably wouldn't have been able to write the novel.

KP: Yes, Godard had that trinity of love, violence, action that he could use as an organizing schema and then proceed to fragmentize.

MM: And I've always liked his fetishistic humor.

Interview with Michael McClure

Inger Thorup Lauridsen and Per Dalgard / 1983

From *The Beat Generation and the Russian New Wave* (Ann Arbor: Ardis, 1990), 113–22.

Born in Marysville, Kansas, 1932. Now living in San Francisco.
McClure has been closely associated with the Beat Generation since his debut in the fifties. Besides being a peculiar experimental poet with a love for biology, he is a well-known playwright.

Major publications include: *Passage* (1956), *Hymns to St. Geryon and Other Poems* (1959), *Ghost Tantras* (1964), *The Beard* (1967), *The Mad Cub* (1970), *September Blackberries* (1974), *Antechamber* (1978), *Scratching the Beat Surface* (1983), *Selected Poems* (1987).

In Russian: "Preduprezhdenie," *Literaturnaia gazeta* (January 31, 1961, 4).
About him: G. Thurley, "The Development of a New Language: Michael McClure, Philip Whalen, and Gregory Corso," in Lee Bartlett (ed.), *The Beats—Essays in Criticism* (London: McFarland, 1981) and *Margins*, no. 18, 3 (1975) (the entire issue is devoted to McClure).
Michael McClure was interviewed in San Francisco, September 5, 1983.

Question: Mr. McClure, do you consider yourself part of the Beat Generation?
Michael McClure: Well, in the broadest sense, yeah. Originally, I think the Beat Generation was a specific, very small group of people. Originally the Beats were Kerouac, Ginsberg, Burroughs, and maybe Corso, and that's the core of the Beat phenomenon. I knew all these people. First time I gave a poetry reading was the first time Allen read "Howl" and the first time I met Kerouac at the Six Gallery in 1955. I was already familiar with the Black Mountain poets before I met Allen. I met him in 1954. So I was familiar with Duncan, Creeley, Olson, and I was already antipolitical in the sense of being an anarchist; and biology had always been my major interest besides poetry and painting. In those days I used to say: "No, I am not part of the

Beat Generation," you know, we were friends. Now, historically, I would say: "Yes, there was a Beat Generation, there is a core Beat Generation, I'm not part of that, but I think that the Beat phenomenon represents a mutation of consciousness, such as the ideal Classic, the ideal Romantic. I think that the Beat also now functions to make a statement about an approach to nature and to reality. So in the broadest sense I would include myself among the Beats, whereas as a kid I was too arrogant to do so." Now I would think that the Beat phenomenon could also include people who prefer to think of themselves as Black Mountain poets. I mean, I think that it could all be put together in a very large pattern, and I certainly feel part of that.

Question: So in the broad sense the Beat Generation was a shift in consciousness which is still valid, it still has consequences?

McClure: Oh yeah! More important now, and it will be more important in the future.

Question: Is it a literary thing only or is it also social and political?

McClure: I think it is primarily environmental. And I think that isn't understood yet. We were more like the literary wing of the people who were biologically and environmentally conscious. We received more attention than they did at the time because we were engaged in a pact of political defiance regarding the Korean War and the Cold War in the US, so we received a lot of negative publicity, but our friends of those days are the environmentalists and the biologists of today who are doing important work. I see it all as one thing.

Question: But isn't it hard to combine, for example, someone like Kerouac with any environmental approach?

McClure: Not very difficult for me. I said "environmental," "biological" would be more appropriate. Kerouac had one of the finest sensoriums, he had the finest use of eyes, ears, nose that I know of, so in that sense he is an example for all of us.

["Poetics" poem follows.]

Although we all see differently, we learn to see as Kerouac sees; and our consciousness and our biological awareness is broadened. In other words, he is not writing from the universe of discourse, he is not writing from ideas that already exist, he is writing from his own perception. And that gives emphasis and energy to biological consciousness, which we see now as close to a broad everyday environmentalism. Rock 'n' roll is part of it too, I mean, the Beatles take their name from the Beats. What does rock 'n' roll have to do with biology and environmental consciousness? In the sixties people started dancing, started using their bodies. People who live in abstract ideas don't use their bodies in a free way and they can't think straight; they can only exist in the one-dimensional society that Marcuse speaks about, until they begin some kind of liberation of their body. And that spread out through society today, so that the concern that we had in those days is now on the front pages of the newspapers, and there is a broad general concern about it.

Question: Do you see this as an international phenomenon?

McClure: Sure, now people want us to come and read in Germany, Holland, or Italy; and they want to get their hands on the things that we had in the fifties and the sixties. It's not that arrogantly and egoistically the Beats started it and everything owes to them. It feeds back. The Green movement in Germany then encourages the antinuclear movement here, so that we have 900,000 people standing in Central Park making a protest a year ago. It's a very complicated process of feedback and counter feedback. It's a very powerful thing that is happening right now.

Question: Do you know anything about the Russian counterparts to the Beats?

McClure: I certainly know about Yevtushenko and Voznesensky. I met Yevtushenko several times, and I know Andrei [Voznesensky] slightly; I've heard them both read and I've read their poetry.

Question: Do you see them as Beats?

McClure: Sure, it's a copycat movement. The Russians decided they needed an Allen Ginsberg, so they set up Yevtushenko. That's a gross oversimplification, but since I don't know what the Russian politics are, I can only see it in a kind of cartoony way; and in a cartoony way that's what it looks like.

Question: How did you experience the fifties?

McClure: The fifties were cold, militaristic. The youth was viewed as cannon fodder; the US was willing to take on the war in Korea for the protection of a vast system that we had created to surround Russia—because the US was in the hands of people who had been in the intelligence service in the Second World War and had come to leadership in the US at the end of the war and were paranoid about Russia. We were in an antagonistic posture and the entire country was in that antagonistic posture. But young poets had taken on the war in Korea and we were all resisting and we were naïve politically. I knew I was an anarchist but I didn't know exactly what an anarchist was, so I found out by living it.

Question: Did you have trouble publishing?

McClure: I wasn't bothered politically, for some reason. My largest censorship trouble was a play of mine called *The Beard*, which was to the theater what Ginsberg's "Howl" was to poetry. The trouble began in 1965. *The Beard* was arrested here for obscenity, they tried to pass a state law against performing it. Then it moved to New York and received two theater awards. Then it moved to London and was received as a theater classic—the play is a confrontation between Billy the Kid and Jean Harlow. Then it went to LA and was arrested by the police nineteen nights in a row. So I went through five years of court cases regarding that. Earlier plays of mine were censored also, productions were canceled; the book of mine that Kerouac was so anxious to have published, *Dark Brown*, had to be published by a small press, even City Lights was afraid to sell it; it was sold under the counters.

Question: Why?

McClure: It's sexual! It's hard for people like you Danes to even comprehend how it was here in the fifties. We were living in a state of a cold war. People were looked at...

Question: Even up in the sixties?

McClure: Censorship in this country began to be broken by "Howl," and Grove Press published Burroughs and Henry Miller and D. H. Lawrence's *Lady Chatterley's Lover*—that began the literary freedom, and then my play came along in the theater. Grove Press produced it in New York City.

Question: Have the Beats become bourgeois?

McClure: I'm trying. I came from the bourgeois, my parents were bourgeois. But then I had no support of any kind; my wife and I lived in utter poverty from 1954 until 1964. It was beautiful poverty, there is nothing wrong with being poor.

["Portrait of a Hipster" poem follows.]

It was a very beautiful, extremely interesting and glamorous life, but I wouldn't mind joining the bourgeois. Does my house look bourgeois to you?

Question: Yes, as a matter of fact it does. Besides, you have received awards, Snyder got the Pulitzer Prize, Ginsberg...

McClure: Allen hasn't received any awards. I think he should have the Nobel Prize! and I hope he gets it! It's odd that Gary got the Pulitzer, I mean, it's usually given to the worst kind of hacks.

People are tremendously impressed by Gary's charisma, so they try to buy him off by prizes.

Question: That's buying him off?

McClure: They're trying to buy off what's happening by giving Gary the prize, a bourgeois prize. I'm glad that he got it, it's terrific.

Question: Who is buying off?

McClure: Oh, the literary establishment.

Question: Of which you're trying to become a part?

McClure: I'm trying to! We should be! In my opinion we are the government in exile; we are the only real poets, too.

Question: Don't you feel that there's a contradiction between your position today and in the fifties and the sixties?

McClure: Why should there be?! I mean, even if I have changed completely, why should it be a contradiction? I think all of us have grown a whole lot. What impresses me is the growth that I have seen in my friends, that is, the soulmaking that goes on, the spiritual growth and the increasing ability to carry out their ideals. When I think of what Gary has done, what Allen has done, what Philip Whalen has done, what Duncan and Creeley have done, then I'm very glad that these men and women have always been my friends.

Question: You mention Mayakovsky in one of your poems....

McClure: I'm certainly a great admirer of Mayakovsky. I guess that's why I'm not impressed by Yevtushenko.

Question: Are you influenced by Mayakovsky?

McClure: I would say so, somewhat. I don't like the term "influence," it's a literary term. The academic American poets in earlier years liked to pretend that they were born fully grown out of Athena's brow. We, on the contrary, have learned very much from one another and we see ourselves as having many sources; but the word "influence" is not appropriate.

Question: Have you heard about the Russian concept of "transrational language"?

McClure: There was a movement in Europe in the twenties and the thirties, in Western Europe centered primarily around the magazine and the group of people called Transition, and they invented languages: Hans Arp, James Joyce, Gertrude Stein, Hugo Ball. Then in France you had a group called the *Lettrisme* and then you had Artaud in his great screaming radio broadcast. I'm aware of all that and I'd be surprised if there wasn't a Russian counterpart. I know a little about Khlebnikov and people like that.

Question: Is the language you use in *Ghost Tantras* also transrational?

McClure: No, it is not.

Question: What is it then?

McClure: It comes from an experience I had. First, I wrote a play in that language, earlier when I was a kid in 1959. Then in 1962 the language came back to me again, and I felt a ball of silence within myself, and in the ball of silence were those sounds, and I knew that there were going to be ninety-nine poems like that and I wrote them out. You want to hear one of them? I just recited this in Rome. It's a night poem [*recites*]: I LOVE TO THINK OF THE RED PURPLE ROSE. . . .

. . . But you see, this is not related to Hugo Ball or to Arp or to Schwitters, I knew nothing about Khlebnikov when I wrote that; but I did grow up reading the Verticalists. It's not that I don't enjoy that kind of poetry, but it's not related. It comes from a different place. My poetry comes from the body and theirs comes from the imagination. Mine comes from the imagination too but theirs has an aspiration that's different. Mine is closer to Artaud. The Verticalists, the Transition group, which you would call them in Europe, were trying to make a transrational language, mine *is* a *body language*. It has nothing to do with transrational or not—that's an idea from the universe of discourse and doesn't have anything to do with what I do. I recite Transition and Verticalist poetry for myself, it entertains me, but I find it mechanical.

Question: Your language is based on English though, and Khlebnikov is, for instance, expressive in a Russian way.

McClure: I call mine "Beast Language." Khlebnikov in translation sounds mechanical.

Question: What role does spontaneity play in your work?

McClure: If I know what I'm going to write I don't write it.

Question: How do you work then without knowing what you are going to do?

McClure: I put my hand on my computer and my typewriter.

Question: How do you know when you are going to write then—do you start every morning at nine o'clock?

McClure: That's pretty personal isn't it?

Question: It's just hard to imagine never writing what you know you are going to write.

McClure: I can't imagine writing something I knew I was gonna write.

Poetry Wars: An Interview with Michael McClure

Barry Miles / 1986

This interview was recorded sitting on the roof terrace of Michael McClure's house in San Francisco, March 19, 1986, for Miles's Allen Ginsberg biography. A shorter version first appeared in *Beat Scene* no. 12 (1990). Reprinted by permission.

Barry Miles: Let's begin with the Six Gallery reading.

Michael McClure: I remember it quite well, although I've heard other variations on the story, which surprise me because it is such a clear memory to me. I was walking down Fillmore Street and Wally Hedrick stopped me as I walked by. At that time he was married to the painter Jay DeFeo, and at that time one or both of them were members of the cooperative gallery the Six Gallery,[1] which was located down at Union and Fillmore, which had earlier been an automobile repair garage. The name came from the fact that originally six artists had rented it and showed themselves and others, cooperatively paying the rent on the gallery. Wally Hedrick asked if I could arrange a reading at the Six Gallery, and I think I said, "I sure would," or "I'll think about it" or "Probably could" or something like that. And, I think I probably had every intention of doing so. It was an intriguing idea and what happened was, maybe a week or two later, I ran into Allen on the street and he asked me what I was up to and I said I had been asked to arrange a poetry reading, as the Six Gallery, but I didn't think I was gonna be able to do it because Joanna was pregnant and I was working at the San Francisco Museum of Art and our lives were simply so busy that I had no possibility of making an arrangement like that, and so Allen said, "Would you like me to do it?" and I said, "Yeah, that'd be great," and the next concrete thing I saw was that postcard. And what had happened was apparently Allen met Gary and Phil, who must have blown into town, because he met them at Rexroth's and I hadn't met Gary and Phil yet. Of course Lamantia I knew because Lamantia was one of the first people I met in San Francisco, and of course I knew Rexroth because I'd been to evenings at his place which probably was where I met Lamantia. The reason that Wally asked me to arrange the poetry reading was that earlier in that year Robert Duncan had staged a reading of his play *Faust Foutu*[2] there and I had been in the play.

It was absolutely my first poetry reading. I wouldn't be surprised if it was Allen's and I wouldn't be surprised if it was Gary's and Phil's. And of course it was the first time I saw Kerouac. Allen brough Jack over, probably the next day, and I got to meet Jack. And I'd read material of Jack's because Allen had showed me letters from Jack and I believe parts of *Mexico City Blues*.

BM: Kenneth Rexroth was the MC. Did you attend his Friday evening meetings?

MM: They were events of mind-awakening profundity. They were opportunities to introduce yourself to subjects, when you're twenty-two years old, you never dreamed existed. These are some of his favorite subjects: the Bureau of American Indian Affairs, Eskimo songs, Buddhism, Jewish mysticism, Jewish Hassidic folklore, Byzantine theology, Californian nature and countryside that would really make you appreciate it, thoughts about what the Pacific Basin meant, what a real bug was, how he'd found a real bug that day and how the true bug differs from other insects, or astonishing perceptions of natural history. He'd descant on the history of China, or maybe on Taoism. A favorite subject was anarchist politics in Spain and anarchist politics in San Francisco and the Bay area. Another favorite subject of his was Stalinism, and the evils of it. Then a very common theme was dirty jokes. The dirty jokes were loud, dirty jokes that he laughed at uproariously and snickered at. I tended to take Kenneth Rexroth as being a creature made out of the whole cloth. Certain people, say Bruce Conner, were never able to accept Kenneth because of the grosser aspects of his. The refined aspects, conversations on the profundity of Morris Graves,[3] would simply be lost when they talked to Kenneth. Rexroth always stayed in the center of these events. There was not really a dialogue, there was no sign of a dialogue. He would hold forth on everything from say Chinese cooking to the poetry of Bill Everson, or Catholicism. Oh, fine printing was another subject. He would stop for questions, but he continued this more or less monologue in a kind of tone that was both eccentric and domineering. And it made him both amazing and in a funny way, lovable. He was extremely fascinating.

There were psychiatrists, working men, students there sometimes, anywhere from twelve to thirty people. I imagine we drank what we called in those days, little red wine, if not little white wine. The situation was genuinely open to the world but it had to be a world that would take Kenneth out of the whole cloth and be submissive on that occasion to Kenneth's ego, because there was no real way to confront it. Consequently really worthy people, many of Kenneth's peers, could not cope. I mean, it would not be possible, say for Robert Duncan to go to an event like that because they would have disagreed about so many things and it would have been impossible.

BM: I understand there were a number of divisions in the poetry scene: the Berkeley Renaissance people, the White Rabbit people. . . .

MM: There had been several poetry scenes previously in the Bay Area. There was the poetry scene that was congealed in the *Ark* magazine [in 1947] that basically came from people coming down from the anarchist camps in Waldport, Oregon. It was Sanders Russell and it was Thomas Parkinson, it was Robert Duncan, it was Ronnie Bladen. . . . That was a very powerful outspeaking against the war machine at a time when there were very few such things. And these people were in various anarchist discussion groups in the city. So that was a core. Then at about the same time a Berkeley Renaissance, and the stars of that were Robin Blaser, young poet Robert Duncan, young poet Jack Spicer.

Then there was a bohemian North Beach poetry scene, people like John Alan Ryan, William Margolis, and mad scribblers with paper bags full of napkins scribbled all over. Then there was a new scene that had come into being in 1954, and that was centered around the Robert Duncan workshop at San Francisco State College, which is now San Francisco State University, so that we were quivering with Robert's genius that was pouring out of him. That would be Helen Adam, Lawrence Bixell, Jack Gilbert, Paul Dreckus, and myself. Then there was a kind of glossier scene which was James Broughton, and Maddy Gleason, more high tea and rhyme, but wholly interesting in itself. They had, of course, connections with Duncan but they weren't part of his new group, and then at the same time Spicer had a group, that was, well this is before the White Rabbit group developed but very soon you run across that White Rabbit group before the fifties had gone much further, people like Stan Persky, come into town, you have George Stanley, you have Harold Dull, you have Joanne Kyger kind of linking herself to that group, Brautigan around the edges of it, Ron Loewinsohn around the edges of it.

Furthermore there was an older, I would call it Marin County–centered group, with Gerd Stern and Victor de Suvero, and they'd actually been out giving poetry readings with bongo drums and girls doing belly dancing in accompaniment with the music. So it isn't like there hadn't ever been any poetry readings before. But I'm not diminishing what the Six Gallery reading did at all, but I want to point out that there was a rich humus that it grew in, a rich, rich humus. For me, the real background to the Six Gallery reading was the Ark group, the anarchist group, as represented in the Ark. For me that's the main line here. In our literature.

Allen very much wanted a group, and he would want it to be Gary [Snyder], himself, Gregory [Corso], when Gregory arrived, and some of his bohemian mad scribblers, like Hube the Cube, whom he saw great virtue in. So Allen not only tried, he did create a group, and I was very welcome to that group if I wanted to be part of it. I couldn't buy the basic tenet of the group, I couldn't; I could buy Allen as an artist with no problem. At that time I wasn't ready to buy Gregory as an artist yet, not till *Happy Birthday of Death* was I in any way convinced about Gregory Corso. I had no doubts about Philip Whalen. And I certainly had an enormous admiration for Jack. But there was a chalk line that had been drawn between [Robert] Duncan and Allen and I was caught by admiration for both. Part of it was homosexuality; but the only homosexuals are Peter and Allen, because Gregory is not, Phil [Whalen] is not outwardly manifesting himself in any sexual form, maybe with ladies if at all. But also [Robert] LaVigne would be part of it too. Of course Robert [Duncan] is homosexual, so it's not homophobia on my part, but the group that Allen was trying to get together smacked of New York, of homosexuality, and on the other hand, something that I admire very much, a social commitment that I did not have within myself. The lines were drawn, the battles were horrific.

BM: Poets shouting at each other in the street?

MM: There were a couple like that. We were pretty macho and staunch. Jesus Christ, we really didn't want to do any damage to each other. I mean, there were only about a dozen of us. No matter how territorial we were or how ferocious our internecine wars might be we had a lot more in common with each other than anybody else out there, so yeah, there was probably some yelling and some name calling but only once or twice. I really only remember one occasion and Jack has that in some novel of his.

So it was a funny Gruppo[4] that Allen was forming. And it wasn't a Gruppo, it was basically the Beats, because I see two definitions of Beats. I see Allen, Gregory Burroughs, Jack—the Beats—that's it. You can add a lot of people to that list. Then I see the Beat movement, the Beat Consciousness. Then I see several of the Black Mountain people, I see myself, I see Snyder in there. We're talking about biology, we're talking about consciousness, we're talking about environment, we're talking about social commitment, we're talking about bringing poetry off the page as well as staying on the page.

We're talking about a new mutation in subject matter in poetry as well as method. So I see two Beats. I literally see the Beat can be taken as romantic classic surreal and Beat. I think it can be taken as one of the larger frameworks of human statement. I saw all of us as comrades, struggling with one another in our vicious delightful comradely macho way, creating new subject matter, and new music and using from one another but with rapacity and genius.

Notes

1. The members of the cooperative were Wally Hedrick, David Simpson, Hayward King, John Allen Ryan, Deborah Remington, and Jack Spicer.
2. Robert Duncan, *Faust Foutu Act 1* (San Francisco: White Rabbit Press, 1958).
3. American Northwest school of painters.
4. After the Italian Gruppo 63 writers associated with *Il Verri* magazine.

An Interview with Michael McClure

S. E. Gontarski / 1990

From the *Review of Contemporary Fiction* 10, no. 3 (Fall 1990): 116–23. Reprinted by permission.

S. E. Gontarski: Perhaps we should just begin with your talking about issue number two of the *Evergreen Review* in 1957 called "The San Francisco Scene," which was put together by Don Allen. In fact Don's cover blurb is rather effusive: "Evergreen Review No. 2 focuses on the exciting phenomenon of a young group in the process of creating a new American culture. With what the *New Yorker* calls 'a pervasive desire to get out into the open in order to breathe fresh creative air . . . looking for some larger poetic form that can accommodate anything and everything-including ordinary rejected and suspect material,' a vigorous new generation of writers, painters and musicians in the Bay Area is revolting against the sterility of American 'academicians.'"

Michael McClure: Well, it was an exciting evening for us all. As I look at the table of contents, I notice that we have a kind of reprise here of the Six Gallery reading. That was the first reading of the Beat Generation. Allen Ginsberg read "Howl" for the first time then. Gary Snyder's "The Berry Feast" was read that night. Here are "Five Poems" by Philip Whalen. . . . We all read at the Six Gallery, and look, our poems are introduced by Kenneth Rexroth who introduced us all at the Six Gallery on October 7, 1955.

SEG: So you were here in San Francisco for a while when this issue of the *Evergreen Review* appeared?

MM: I arrived here in 1954. I met Ginsberg after the first reading given at the San Francisco Poetry Center, at a party for W. H. Auden. Kerouac was at the Six Gallery reading as well. Isn't this the issue that has Kerouac's "In the Railroad Earth" in it?

SEG: Yes, "October in the Railroad Earth."

MM: You have an interesting concurrence of names here. You have "us-ens" who were the Six Gallery reading people and then you have the older generation of poets and anarchists, including Rexroth of course, Robert

Duncan, William Everson who later called himself Brother Antoninus, and then you have a related but slightly different group, James Broughton and. . . . What you have is a kind of shimmer, several overlapping groups. It encompasses an intellectual atmosphere. . . .

I remember that Robert Duncan was instrumental in my appearing in *Evergreen*. He spoke strongly on my behalf, and, young as I was, I was thrilled. One of my few previous publications was in *Poetry* magazine in January of 1956; they printed two old poems of mine—two villanelles—perfect, rhyming, iambic pentameter—which were actually exercises. I'd been published in *Poetry* magazine and I'd been published in a magazine I edited called *Ark II/Moby I*, which was a resource for *Evergreen*. In the magazine James Harmon and I brought together the San Francisco poets and the Black Mountain poets and the older generation, *Ark II/Moby I* was the earliest to do that. The magazine included Ginsberg, Duncan, Whalen, Snyder, Levertov, Rexroth, Ferlinghetti, Louis Zukofsky, Olson, Creeley, Dorn, Kerouac. It contains the first publication of a chorus from *Mexico City Blues*.

SEG: Well, that sounds like anticipation of this whole issue. What kind of circulation did that have?

MM: I believe we printed eight hundred, and they sold almost immediately. They came out when people were passionately interested, and they sold easily. Looking back I remember that Donald Allen was already a player on the scene. I think it was Don who translated *The Bald Soprano*. . . . He may be the first English translator of Ionesco. He also edited and selected *Lorca*, which was an almost visionary work, published by New Directions. The selected *Lorca* was a marvelous edition with a wide variety of translations. I'd been watching Grove Press, and Grove was interesting. Grove started out with a strange list. Seems to me it had Saint John of the Cross and Gerard de Nerval and Melville's *Pierre*. As I remember, the books were curious, and tended to be deep, or mystical, or dark.

SEG: And *The Monk*.

MM: Yeah. That's right. It was a marvelous list to begin with.

SEG: It was really quirky in some respects. . . .

MM: And then Barney started to add to it. It had already caught people's eye because there was nothing much of interest going on at the time. Barry Silesky, who is writing a biography of Ferlinghetti, asked me about editing the magazine that Lawrence Ferlinghetti and I edited: the *Journal for the Protection of All Beings*. That was about 1960. Our proposal for the magazine was, "Give us something that you'd strongly like to say, that you can't say anywhere else." The magazine became legendary, but we didn't get the spectrum of material that I wanted. We talked to everybody from Steve Allen to Harpo Marx and Linus Pauling. We ended up with stars like Gary Snyder and Norman Mailer but not the breadth of people we wanted from the sciences and popular arts. There was a dull, black scene going on—except for the literary scene—in terms of what was being published. . . . It was a flat world, the cold fifties; gray-flannel suits, tract homes and the Buick scene going on. *Evergreen Review*, under the captaining of Don Allen and Barney Rosset, and Fred Jordan, started steering a wide strip right through the middle of it and leaving opals and diamonds of insight.

ER began exploring areas I was vitally interested in. They published Henri Michaux's "Miserable Miracle." Seeing that Michaux piece was one of the things that caused me to begin writing my essays on drugs, because I thought that if Michaux could not describe drugs honestly, who could? I'd try! Michaux's beauty and lucidity was still a twisted picture of what was going on in the mescaline experience. Michaux was one of the most direct pushes for me to begin my own series of drug writings, which later became *Meat Science Essays*. Michaux was the impetus it took for me to begin writing my prose pieces on peyote and drugs. Then, when I wrote my drug notes they were published by Ferlinghetti, who's also published in the San Francisco issue of *ER*. Another thing, it helped that *ER* was stitching up a very big bundle. The "artist-intellectuals"—and I say that to distinguish them from "intellectuals"—the artist-intellectuals on the East and West Coasts came together and were interested in each other.

SEG: When you talk about the San Francisco poets publishing before the "San Francisco Scene" issue of *Evergreen Review*, you're talking mostly about regional publication, aren't you?

MM: Right. My first two books were published by a friend of mine, Dave Haselwood, who started a press called Auerhahn Press. He also published Philip Lamantia, John Wieners, William Burroughs, and Olson. He published my first two books, *Hymns to St. Geryon* and *Dark Brown*. He was getting some East Coast distribution but the books were hard to find. They were handprinted, beautifully done and difficult to distribute.

SEG: So *Evergreen Review* number two was the first really national publishing of the San Francisco group.

MM: For our generation it was certainly the first. It was the premier. Before that, as you know, we had little magazines like *Origin* which were important. I'd never participated in *Origin*. . . . I was not a participant in that magazine's "soul-building experiment." My soul-building magazine was Baraka's *Yugen*, which began to come out about the same time as *Evergreen* . . .

SEG: What followed from this *ER* publication?

MM: What followed was something midway between notoriety and fame, on a small scale, but on the only scale there was. I could talk to someone in Camden or France or Florida, who had seen my picture and read my poems. A piquant selection of authors' photos and their writings were represented, though a number of us, including myself, had been written up in *Life* and the *New York Times*. *Evergreen Review* and the New Directions books and annuals were the first above-ground literary events for those who were truly against the establishment. And they were major. J. Laughlin was the first great pioneer of modernism in literature and then after that Barney confronted the censorship apparat.

SEG: Was it easier, then, to get published? After that?

MM: Yeah, and it also encouraged a host of smaller literary magazines to print serious strivings. So, not only was *ER* in itself a surfacing, it encouraged the underground. So often when something surfaces, it tends to destroy the underground. The surfacing of something can do away with the subsurface, whereas *Evergreen Review* sprang generously. I have to say this—there is always something generous about everything Barney Rosset has done. As Goethe said, "You can expect me to be sincere, but not impartial." I can't be impartial where Barney is concerned. He is a terrific human being. Because of what he did—basically because of his generosity and his vision, his willingness to accept advice, his taking advice from the right people, his absolute bravery about taking his gamble, his politics, with which I generally agree, and his lack of fear. When I think of Barney, I think of a man who defied the US censorship system and he did it not once, but three or four times.

SEG: He put the company on the line every time.

MM: Put the company on the line every time. Also, I've seen Barney do one of the most personally physically brave things that I've witnessed. Years ago at a drunken and severely stressed party a man was injured—and then, weirdly, the injured man was attacked by a number of other men at the party, like a dog pack. The men who were doing the pounding were good-sized men, and it was crazed. It was Barney, who is about five and a half feet tall, like Keats was, who stood against the mob and started pulling the thug-sized fellows away from the melee and ordering them to stop. Then another man and I joined in and helped Barney. There was the smell of real blood in the air and Barney was apparently fearless and acted quickly. Barney is without fear physically and intellectually—he's a man of great courage. He's idealistic . . . who else would have printed the unexpurgated

Lady Chatterley's Lover? And when my play *The Beard* was having all those censorship problems in San Francisco and Berkeley, he took it to New York.

SEG: Why don't we just go into that?

MM: Okay. *The Beard* had been performed here in San Francisco—and we were busted—and it had been defended by the ACLU. It took a long time, but we finally won our case. And then we produced *The Beard* at the Encore Theatre where the Actor's Workshop had its base—as a matter of fact, that is where the play had originally played. In the earliest beginning *The Beard* had been allowed only a one-night performance but, in fact, the Actor's Workshop tried to stop the production completely. Let me just tell you how they got *The Beard*. I had been showing my plays to Herb Blau. I had been trying to show my plays to him for a long time. It was the late fifties and Blau was doing Pinter and he was doing Beckett, and I was impressed. At that time I didn't like Beckett. I thought Beckett was an absolute cynical monster.... And it was *Endgame* which overwhelmed me, changed my estimation. Earlier I had liked the style of Beckett but not the content.

SEG: You saw the Workshop production of *Endgame*?

MM: Yeah. Those were the only ones around. They were good too. And so I took my plays to the Workshop, but they were not interested. I thought, "Why will they stage these people who live in Paris and London and not me?" And then one day someone told me that Harold Pinter was in town and didn't know anybody in San Francisco. So I called Pinter at the hotel where he was staying and told him, "I heard you don't have any company here and I thought maybe I could show you what there is to see." "But I'm leaving tonight—have to fly back to London," he said. So we had a drink and talked. I probably talked about my poetry. Pinter wrote Alan Mandel at the Actor's Workshop and said why don't you get some plays by Michael McClure? He lives right there in San Francisco. So they asked me for a play, and I'd just written *The Beard*. I took a copy to Mandel and that's the last I heard of it until maybe a year or so later; a young director phoned: he said that he had found *The Beard*. I said, "Where did you find it?" And he later showed me.... It was a kind of subbasement in the Actor's Workshop—sort of in the bottom drawer of the filing cabinet in the darkest room of the subbasement.

SEG: But he dug it out?

MM: Marc Estrin dug it out. And the play was done.

SEG: So he was doing it independently or as part of the Actor's Workshop season?

MM: Part of the Workshop. And I got a call from the artistic director who followed Blau saying, "I've seen what they're doing with that play of yours—it's been canceled." I said, "God, I've invited everyone I know." So we argued about the show. "Okay," he said, "you can have one performance at midnight—we'll schedule it for then—there'll be one performance. I won't cancel the show, but you have to cancel the reviewers." I did it in all honesty. I canceled all the reviewers. But John Hancock and I both were very surprised the following Tuesday to find a major review of it in the *San Francisco Chronicle*. I had not canceled my invitation to Michael Grieg, who is a liberal thinker and staff writer for the paper. That let the cat out of the bag. The Actor's Workshop was in the middle of a fundraiser at the time, and they believed that a play like *The Beard* would destroy the workshop. This was a real misreading. It was the kind of "scandal" that San Francisco loved at that time.

Then we performed *The Beard* at the Fillmore Auditorium, which was the rock 'n' roll palace, and we did one performance there too. We were scheduled to do another. We did it at the Fillmore Auditorium with handheld microphones and a big light show—it was marvelous, truly a spectacle. And Bill Graham said, "Okay, Michael, you guys, sorry, but I've canceled the next performance." Why? "The police have said if we do another production, I'll lose my license."

SEG: So how did Barney hear about this, do you know?

MM: The arrest of the next performance was pretty famous. But not only were we busted in San Francisco, we said, "Okay—we're not going to stop performing the play," and the actors and I formed a production company. Richard Bright who played Billy the Kid was in charge of finding the next venue. He rented a little theater in Berkeley, but he didn't realize it was the Board of Education's theater. We didn't know it! And that turned into one of the great Bay area intellectual events.... We decided to go ahead and do the play. We thought the busts were really crazy! We believed the play was a work of art and we didn't really understand the mechanisms of censorship. Then we got a letter from the Berkeley chief of police telling us if we performed, we'd be arrested on sight. I said to the actors, "You want to do this, you'll probably get arrested." They said, "Oh, yeah, we believe in this—it's a work of art." Richard Bright and Billie Dixon who played Jean Harlow are the real heroes of the story. I said, "Okay. We're going to do it. We're really going to be hard to bust." I got everybody from Mark Schorer and Lawrence Ferlinghetti, to Don Allen, to Zen priests and Alan Watts—every intellectual and religious leader available. And I seated them in the front rows of the theater. The police were there with tape recorders, and I had people there with tape recorders taping the police. Beforehand I stood up and read the letter from the chief of police, saying we couldn't use the theater. They didn't bust Billy and Richie that night . . . but they did the next day.

That was our second bust, and the ACLU defended us on both of those, and after that eventually we won the cases, which took a great deal of time. We formed a production company, Rare Angel Productions. The play was running its course. But it was badly in need of redirection. Barney published it in *Evergreen Review* and made arrangements to publish the book, and to produce the play in New York City. Later, *The Beard* was arrested fourteen performances in a row by the LA police department. The only other play arrested under that law was Aristophanes's *Lysistrata*.

SEG: Now Barney had published a book of yours before that?

MM: Yes.

SEG: Some poetry?

MM: The *Evergreen Review* had led to the publication of my third book of poems. In 1961 Grove published *The New Book/Book of Torture*.

SEG: Had Don Allen been at the Berkeley production of *The Beard*?

MM: I'm sure it's possible.

SEG: So he may have brought the work to Barney's attention.

MM: I don't remember. That's possible. So anyway, Barney had bought that space on University Place and was in the process of converting it into a theater, the Evergreen Theatre. It had a bar in front.

SEG: I remember it.

MM: The bar was done in black Naugahyde and all very slinky. We commissioned USCO to do the light show for the play. We not only had a light show (we'd always done *The Beard* with a light show), but the whole theater itself became a kind of pulsating organism of light, projections all over the cavelike walls and ceiling. I went back to New York—I'd written songs—a series of Blake songs—and I had an outlaw motorcyclist, a cowboy and an angel come in before the play, during the light show, and sing songs by Blake. And out front in the lobby we had cages of live ferrets and doves stacked up on one another.

Earlier Rip Torn flew out to San Francisco and caught what was the tail end of our West Coast production. It had been too long without direction, so Rip stayed with me here—took a look at it, and said, yeah, he'd like to direct the play. So we went to New York. The New York production broke up our production company because then Bill and Richard became union actors and were getting paid a wage. And I started taking author's royalties. Up till the New York production it was all Rare Angel Productions and an even split.

SEG: Barney suggested that even rehearsals got pretty wild.

MM: Rip used to throw me out regularly! Jim Walsh would go running through the theater and try to make everything right. We had a costume designer; she wasted more of our time than we got to spend in rehearsal. She's famous. USCO was around all the time. They were using up all the rest of our time. Rip was getting desperate to get enough time with Billy and Richie on stage. And he did an excellent job. But we had to struggle to get any time between the light show, the animal handlers for the doves and ferrets, and costume designer and. . . . Yeah—there was lots of yelling and shouting, and Rip and I going out and getting drunk afterwards. . . . Rip and I were also working on that first Mailer film at the time, *Wild 90*.
SEG: So you had some connections with that?
MM: Yeah . . . Rip and I played outlaw motorcyclists.
SEG: How long did *The Beard* run?
MM: Long enough. The reviews went from absolutely understanding, profound reviews by Jack Kroll to god-awful dink reviews from those little New Jersey papers that housewives bought to decide what piece of theater to go see. . . . Pretty good reviews in the *New York Times* and good reviews in *Newsweek*. We had the guy from *Time* magazine come in to review it and then no review appeared. A few weeks later another reviewer from *Time* came in, and we got an extremely ugly review. About ten years ago, I met the first reviewer from *Time* magazine, and I got a chance to talk to him. He said, "Yes, I went to *The Beard*; I loved it. I went back and wrote a fine review of it and they told me they wouldn't print it."
SEG: Let me also ask you one final if impossible, question. Can you try to assess whether or not a press like Grove—or even say New Directions, or a literary journal like the *Evergreen Review*—can they really have any sort of direct cultural impact or do they just pick up trends already well developed in the culture, pick up movements already in progress and just reflect them? Bring them to the fore?
MM: In rare instances, presses like New Directions or City Lights or Grove became a viable, cultural organism. But, of course, it requires a visionary captaining and the directing of people like Barney, Fred, Don Allen, J. Laughlin, or Ferlinghetti. These venues take on a life of their own, and they are as precious and as urgent to a poet as food or breath and the time and space to write. To be an editor of such a press or magazine requires nerve, self-reliance, belief in the art, and the energy to make a long-term commitment. There is no scale of proportion in such a venture. Di Prima and Baraka's *Floating Bear* newsletter is as heroic an act as *Evergreen*. There isn't any scale one can apply—to believe in and love poetry gives luster to the world.

An Interview with Michael McClure

Steve Luttrell / 1994

From *Café Review* 5 (Spring 1994): 24–35. Transcribed by Roger Dutton (December 31, 1993). Reprinted by permission.

Steve Luttrell: What is your take on the interview as a possible new art form as such? Do you like that idea of the interview as a "new art form"? Are you comfortable with that?

Michael McClure: As a form it's a powerful package of information, because it has ways of being both more formal and less formal than the prose that's written to be read. For instance, when I read a major interview with Francesco Clemente, I understood more about his painting that I had before, and I realized the structure and the shape of the thought behind the painting.

Luttrell: So, it opens things up for you, more or less?

McClure: Absolutely, and I like being interviewed and I also like doing interviews. Mary Caroline Richards visited us and I thought after asking M. C. what brought her to do the first translation of Artaud into English which was *The Theatre and Its Double*, how much I would like to interview her about her life. Another person to interview would be the painter Jess, who was Robert Duncan's companion.

Luttrell: Jess Collins, yeah. Speaking of Duncan, in an interview that you had done with Robert Duncan, from *Conjunctions*, you had said somewhere in the body of that interview that all souls are equal in childhood. Would you say that the experience of childhood tends to shape a poet's direction in sort of an organic way? For example, some of your early poems entitled *Fleas* seem to maybe suggest that.

McClure: Yeah. I'm always thinking about the idea of soul. Duncan gave me a great clue to Shakespeare by saying that all souls are equal in Shakespeare. He did not mean that all individuals were equal as men and women, or that they did not fit social hierarchies, but that there was another non-hierarchical, anarchistic, liberational stance of seeing and feeling beyond all that in which everyone is equal. Everyone in Shakespeare is building a soul; everyone does have a soul to build. Of course, the soul is *out there*. It is not something inside of ourselves, but it's something that we create or discover around us, because it's everything from our own fingerprints to the distant stars. One of the things that concerns me recently is young people who have no contact with biology or nature in their childhood. People who never grow up seeing a tadpole in a vacant lot or seeing a corner garden where apple trees and cherry trees are growing, or maybe not even seeing a cow. I am especially concerned that the vocabulary of youth is being given to them by the television. That vocabulary is the voice of what we blandly call consumerism, which is, in fact, what Marcuse defined as one dimensionality, wherein the outer world is introjected into the self, and finally there is no difference between the inner dimension and the outer dimension. It's urgent to have a rich inner life that connects in as many ways as possible with the universe of nature as well as with the human universe. If one, as a child, is smothered by the human universe and misses one's roots in nature, the results are clear in the disasters of lives around us.

Luttrell: It would seem to be an estrangement from our basic nature. A disconnectedness with our ground of being, perhaps.

McClure: Yes, part of being an artist is using your art, whether you're a poet, or a painter, or, in fact, whether you're an explorer or a biologist for that matter. Part of one's art is to use the self as a means of exploring, whether it's to look for the origin of matter or whether it's to seek myriad mindedness. Without a rich childhood these searches aren't possible. I don't think a childhood is rich unless there's a sizable overlapping and simultaneity of the human universe and the universe of nature. I make that distinction because cultural forebears like Sartre and Camus were primarily sunken into the human universe. I don't mean there cannot be thoughts or experiences to be primarily absorbed from the human universe, but it means that there are clear limitations to it. One has to live beyond the urban and the urbane to fully be the ape or the lion or the "meatly" human being that one is.

Luttrell: How, in your view, is the poem physical?

McClure: Let me give you two answers to that. I used to say that the poem was physical because it was like the gesture of a gestural painter in the sense that Jackson Pollock's paintings were a continuation of Jackson Pollock and were real parts of his living organism. Also the poems of William Blake looked that way to me. Now I see it in a slightly different way: we are simultaneously physical, "mystical," and real. I see myself as being the flesh that I am, which is utterly no different from the consciousness that

I am. They're the same thing. The poem is one of the most useful edges of who I am to myself. It is not less than an artifact and it is an actual "edge." The poem is physical in the sense that I am physical and it's part of the edge in me. I realize my poems are difficult to understand for that reason. I'm almost at the point where I recommend that people come and hear Ray Manzarek and me. With music it's much easier to hear what the poem is about.

Luttrell: You mentioned Ray Manzarek, which leads me to the question: Would you say that the performances that you and Ray Manzarek are doing, maybe, find their roots in the baric tradition?

McClure: Not directly. Directly, the roots are found in Ray's work in blues (whether it's Howlin' Wolf or Willie Dixon), and in rhythm and blues and in the classic music that he also studied. Also in rock 'n roll and working with Jim Morrison. My roots in what Ray and I are doing go back to my first poetry reading at the Six Gallery, where Allen Ginsberg, Gary Snyder, Philip Whalen, Philip Lamantia, Rexroth, and I had all decided that we no longer wanted our poems solely on the page; we wanted them out into the air to go directly into people's consciousness by the ear as well as the eye. By none of this do I mean to denigrate the page. I'm a lover of the page and the beauty of it and of the book, just as Mallarme loved the book. Ray and I recognize and often talk about the tradition of poetry and music; we have examples ranging from the very early Greeks to the sixth century BC in China, when Confucius sat by the river playing his small lute, which sounded like a Delta blues guitar—only very quiet. The early Chinese, like Robert Burns much later, were playing and singing poems, set to folk songs, that were sometimes hundreds of years earlier in their origin. Sometimes, we talk about troubadour poets of the tenth, eleventh and twelfth century in Southern France. We also remember Vachel Lindsay and we think about the poetry and jazz in the fifties, which I was aware of and interested in, but didn't partake in because I saw, with major exceptions, poets reading their poetry with happily willing musicians who were just backing them up. What Ray and I do is something entirely different. It's a real symbiosis. We're creating another work of art. It's not Ray's nor mine. I think it's probably more like what the Greeks were doing and more like what the Chinese were doing. Although, on the other hand, it's related to rock 'n' roll and Howlin' Wolf and Miles Davis.

Luttrell: Yeah, that's how it comes across to me when I hear it, you know. It's got that long tradition going back, but at the same time it's very contemporary in its approach.

McClure: Sometime soon we'll do a big event of American Bards. I'm not sure what "Bardic" is. We talked about it in the fifties and I'm not sure I ever understood it. There's always been a tradition of poetry and music and it's rich and it's completely normal. It largely springs up of its own energy because, one side of the brain hears pitch and the other side hears words and then orders them and deals with them as acts of consciousness. When pitch and words happen simultaneously, it's a richer experience, both for the person doing it and for the person listening or taking in the event as a spectator.

Luttrell: In distinction to the poem heard and experienced, what's your take on the so-called language poetry? And, do you think that it maybe glorifies structure too much?

McClure: Making a generality about the language poets is kinda like making a generality about the Hells Angels. When I had my motorcycle and was riding with Freewheelin Frank who was the secretary of the Angels, I got to know the Hells Angels well, the San Francisco chapter of the Hells Angels. And people would ask what the Hells Angels are like and I'd say, "Well, they're completely individualistic. One is a lawyer and a kind of an intellectual and another one is a proletarian who delivers auto parts on a three-wheeler and another one is something else and it's the brotherhood of the Angels that holds them together." It's hard to make a generality; I'd say that about the language poets. Lewis Turco speaks of an abstract language poetry movement that has a beginning, in its American form, with Frank O'Hara and John Ashbery. They're not language poets, but a poet like Ron Silliman I find most interesting. I'm often interested in the sheer beauty of experiment. Some language poets are abstract poets and some of them are experimentalists and some of them are both. Some of them do one thing one time and another, another time. I go through some of the language poets and find nuggets of experimental work that bring facts of consciousness to me.

Luttrell: Well, touching on what you said at the beginning of that question on language poetry, you mentioned the book that you had done on Freewheelin Frank and the Hells Angels, which for me that area of San Francisco is implicit in. So, I would ask, how has the city of San Francisco, as an area, shaped you as a poet?

McClure: I came here when I was twenty-two. San Francisco was like a cow town, a combination of harbor town and a cow town. I think the tallest building on Market Street was sixteen or twenty stories then. "Frisco" was right by the side of the Pacific Ocean and up on the top of the peaks, and there were still some horses out to pasture on Twin Peaks. You walked down through Chinatown and there were the wonderful Asian faces, the sounds of the Asian languages, beautiful things to eat. And you walked on a little further and you got into the Mediterranean section of town, North Beach, and there'd be old Italians with a different history and a lot of fresh political ideas which were here because of the Italian anarchists and, also, because of the Wobbles, the members of the I.W.W. from up the coast around Seattle and Oregon. In those times I could get in my car and drive through the fog across the city, across the bridge, over to Mount Tamalpais. In those decades before traffic you could be on top of Mount Tamalpais, a relatively wild mountain, in thirty minutes. Or, you could get into your old car and drive a few hours to the south and go to Big Sur which was not yet covered with houses and still wild. Henry Miller lived there. Or, you could drive a little longer and get to Death Valley, around Easter time, and see the amazing crops of spring wildflowers, with ravens walking around among them, picking out roots and seeds.

Luttrell: So, the beauty of the area definitely comes through in your poetry?

McClure: Yes. It was a combination of being able to go to so many vibrant places—from seashore to desert to mountain—and at the same time what I am kinda haphazardly calling the universe of nature and the human universe in a rich mix, in the same locale. There were great thinkers here, great artist thinkers, like Robert Duncan and Kenneth Rexroth and film artists like James Broughton and people like Jack Spicer and it was dense artistically. It was not overcrowded because the San Francisco that I think of was in a US where the population was a third of what it is now.

Luttrell: Yeah. Well, you know, that touches upon a question I wanted to ask in regards to the fact that I know you collaborated with many well-known artists, such as Wallace Berman and George Herms and, more recently, Francesco Clemente. How do you feel that working with visual artists has influenced your work?

McClure: Before I discovered poetry, when I was very young, I was interested in anthropology. First natural history and then anthropology. I was about twelve years old. I was also lucky at an early age to find artists and painters that intrigued me. I was quite taken with Salvador Dalí, quite taken with Picasso, and was amazed when I got a little older and saw the appearance of the abstract expressionists. But the time I was sixteen, I was seeing Pollock reproduced in magazines. And a brilliant young painter my own age named Bruce Conner showed me more of what other painters like Motherwell and de Kooning and Guston were doing. My ambition as a poet, my primary one at that point, was to utilize what I understood the physical philosophy of abstract expressionist painting to be and to bring it into the art of poetry. And, I was able to go further with that ambition when I discovered projective verse and was able to begin writing and creating my own form of projective verse.

Luttrell: In your own personal universe, what would you say are a few of your own "drive words" that particularly are from your own universe? At least in a current sense.

McClure: *Ink, swim, turquoise, rose, thunder, lion, wave*: words like that.

Luttrell: I've made several of my own personal universe decks and I've noticed that they change from period to period.

McClure: Every time I make a word deck it changes. When you asked me that question, several of the decks I made slipped through my mind and I took words that tend to be in all the decks.

Luttrell: Well, maybe that's a good way of working.

McClure: But, those are all "good" words. *Envy* should be in the list, because one of the things I warn about in the deck is that one might only present their sweet, angel-food-cake persona. And I presented a power aspect in the words I gave you, like *turquoise, swim, lion*. On the other hand, probably *ape* should be there, *envy* should be there, *moth* should be there and *hunger* should be on the list.

Luttrell: I suppose that it's the immediacy of where we are that dictates, at least in part, what those words are at any given time.

McClure: Also, having powerful examples. If we read Federico García Lorca, we look at a poem like "Nobody understood the perfume of the dark magnolia of your womb / —No one knew that you tormented a hummingbird of love between your teeth / —A thousand Persian ponies feel asleep at the moonlight plaza of your forehead." The poem is almost all *drive* words: *Nobody, understood, perfume, dark, magnolia, womb, hummingbird, tormented, teeth, thousand, Persian, ponies, asleep, moonlight, plaza, forehead*.

Luttrell: Yeah. Those are all drive words. I see what you mean.

McClure: Yeah. So that Lorca, sometimes, is almost surely drive words.

Luttrell: Which, maybe, gets to, at least as far as Lorca and the drive word, it gets to a sense of that *duende*.

McClure: Lorca was able to conceive of the *duende* in poetry because he's living on top of a vibrant, dangling, viny growth of his own drive words. When I say drive words I mean his consciousness. You know, there are emblems of consciousness. Because his consciousness is so myriad minded, he's able to open himself up to be a large enough person to become aware that the *duende* is not simply the force coming up through the soles of the feet like in the flamenco dance, but is also an understanding of a demon of power, a demon that's physical to poets and apparent in poets.

Luttrell: What do you think are the emblems of our age?

McClure: The emblems of our age are being created for the people younger than us by television and they're transient. When kids say things like "Nike," they don't mean the goddess, but the tennis shoe. And "Honda" is not a Japanese family but an automobile corporation.

Luttrell: Yeah, it's sort of a perversion. The emblems of our age are perverted.

McClure: It's deleterious if one wishes to grow a soul.

Luttrell: Yeah, I would think that in what Keats refers to as that "Vale of Soul Making," that television is the enemy.

McClure: That's clear at this point.

Luttrell: In the sixties I know that you edited a small-press magazine called *Ark II/Moby I*.

McClure: Yeah. Actually, it was in the midfifties.

Luttrell: Well, given that experience, what's your take on the role of the small press poetry mags, now and then, and have they changed and, if so, maybe, how?

McClure: The most important thing for a small magazine is to have a strong editor. People complain about the quality of poetry being printed in magazines. Let's go to the negative aspect here for a while. When readers disparage the small-press magazine, they talk about the quality of the poetry. They disparage the magazine because of the quality of the poetry and that's wrong. I think when one looks sourly at a small-press magazine, rather than disparaging the poetry one must ask what the editor is doing. It takes a strong editor to create a magazine that has meaning. I see the editor as the most important part of the magazine. A magazine can be a real state of consciousness, a real important thing for the development of awareness and thinking and perceptions. It's what the editor puts into the magazine that gives the magazine its strengths and weaknesses. It's not what's out there or even what appears in the magazine, it's what the editor did. Poets should be willing to be accepted as well as rejected and they should view magazines as objects of importance in politics, not just literary politics. My favorite magazines are *Black Mountain Review* and *Origin* and *Yugen*. . . . also *Floating Bear*. And those magazines were functions of Robert Creeley and Baraka and di Prima and for *Origin* it was Cid Corman. And another thing is, Corman didn't actually do it all himself, not to detract from his distinction in any way, but he had his advisors, Creeley and Olson. It was a triumvirate. They were really "shapers," this powerful triumvirate, and were making a platform for poets like Paul Blackburn and Larry Eigner.

Luttrell: Speaking of poets, what poets are you reading at the moment?

McClure: I'm reading Mallarmé. I go to him because I'm interested in what he says about the book as universe.

Luttrell: In your first published work in *Poetry Magazine* in 1956, those poems were dedicated to the late poet Theodore Roethke. I wonder what influence, looking back on it from now, he had on your work?

McClure: It was powerfully liberational for me when I was in high school. I discovered his book *The Lost Son and Other Poems*, which I think was either his first or second book. In it I found a man who was deeply involved with the biological world. It was is if he was walking around up to his knees in tadpoles and flowers and I guess that's the way I felt I was. I felt a great kinship. "The size of a rat, it's bigger than that, it's less than a leg, it's more than a nose, just under the water it usually goes: Gillyflower ha, gillyflower o, my love's locked in the old silo . . . she cries to the hen, she waves to the goose, but none will come to let her loose." I loved those poems. I still do.

Luttrell: Well, I know that in Roethke a lot of his metaphors are greenhouse oriented, and flowers, lots of flowers and I don't know that if, in fact, maybe his father or someone actually had a greenhouse?

McClure: Yes, his father did have a greenhouse. His father was German. He talked about his father shouting, and one of the lines of the poem goes, "Ordnung, Ordnung, papa's coming." Ordnung means order, order, attention, get yourself together, Papa's coming.

Luttrell: So, I suppose, to a certain extent, at least, our immediate surroundings are extremely important, almost in an unconscious way, maybe.

McClure: Of course, Roethke's environment was his own soul, the voices coming out of it and the voices he heard coming from the primordial stuff that was springing to life in the greenhouse and in the lawns, the pools. Yeah, I can still see what I saw in Roethke.

Luttrell: Michael, thanks for your insights and inspiration. I'm sure our readers will appreciate them.

McClure: Cool.

Craft Interview with Michael McClure

New York Quarterly / 1995

From *New York Quarterly*, no. 55 (1995).

New York Quarterly: You say that consciousness is a real thing, like the hoof of a deer. Is consciousness a physical thing for you? If so, how do you put it into poetry, or vice-versa? Is poetry physical too?

Michael McClure: When I hold my hand up in the air and just let the fingers hang down and look at it, I realize that the fingers, the hand, the whole thing that I see—all of the flesh hanging there—is consciousness. The body is consciousness. The mind is an extension of the body. So what we usually think of as consciousness is like foam over the edge of the wave. It is the body itself that is consciousness. The hand holding the pen which moves across the page or typing the keys of the computer or holding the stubby pencil and writing on the brown paper bag, however we do it, is a physical piece of consciousness and it is creating the poem which is an extension of that consciousness and is utterly physical. The poem exists in the air when we speak it, or exists on the page when another part of the consciousness writes it down, whether with lead or with jetted ink from a spray printer or out of the tip of a fountain pen.

NYQ: So having many poems in your head is like having the consciousness of many great poet spirits in your head.

MC: Yeah. If I recite to myself a poem by Blake, or a nursery rhyme, or a poem by Emily Dickinson—if I say "Split the Lark—and you'll find the Music— / Bulb after Bulb, in Silver rolled," or begin a poem of Blake's, "I low sweet I roamed from field to field, / And tasted all the summer's pride"—or if I say a nursery rhyme, "Hark, hark, the dogs do bark / The beggars are coming to town"—you know, those are all acts of consciousness that I'm privileged to have within my own. And they have become me. It is like the hoof of the deer: the neuronal substrate that contains that information is as real as the hoof of a deer.

NYQ: Mailer says you, Michael, are always your own voice, yet we find one of the most interesting things about your work is that we never know what to expect from it. We don't think of there being a single McClure voice. What is your view? Do you have one voice, or many?

MC: A moment ago, I started a poem by Emily Dickinson, "Split the Lark and you'll find the Music— / Bulb after Bulb in Silver rolled— / Scantily dealt to the Summer Morning / Saved for your Ear when Lutes be old." What Emily Dickinson is describing is the onions that used to grow in Grandma's garden, when you cut them in half you see the separation of the spheres within spheres within spheres, oftentimes divided by a kind of silvery or golden membrane. So in a sense, all of those layers of onion are alike, are the same thing. That's one answer. The other is: I think it's more clear that my work is all one voice the more one knows of my work. If one were able to read my essays and my novels, and to see some of my plays in production, and hear the performances that I do with Ray Manzarek, then I think one would begin to see the holism of it all. I feel it's all one voice.

I don't publish a large amount of what I write. When I write, I don't inhibit myself about what I may *not* say, although I have many rules about what I may say—many rules of projectivity and projective voice. I don't inhibit myself about what I *must* say, but I try to speak as widely as I can. And then when I've written what I've written, I say: "*Is* that my voice? *Is* that me? *Is* that authentically what I say?"

NYQ: You have had many personal transformations: sober poetry apprentice, husband, father, psychic explorer, experimenter with drugs, Hells Angel, wild man, icon of sixties male beauty along with Jim Morrison, musical performer, serious scholar, dedicated professor. And there have been at least as many transformations in your poetry. We're wondering how the two are related, the transformations in your poetry and the transformations in who you are, in your many personae.

MC: Let me add one persona to that, one more layer to that. Let me say "grandfather." Because I'm a grandfather. No one ever told me that when I was a grandfather that I would be dreaming about my grandfather or thinking about my grandfather. Or thinking about my grandmother. I wonder if this is true for many people, when they reach this age or become a grandparent.

In which case there's a huge linkage of family and person that we do not consider when we're younger. If I could bring one person back from the dead to speak to right now, it would be my stepgrandmother. I'd like to talk to her. I was too young to really know her deeply, and I think she had a great deal to tell me. I wouldn't have guessed that that would be the case, or she'd be the person I'd want to bring back, fifteen years ago.

We used the word "personae"; I don't really think that any of the things you've mentioned are personae as much as they were simply the things that I was doing at the time. I am much related to what's going on around me. If I'm writing the autobiography of a friend of mine who's a Hells Angel, I can't help but become involved. I was writing the autobiography of Freewheelin Frank. The book was called *Freewheelin Frank, Secretary of the Angels, as Told to Michael McClure*, and if I hadn't gotten a motorcycle that was the twin of Frank's motorcycle, and had it built by his Hells Angel friends, and learned to ride it, I would have felt like a voyeur. I would have felt unauthentic. So I came to it out of my respect and love and honoring Frank Reynolds's gift of storytelling and language, and his interest in life. I was drawn by that into finding myself astride a motorcycle, so to speak. So I see it all as simply those things that one explores, in the creation of their soul.

NYQ: And does your poetry keep pace with where you're going, where your psychic changes are going, where your mind is going?

MC: Sometimes my poetry leads, and I have to figure out what I wanted to come to—the poetry expresses where I wanted to go; sometimes the poetry's right where I'm at, which is what's happening right now, because I'm deeper in my body than I've ever been before, and I'm writing long poems of the body. So the poems are right where I'm at. And other times I'm looking back and writing an earlier kind of poetry, and I try to discard that. It doesn't seem as impetuously important to me as an artist.

NYQ: What will become of this writing that's not being published? Do you see it as someday possibly being published, or is it just for people that are curious about your work—?

MC: Some of the unpublished work is practice. Some is field notes. Some is experimental. Some is misbegotten; some of it is interesting and *should* be published. However, the requirements of books as one publishes them limits what can be printed, so you select for the brightest that follows a particular vibration. You can't allow the work to expand in a book as much as it has expanded in your writing and in your consciousness, in your life. You can see that in Shelley.

NYQ: How do you know when a poem is working? Is there any secret?

MC: I can tell instantly. Sometimes I'm wrong. But there is an ebullience to a poem that is a true work of art which resembles the life one would see in a chipmunk or a jellyfish or a penguin or a marmoset, or a madrone tree. There's a vibrancy. Sometimes it's a low-timbre vibrancy, as one might see in a tree, and other times it is a kind of sprightliness that one feels in some swiftly moving warm-blooded animal. But I recognize it, and that's also what I look for in poems by other artists. Everybody has their own exuberance, or their own vitality, or their own life-ness in their work. Amiri Baraka has one kind, Allen Ginsberg has another life-ness that's in his poetry, Artaud has another.

NYQ: Do you revise a lot, or if you see that a poem has that kind of ebullience, is it pretty much there and doesn't really need much tampering with?

MC: Sometimes I revise endlessly. I spent four years writing a poem called "LOVE LION BOOK." Other times I revise endlessly and then go back to almost the original work. Sometimes when I write a work it's as clear and spontaneous and true to itself as one could hope for, and there'll be no changes, or perhaps only a change here and there. I enjoy poems that come out and don't require any changes; I also enjoy working over a long period of time with a long poem. Or working over a long period of time with a short poem. I like each process very much. One is like spontaneously writing a sonata, and the other is creating over a long period of time, in some instances even building up—in some instances even layering, or oftentimes searching for what the original word would have been: to find it in its original spontaneous shape, it's like working on a string quartet.

NYQ: When you're revising, what do you go for? You say sometimes you're layering, and sometimes you're just searching.

MC: Usually, I like to think that I'm looking for the original impulse, but this is not true. As much as I would like it to be true, that in itself is a fiction, because oftentimes in going back, looking for what I thought was the original impulse, I find whole areas of perception and consciousness and imagination that I can follow which are as true as the ones that I was looking for originally. And *those* are really baksheesh. That's the word Ford Maddox Ford used: those are the real gift.

NYQ: You said in the preface to *Rebel Lions* that poetry comes from the body. How has your poetry changed as you've gotten older and your body has changed?

MC: Several things about growing older are of much importance. One is that age allows the possibility of becoming more radical. Many people do not become more radical as they grow older, but age opens the possibility for those who choose to do so. I see myself becoming more radical. I would like to see greater concern with radical conception, whether it's political or environmental or soul-building. When one grows older, one has the possibility of dropping some of one's personality. And the more personality we're able to lose, the more whole we are. The personality is the result of things that have happened to us during our lives, that have accrued to us. As we get older some of us are fortunate enough to need those parts of the personality less, we're able to drop them away, and we're able to think, feel, perceive, in a way that's fresh again—that's like youth, only perhaps richer than youth. I'd like to have those elements in my poetry; I think I do have them in some poetry.

NYQ: Does any of that connect with the body, though, with the aging of the poet's body as he gets older?

MC: Oh, yes. The personality is the postures that we hold with our body, and the way we act or move or speak from those postures. And those postures are to some degree inherent, genetic, those are fine, there's nothing we can do about those except layer on top of them—and it's the layering on top of them that is the personality. The personality is the sum total of the things that have happened to us. And by that I also mean things that we're involved in, that have happened to us, or that we create. And much of that is illusory.

NYQ: And you seem to be saying that some of it drops away.

MC: It is possible, with effort, to drop some of it away, and I have been making the effort to let some of slip away.

NYQ: In comparison to Kerouac, you talked about how as a young man you had a kind of stiff self-consciousness.

MC: Absolutely.

NYQ: And has some of that dropped away or been discarded?

MC: Much of my self-consciousness has. The self-consciousness that is self-conscious about being self-conscious about being self-conscious is dropping away. And I must say a lot of that is the privilege of working with Ray Manzarek. Particularly, it's been able to drop away in the last six or seven years of working with Ray—and of other major changes that have happened in my life.

NYQ: Why is that? What is it about working, doing the musical performances with Ray that has made you less self-conscious?

MC: Let's say less self-conscious in the pejorative way, because I believe there's a genetic self-consciousness that has not changed a bit. Being in a space, on a stage, with a fellow creative artist, and creating a symbiotic work of art, a work of art that comes fully and completely from both persons and operates from the energies and imaginations of both people, and being able to do that for an audience, is one of the thrills in life. It has allowed me to exercise some of the radical potentialities that I told you about. Manzarek and I, as a duo, have been able to go to music halls and colleges and even to blue-collar blues clubs in places like Detroit and present heavy-duty visionary environmental poems, have been able to go into those places and do outspoken political poems, and have them heard, because it's in conjunction with the music. And we've often received standing ovations, by people who understood what we said. There are physiological reasons for that kind of reception, too.

NYQ: What do you mean?

MC: Well, we began by talking about consciousness being physiological. The fact is that people can listen to poetry and music in a different way than reading poetry on the page (by the way, I honor both, completely). More people can understand more at this point by hearing poetry with music—in my case, with Ray Manzarek's music. The left side of the brain is the word side and responds to words; the right side is the pitch side and responds to pitch. This is not a right/left brain thing, I'm not talking about Ornstein's theories of the right and left brain. I'm speaking about where these organs are located in the brain. When both sides of the brain are used, the listener experiences a more complex event and becomes more physiologically involved in the event. In other words, the auditor or the spectator/auditor is experiencing herself or himself more and takes more away after the event. It has to do with the amount of action, of meat action, that the auditor has in harmony with the event. If one reads verse on the page, one has to give huge amounts of oneself to the experience—which I deeply enjoy doing. I love poetry on the page—but when I listen to a poet reading, I'm able to say, "Ah! *This* is what she meant! Oh I get it now." It might have taken me years to know her voice that clearly, or maybe I never would have gotten there. That doesn't mean I think everybody ought to work with music.

NYQ: There seems to be an implication that by the audience taking away more; it's somehow redounding to you and expanding you as well. How is that?

MC: It becomes me creating a soul out there, but actions that I make, that I can incorporate into my inner life. Because we don't build a soul on the inside. The work of soulmaking has to be outside. As Keats said, it's a vale of soulmaking; you've got to be in that vale. The vale isn't in you, you can draw upon it and make it part of your inner life.

NYQ: In the preface to *Rebel Lions*, you said that poetry is the voice's athletic action. Action painting comes to mind, and we're also wondering how this is related to Olson's projective verse. The athletic principle of poetry, is that related to Olson in any way?

MC: Absolutely. It's related to Olson and it's related to the work of Jackson Pollock. My work was sourced at an earlier time in Olson's idea of projective verse, in the object of perception creating an energy in the artist which then comes out through the tip of the pen or the computer again, almost like a *pounce* onto the field of the page or the mind. That's projective verse. In addition, one listens not for the meaning of the poem—which ties in with Goethe saying that poetry to be great must be both incomprehensible and incommensurable. One listens not for the meaning of the poem, but for the music of the syllable. That's projective verse.

With action painting, with spiritual autobiography as practiced by Pollock and the abstract expressionist painters, one creates, through the physical movements of the body, an act of consciousness which remains extant on a canvas, on a wall, or a piece of paper. And as with the American Indians or with other sophisticated peoples, one does not deal with the small events which happen in our lives, which are utterly like everyone else's events in their lives—the garbageman comes and picks up the garbage, we drive our automobiles and burn petroleum; we have our families, we have our feelings, all of these things are in common—but the spiritual events for the abstract expressionist are modes of perception; as in the case of American Indians they were dreams and visions that they had. If you asked Native Americans of the California tribes, fifty years ago, what were their great events, they felt that their lives were like everyone else's lives. And of course, in a tribe, each life is very much like everyone else's lives. So they'd tell you about the great dreams they had, or they'd tell you about the perceptions they had.

NYQ: Do you feel that's at least partly true for you? Although you've had an interesting life in the physical world, would you feel that some of your most interesting moments are your spiritual revelations, or poetic revelations, or dreams?

MC: It's a model for me. Whitehead said: we think in generalities, but we live in detail. The details of our lives are of great interest, but it is the pattern of the wholeness, the field we move on, to which we are committed. Maybe the personality fools us, yet we don't believe that's the case. Corporations create personalities for us so they can sell beer and tennis shoes and murderous movies to our personalities. As our personalities develop and become more illusionistic, we forget the whole field of our lives, and we think that we are those smaller things that we do, and then they become overwhelmingly interesting. We're fooled.

NYQ: So when you think back on the most interesting passages of your life, or experiences of your life, do you think about physical times like hanging out with Freewheelin Frank or do you think about the mental changes, the revelations, the things that went on inside?

MC: Oh, I remember the physical details. I remember the way someone's voice was, and the way something smelled. I remember the spot of oil I slipped on when I was riding the motorcycle. Absolutely. We reexperience those things in details. But Goethe said experience is only half of experience.

NYQ: Your poetry tends to be more accessible not only than Olson's but also than a lot of Robert Duncan's poetry.

MC: It's only been the last few years that people have considered my poetry accessible. I'm quite surprised to hear it, because I've always thought my poetry was open and accessible but it's only been recently that other people have agreed with me. Olson and Duncan are doing things that I'm not doing. I'm doing a third thing. Olson immersed himself so deeply in history, first history that he'd studied and then history as a palpable sensory concept, that he himself became history. You have to become involved with his stream of perceptions and revelations and experiences that he's embodying to understand. In the case of Duncan, Duncan has become one with language. Duncan has immersed himself so deeply in language that he is part of an ocean and river and waterfalls and cataracts of language, and one must say, "Yes, is that interesting to me? If so, I will flow with Robert over these rocks and through these channels and with these tides." My own work has been with nature and with physical experience and with my friends and with my body, which is sometimes more open and accessible.

NYQ: Your book of memoirs and essays, *Lighting the Corners*, shows the large number of people that you've had very close, and almost soul-connecting relationships with. Very close-up, intimate portraits, of Richard Brautigan, Robert Duncan, Jim Morrison, Jack Spicer, and many, many others. Yet in some respects you've been portrayed as a loner. You're not part of the famous group photographs of Ginsberg and Corso and Kerouac and Burroughs and so on. Yet your life among other people, and your deep friendships, are a vital part of who you are, and possibly also a part of your poetry.

MC: At various points in my life I have been a loner, as people say, and at all times in my life I require large amounts of solitude, almost every day. On the other hand, I am the result of my friendships. Not wholly, but my friendships have been important. My friendships with the people who are spoken of in *Lighting the Corners* were with those who in many cases became like brothers, or in the case of Robert Duncan, a family mentor. I would not be who I am today without my relationships to those people. But I didn't feel that they were solely contributing to the creation of my person.

They were contributing to their creation of their spirit and their soul. I've had warm friendships with many people, and with my family, and they've been extremely important to me. I don't think I would be the poet that I am today—not in any way to diminish my own originality, but I certainly would not be the poet I am today if it had not been for Artaud, or Allen Ginsberg, or Robert Creeley or Robert Duncan. Or Amiri Baraka or Diane di Prima or D. H. Lawrence or William Blake.

NYQ: There is a certain amount of anger and political rage in your poetry much like Allen Ginsberg's—"the stench of human cruelty creates a cloud that does not pass," or another line of yours, "the grief of every beggar hurts me in my seams." Yet we tend to think of your work as being more private, a private visionary dialogue with yourself, and not at all public in the sense of Allen's political poetry.

MC: My political poems are forced out of me. I don't have any intention of writing them. They're a response. "The grief of every beggar hurts me in my seams" is what I write after seeing the street people on the grimy streets of Berkeley.

The other line you quoted is my very deepest—I didn't wish to make a response to a series of atrocity murders in Calaveras County that were so horrible they shouldn't be publicized but I had to. The political poetry that I wrote when I was young was the outrage of the young man at NATO soldiers and sailors killing a hundred whales off the coast of Iceland in 1954. In my poetry I have that early rage at the injustice and biocidal frenzy that was clearly visible during the Cold War. And in my later poetry there is the privilege of the maturing man or woman to become more radical. It is a privilege to see that suffering and be able to speak against it. Not a privilege to see it, but to be able to speak against it. And to do more than speak against it: if one can make another kind of gesture, to make that too.

When Allen and I first read our poetry together in 1955, when six of us were at the Six Gallery on October 12, 1955, Allen's politics was "Howl." "Howl" changed all of us at that reading, whether we were young bourgeois anarchists or young Marxist socialist radicals, because we were all of one stripe or another in a dissident camp. We could not draw back.

Since then, most of what I would call my political poetry has been "environmental." Lately, though I've been able to speak from another deeper set of feelings.

NYQ: Your writing comes out of a deep personal connection with nature, with animals—you love animals very dearly, and we often think of you as much like Thoreau, who had a kind of soulful connection with trees and bushes and animals and birds. So it's not so much political, environmental, whatever the trendy level is, but that it's coming out of some personal need or connection in you.

MC: My deepest feelings have always been connected with nature. And you're absolutely right that "environmental" has become a stolen term. The concept of environmentalism has been coopted, and the corporations use it as a way of selling guilt and toxins and confusion.

NYQ: With you there's that kind of immediate, physical, gut response of connection, with other living creatures.

MC: I am part of one huge molecule that incorporates all forms of life that ever existed or ever will exist. I am a mammal patriot, in particular. I travel to what people call Third-World countries, to Kenya or Tanzania or Mexico, but the integral, basic reason I'm there is to see birds, plants, animals, and the environment of those areas. Much of the traveling I do is to deepen my understanding of the life around me. Whether it's in early poems, when I write "It's the mystery of the hunt that intrigues me / That drives us like lemmings but cautiously" or in the most recent haiku about a rabbit running down the driveway in a neighbor's yard.

NYQ: It's much more than an intellectual apprehension with you; it's who you are and your physical love for other beings.

MC: Much of what I know about nature and biology comes from, not my reading, but from traveling and associating with biologists and botanists in various places, or taking walks with them, or having dinner with them or having conversations with them, or going out to look at eagles, or trails, or jungles, or cacti with them. So it's not a result of reading, although I'm self-educated to a large extent in some fields, but it is travel to see, to feel, to perceive, to smell, to be there, to actually look into the tidepool and see the sea anemone.

NYQ: The English poet and critic George Dowdon makes a strong case that Allen Ginsberg is hardly a visionary poet at all, and his basis is saying that truly visionary poets write a lot about nature, identify with nature. And he doesn't find a lot of that in Allen's work. And yet in your work it seems to be there all the time, this identification with nature. So do you feel that puts you much more strongly in the visionary camp of poetry?

MC: I recommend to the English poet and critic who said that about Allen, that he take another look at Allen's work. We are so impressed by Allen's political work, and the honest-to-god real world research that he's put into the facts that he uses, and the brilliance that he puts into writing it all out as ballads and singing it with his harmonium, that we tend to overlook other poems of his. Look at the major beautiful poem that he wrote on the wildflowers in Big Sur. Also, I would point out that for Allen the natural world has always been what we think of as "consciousness." Nature is, for Allen, consciousness in the sense of mentation. Allen is more deeply involved with the human universe that the universe of nature. This is a fact. But he's not uninvolved with the universe of nature.

NYQ: More than most of the so-called Beat writers, you use traditional forms: odes, sonnets, sestinas, old-fashioned poetic devices such as rhyme and rhyming couplets. . . . Do you consciously use these in an attempt to give your poetry more of a formal shape, or are these devices something that's somehow coming naturally out of a physical extension of yourself?

MC: When I was a child, I grew up listening to songs that were written in the ballad form. Also I remember my mother reciting humorous poems of Kipling to me: "Ere the steamer bore him eastward / Sleary was engaged to marry / An attractive girl in Tunbridge / whom he called 'my little Carrie.'" And I remember a lot of comic verse, written in structured forms; also the *Rubaiyat of Omar Khayyam*, written in quatrains. As I became an adolescent I discovered free verse, from e.e. cummings to Pound, when I was in high school. When I first started writing poetry it was extremely free verse, almost pictographic. Then I realized while reading Baudelaire and Blake that something large was missing in my work, and I taught myself forms and meter and wrote Miltonic and Petrarchan sonnets and villanelles and sestinas and ballads and Spenserian stanzas and Sapphics, and enjoyed working with them, but they were too constraining. As I gained skill, I began to realize that the forms I was teaching myself were too constraining for what I had to say. They were beautiful: it's a beautiful thing to read Hart Crane's "A Name for All"—gorgeous things can be done with strict rhyme and meter and form. But if you look at the unreworked poems of Crane, they may be less beautiful, but they say so much more. They may be not such shimmering or conceited works of art, and I use "conceited" in the literary sense, but they are more profound. His posthumous poems, that he didn't rewrite, those are the deeper ones. I could see then that forms were strangling the essential imagination into structured elegance, whereas with projective verse, one had the possibility of giving beautiful rules to the imagination and to the creative power that one has so that they might shape more profound structures in the field of consciousness. Yet I could not say goodbye to those beautiful forms I had grown up with. Those were part of me also, and I enjoy having them appear. I particularly enjoy finding lines of iambic pentameter, or maybe even a rhyming iambic pentameter couplet, in a poem that is my own projective verse. It is utterly natural. It belongs there. It delights me. Sometimes years later I'll say, "Oh look! If you just rearrange that on the page, it's a rhyming couplet." Or maybe I'll find a ballad, or a ballad stanza that I'd hidden from myself, and maybe even from the reader, by having it on the page in a different way.

NYQ: You use the word "beauty" a lot. Is beauty a really important factor for you in the writing of poetry and the appreciation of art?

MC: Absolutely. I believe in the importance of beauty. I find many kinds of beauty, whether it's the beauty of projective verse, or the beauty that one would hear in Kurt Schwitters's sound poetry, or see in the distraught and elegant assemblages of Bruce Conner, or the laughing agonized profound pastels of Francesco Clemente. There are many kinds of beauty, and I do believe that it's important.

NYQ: What is beauty? Keats said it was truth. Do you have a simple definition?

MC: I'll go with Keats. Since Keats and Whitehead both said the same thing, I'll take their word for it. In the late fifties and in the sixties, I was concerned that beauty was a commodity, and that we were handing people beauty, and I reacted strongly against it because I was capable of writing poems of enormous beauty. Then I was radicalized by Antonin Artaud's use of his psychosis as a means of exploring what is knowable and to be explored, and began writing another poetry. And I denounced beauty in those poems, the same way I hear people today denouncing beauty as a commodity and a product. But having been through that thirty years ago, I don't go through it anymore, and I look back on those reactive poems and those poems are now beautiful.

"What Are Souls?": An Interview with Michael McClure

Jack Foley / 2001

Interview taped in Jack Foley's home in Oakland, California on Mary 24, 2001 and July 16, 2001. Reprinted by permission.

[San Francisco's] geographical distance from New York encouraged aesthetic independence, and its connection to anarchist politics contributed an edge of social engagement.
—Steven Watson, "Chronology," Beat Culture and the New America 1950–1965

Poetry is a muscular principle—an athletic song or whisper of fleshly thought.
—Michael McClure, Jaguar Skies (1975)

Part I

Jack Foley: Michael, let's talk about your life. Before we begin that, though, would you read a letter and a poem—significantly titled "Souls"—to Ernesto Cardenal. You wrote the poem in May after seeing Cardenal speak.

Michael McClure: Cardenal's reading was a celebration. There were eight hundred people there! He's one of the great Nicaraguan revolutionaries of his generation as well as the liberation theologian who has galled the Church the most intensely. He's smaller physically now and his hair and beard have become silvery white. OK, here's the letter:

Dear Ernesto:

You are a sun sprite, all whiteness and light—what an enormous pleasure to see you and hear you again. What a deep and flying poem of revolution, liberation theology, socialism, love, environment, microbiology, and astrophysics! Three

days later I found COSMIC CANTICLE and am reading it. Thanks to you for being Ernesto Cardenal—we need you. And thanks to Alexandro Murguia for his strong and sensitive reading of the English translation.
Enclosed is a poem you inspired.
Love to you and yours.

And now the poem. [*Reads "Souls."*]
Jack, the poem "Souls" has opened a circuit of antibrutality poems, raw things, something like the grim and comic late paintings of Philip Guston or Goya's *Horrors of War*. The "grahhr" at the end comes back from "Poisoned Wheat," my long poem contra the Vietnam War—the first long poem written contra the Vietnam War. It was republished in *Huge Dreams* (Penguin, 1999). Rod Phillips, author of *Urban Thoreaus and Forest Beatniks*, a book about me, Gary Snyder and Lew Welch, just did a paper on "Poisoned Wheat" and brought that "grahhr" of my old Beast Language back to me. The poem opens with some "Beast Language."

JF: "Odem, not Geist," you write in the preface to your first book, *Hymns to St. Geryon* (1959). You say you write "to free the Beast Spirit": "there is no logic but sequence."

MM: Yeah, Odem and Geist are German. Odem is the Beast Soul, the undersoul. Geist is the same word as "ghost" in English—sort of. The "ghost" that leaves the body at death, theoretically. We don't make those distinctions in modern English.

JF: That statement was made in a journal you wrote in 1957.

MM: Yes. It became the foundation for an exploratory and declamatory poem called "Rant Block," which begins, "THERE IS NO FORM BUT SHAPE! NO LOGIC BUT SEQUENCE!" "Rant Block" was published in 1957 in *Yugen*, a magazine edited by LeRoi Jones (Amiri Baraka). That was the magazine I matured with. Everybody in those days had a magazine to mature with—one with an editor who was furious and ferocious and prejudiced for you and against you and had deep feelings about everything that went into his magazine. Robert Creeley and Charles Olson had Cid Corman's magazine, *Origin*. I had *Yugen*, and *Semina*.

JF: There's a word, along with "grahhr," that shows up in both of the new poems you read today, and it's a word that goes deep into your poetry: it's the word "soul." You ask, "What are souls?" You take the term "soul-making" from Keats but use it in your own special way. That's an issue of your poetry.

MM: My wife and friend Amy is a person with a richness of soul, and it shows in her eyes and hands as they give some of their soul to the way she shapes figures of Buddhas and horseheads. It's stimulating to me to see art like that grow from "soul." Robert Duncan said that one great thing about Shakespeare was that he gave every *persona* from gravedigger to king, every character in his plays a soul. I take it that's what "soul" means—to have the richness of spirit as in Shakespeare. We're born with the capacity for soul-making, and we learn to enrich it and to make it be meaningful—and to allow it to be ourselves.

JF: I think that part of the interest in your work is just that. "Identity" is to be made; celebrated (as in your praise of Cardenal) but continually to be made, over and over again.

MM: There's too much emphasis on process. I believe there is essentially *restlessness*. And the restlessness that creates more space for restlessness creates more space. And the more space there is, the more it is an act of creation. There's restlessness. And then more restlessnesses. And then more *restlessnesses* move in that space.

JF: Is it like what one would think of as mental evolution—not evolution towards a goal but movement, mental movement. Mental movement is perhaps a mirror of the evolutionary mode of the world—of people, of beasts.

MM: I was thinking it's like a family of foxes running in a field! [*Laughing*]

JF: [*Laughing*] And all over the place!

MM: Yeah.

JF: Let's go back a ways. You were born in Kansas. . . .

MM: I was born in the wheat and oil state of Kansas in 1932.

JF: There's your "poisoned wheat"!

MM: Nineteen thirty-two was the year that was the height of the Great Drought.

JF: You come in when there is no water.

MM: There were rivers and streams but there was plenty of topsoil blown deep and dry on everything. It was the "Dust Bowl"—the center of the "Dust Bowl."

JF: Going through my various dates of your activities throughout your career, I noticed how much you connect with other people. So much of what you're about is your friendships and your connections with fellow artists. The summer in Kansas is dry and "dusty" in *many* ways. . . .

MM: It was the Kansas of the Flint Hills on which [L. Frank Baum's] Oz is based—but that was only for the few of us who went into the Flint Hills and found those little Munchkin towns and drove around in them and explored limestone caves. Kansas was a place of tent revivals—Fundamentalist Pentecostal Tent Revivals—and the praise-shouting and preaching was heard on the street as you walked by. People were drawn in and "saved." And it's also the Kansas of bar fights. Artist Bruce Conner used to go into the tent revivals: Bruce was saved a number of times! [*Laughing*] I thought it was flamboyant of him! It was a primitive place. Farmers with their red, suncracked necks were moving from being reapers to being people wearing sombreros and riding on power harvesters. In "THE BULKS OF HEARTS" in *Rebel Lions* (1991) I wrote,

> Sun beating yellow fields of wheat
> and reapers' shadows reaping
> while the women cook up pies and stews.

I'm not sure how many power harvesters I saw as a boy. I think most were drawn by horses. At the same time, there were old men farmers with pet monkeys in their barns. I remember my father driving out with a new car to see one of them and I remember being fascinated by seeing a monkey for the first time. But the cities of Kansas—I'm thinking in particular of Wichita, which is the setting of the first half of my novel, *The Mad Cub* (written 1964). Wichita had an unprimitive quality. The people there had to be tough to survive the four seasons—violent snow, violent rain, very violent winds: powerful, powerful seasons—*and* all the electrolytes in the soil which are constantly being stirred by the wind across the plains. Before the days of factory farming, the electrolytes had a tremendous biological impact on the grasses there, so that horses and animals were often stronger, more powerful. This was believed to be caused by the electrolytes in the soil, which were picked up in the fodder that the animals ate. There are books on the subject.

JF: Does this apply to people as well?

MM: Yes—to the enormous energy that so many of us had. But it was the misdirection of that energy into crude purposes that made us feel outlawed there. And it made the people who were my friends feel like desperados too.

I'm talking about high school now, and the first year of college, when I was in Wichita. In fact, I grew up in Seattle, Washington, by the side of the Pacific Ocean—really black ocean—looking at tiny crabs squinting at me from under rocks on the beach and walking through panoplies of forests. There's nothing but buildings in Seattle now. I was there a couple of weeks ago driving around in one of those areas I used to live in as a kid: the forests and lakes were gone. I went to the Seattle Museum, which was an influence on my childhood—the Asian collection there.

But to return to Kansas: The friends that I had there had to stick together, and I was tight with them because we really felt like—seriously—desperadoes. Partly because we weren't liked but equally because we did not like the others. It was a no-holds-barred world. We were giraffes in a flock of sheep. There was rigid conformity and social stratification. We stood out. I had occasion to look at our high school yearbook lately; the group of us that graduated together and were friends are extraordinary compared to the others. In comparison we look like images on most-wanted posters. Some strong souls like Lee Streiff stayed and held the fort, but most of us left.

JF: One of the words that shows up again and again in your work is "kid." Billy the "Kid," the kid in "Simple Eyes," who is also the Christ child and the "inner child." All of these influences that you were taking in at the time contribute to this theme.

MM: I also think about the way I lost my "kidship." I had to bargain heavily to have anything I had. I was essentially abandoned—I was sent away by my mother when I was five. Fortunately, I went to live with my grandfather in Seattle. But I went through the hell that baby primates do—as in the famous experiments on isolating baby monkeys. I remember standing in the caves of Hell bargaining with the Saber-Toothed Tiger, the Lone Ranger, Mona Lisa, and Isis, at the age of five to bring back my universe to me—despite the fact that I was with my grandparents, whom I felt love for.

JF: One of the things we've talked about—and it's also in one of your new poems, the poem about alchemy—is your statement that "I LOVE THIS!" The most horrific and traumatic of events which show up in your poetry are something you can turn around and respond to by saying, "I'm accepting this." That's one of the great strengths of your poetry and must have been one of the great strengths of your childhood.

MM: I had more problems than being sent away. I was cross-eyed, and with a growing cross-eyedness! My doctor grandfather helped by teaching me eye exercises. I also had asthma and hay fever in Kansas—which was no doubt associated with the Dust Bowl at that time. I'd had my ear drums break several times, so I did not hear well. At one point I was offered lip-reading classes. I had physical debilities that made me even more of an outsider—and a sort of advanced chubbiness when everybody else was Depression-era skinny: it was the end of the Depression. Somehow I was a "robust" kid.

JF: I've known you for over ten years, and I've seen photos of you from before that: you never look fat.

MM: I'm talking about before the age of fourteen.

JF: You're talking about "kid," about what they call "baby fat."

MM: Yeah, but serious enough to be, with the other problems, socially crippling if I let it be.

JF: Part of what's remarkable here is that everybody—including Jack Kerouac in his novel, *Big Sur* (1962)—speaks of your physical beauty as a young man. When you're in your twenties, all of those problems are behind you.

MM: I don't mean to be immodest, but I'm coming to realize now that that business about my "beauty" was true.

JF: It certainly was!

MM: It was an embarrassing fact, like a blister. But it was also of use to me: I played it. I tried to play it fair, but nobody ever plays an advantage fair when they've been fucked over when they were young. Now I see old videos of me and I realize that people were right! But I never believed it. I'd keep looking in mirrors to see what they were talking about. Probably sublimated narcissism!

JF: I have a photo of you from 1960 as you're watching your play *!The Feast!* being performed at the Batman Gallery. You were twenty-eight years old and you were absolutely gorgeous.

MM: That's a long time after fourteen.

JF: I understand that. But the transformation is extraordinary. Here's how Jack Kerouac describes you in *Big Sur*. You had read the manuscript of your book, *Dark Brown* to Kerouac, and he was very impressed with it:

> [McClure] is one of if not THE most handsome man I've ever seen—Strange that he's announced in a preface to his poems that his heroes, his Triumvirate, are Jean Harlow, Rimbaud and Billy the Kid because he himself is handsome enough to play Billy the Kid in the movies.... McLear [McClure] exhibits another strange facet of his handsome but faintly "decadent" Rimbaud-type personality at his summer camp by coming out in the livingroom with a goddamn HAWK on his shoulder—It's his pet hawk, of all things, the hawk is black as night and sits there on his shoulder pecking nastily at a clunk of hamburg he holds up to it—In fact the sight of that is so rarely poetic, McLear whose poetry is really like a black hawk, he's always writing about darkness, dark brown, dark bedrooms, moving curtains, chemical fire dark pillows, love in chemical fiery red darkness, and writes all that in beautiful long lines that go across the page irregularly and aptly somehow—Handsome Hawk McLear....

MM: Bless you, Kerouac. [*Laughing*] Jack was a generous man.

JF: You wouldn't say that "McLear" came from Kansas and the Dust Bowl!

MM: No, that sounds more like I came from Charleville, France, where Rimbaud came from! [The date of McClure's birth, October 20, is also the date of Rimbaud's birth—ed.] McClure is a name associated with the Scotch-Irish—the pre-Celtic group called Cruthins. As a child my mother lost her mother, who was a Seward descended from Lincoln's Secretary of State who bought Alaska. Through the Seward connection it's likely that I'm related to William Burroughs.

JF: There are so many reports on the impact you had on people in San Francisco. But it's interesting that you didn't think of yourself as brilliant or beautiful. And you came from a childhood in which you were told anything but that.

MM: I was told the opposite. I supposed I was a dripping and coughing mess. You mentioned that I must have felt like I transformed myself. On the one hand, there's the story of the ugly duckling becoming the swan: he just wakes up one day and has grown a long neck and elegant feathers. On the other hand, I remember when I was interviewed about Jack Kerouac, Gerry Nicosia asked me how I thought Kerouac *became* a novelist. I said I didn't think Jack could have *become* anything *but* a novelist. I don't think he transformed himself in any way. I think it's the way a baby kitten grows up into a cat or an eagle chick grows up into an eagle. That's how Jack grew into a novelist. So, on the one hand, I could say I transformed myself—and I think I used to *feel* like I transformed myself. Now, I don't believe I transformed myself so much as perhaps, in the Zen sense, I became the recipient of the situation; the situation manifested itself in me. That's dense Buddhist talk out of Trungpa, Ginsberg's guru or even more so from Dōgen. Let me take it a step further. I was on the Internet looking at a piece Levi Asher had written. It was on the "Literary Kicks" site. The piece was quite knowledgeable, but there was one thing that wasn't true. It said that Michael McClure "hung around" the Summer of Love in San Francisco in 1967. That's not what happened at all. What happened was that in 1961, when I was coming back after a time of living in New York, Joanna and Jane, my daughter, and I moved into a flat on the third floor of a house on a hill in the Haight-Ashbury district. It was then a district of Blacks, the elderly, and Russians. I lived there watching the Haight-Ashbury event take shape. It didn't really begin until a couple of years after we were there. I began to notice that it was the "Haight-Ashbury" when my favorite group the Charlatans moved in and started practicing five doors down the street from me. Country Joe MacDonald of Country Joe and the Fish moved in across the street and we introduced ourselves. Then the Psychedelic Shop on Haight Street opened up. It's not like I "hung around." It's like these things happened around me. I believe that these things happen around me, not that I come upon them. The Human Be-In in January of the Summer of Love in 1967 was planned in my apartment. The planning session is described in Jane Kramer's biography of Allen Ginsberg. Allen and Gary Snyder and I and several others were setting up a balanced plan for the event.

JF: There's a sense in your work that poetry is the making of something beautiful, an esthetic, almost Oscar-Wilde-like beauty. Beauty means beauty of body, beauty of surroundings. You hung art where you lived. There were rituals which you followed. One finds this also in Yeats, who was directly influenced by the aesthetic movement in England.

MM: The outlaw-gypsy-San Francisco community believed in art. They did what they did because they were artists. They never believed that they would sell a poem. They never believed that they would have a book published unless they published it themselves. They never believed that they would have a car other than the one with the door tied shut with a rope. They were set on creating their own—it's a bit like Gary Snyder's idea—wildness. In the city, you create an airy, uncrowded, aesthetic field that you live in; you're creating space by creating art. I don't mean just "inner space"; you're also creating the space of the discussion of this art. And, for me, the other thing that comes in there is that, early—in 1959—I'm saying I will not give you Beauty in my poems, yet the poems in which I'm saying that are obviously beautiful today forty years later.

JF: Yes!

MM: They're saying, "*At the right time I believe*, I'm not fucking gonna give you Beauty"—because we'd had too much of it and it's backfiring, it's commodity. That was important: the *redefinition* of Beauty first by the abstract expressionist painters, then by the assemblage artists, then by the Pop artists. All that happened at that time, and it was exciting. Art can try to be a substitution for nature. Except that, in *this* case, in San Francisco, we all had nature available to us: oceans, mountains, foothills, desert, close at hand.

JF: Both you and your Kansas friends become exotic figures—not "American as apple pie," not the wheat belt.

MM: Where we came from *is* apple-pie America. None of my friends ended up apple pie. But they ended up with the strength and the power that Kansas gave them. Electrolytes in the soil, violent extremes of weather. Look at Kansans like filmmakers Stan Brakhage and Dennis Hopper.

JF: And resistance. "Revolt" is a word you use.

MM: We were in revolt against everyone who had been socially propagandized. And the locals were revolted by our freedom in the midst of their post–World War II conformity and Cold War fear.

JF: You make an important distinction between "revolt" and "revolution."

MM: Revolution is the system going around and somebody else coming up on top. Revolt gets something done. Maybe you won't *like* what gets done—but it gets something done. It makes a change.

JF: It also doesn't stop. You continue it. Why did your friend Bruce Conner come to San Francisco?

MM: Bruce Conner came to San Francisco a couple of years after I homed in here. Bruce is about a year younger than I. He was in high school the same time I was. We had the first year of college together at the University of Wichita. Bruce is Leonardo-like: he has mastered so many media that when museums give him a retrospective show, they barely know what to show: his films, his amazing drawings, his paintings (he gave up painting quite early), his assemblages (incredible pieces—he's best known in the art world for them). They're like Rimbaud's works—but not "decadent": they're healthy, creepy, dark, sweet, laughing works of art.

JF: The marvelous title for his recent retrospective was "2000 BC."

MM: Yes, BC/Bruce Conner. Early on we discovered that this sixteen-year-old kid Bruce was a real painter. And we recognized it. And everybody started acquiring his paintings! I knew Jackson Pollock's work and was interested in Pollock. I had found the article about him in *Life* magazine in 1948 [actually, 1949—ed.], and I said, "My God! I knew there was something out there! Let's get moving!"

JF: It's amazing that you came to Pollock by *Life* magazine, which eleven years later would run unflattering stories about the Beats.

MM: "Unflattering" is the pleasantest description I've ever heard of *Life*'s coverage. *Life* magazine was the television of the day. In 1948 there was no television on the scene. *Life* magazine was the high point of the week for people . . . Bruce introduced me to the works of Robert Motherwell, to Gottlieb, to Clyfford Still—I could go on with the list for quite a while. Now they're seen as major artists. Here we were early in the fifties watching them. I became deeply interested in some of those artists, particularly Mark Rothko and Clyfford Still. I was in Tucson going to college, taking—oddly enough—advanced painting techniques, postgraduate physical anthropology, and German!

JF: "Odem, not geist!"

MM: These were the only things I could work up the patience for. I was reading any book of Céline's I could get my hands on and studying the research I could get from the library about peyote, which I hadn't even seen yet. I found a catalog for the San Francisco Art Institute and wow!—there was Clyfford Still and Mark Rothko. I said, "That's the place for me!"—so I went there. The first thing I found out, of course, was that Mark Rothko and Clyfford Still hadn't been there for a few years. I hadn't checked the catalog date. Isn't that *exactly* what kids do! Some of the friends I'd been with in high school had gotten to San Francisco first, and they were studying Alan Watts, who was thinking and speaking about Eastern religion and philosophy in new ways. Watts did broadcasts on Berkeley radio station KPFA. After I found out that the painters weren't around, I discovered that I could get into San Francisco State College. Going through the catalog I found somebody I'd never heard of: the poet Robert Duncan. He was giving the first poetry writing class he had ever taught.

JF: At this point you conceived of yourself as a writer.

MM: Absolutely. The interest in painting was ancillary to the fact that, from the middle of high school on, I conceived of myself as a poet.

JF: OK, it's 1954, and you have just moved to San Francisco. In "Painting Beat by Numbers" in *The Rolling Stone Book of the Beats*, you write,

> I arrived in San Francisco from Tucson on December 31, 1954. My first night, New Year's Eve, I was thrown out of a club onto Columbus Avenue, across from City Lights, for trying to make it with a girl on the bandstand. I was drinking and blurred on benzedrine—I didn't notice it was a lesbian bar. Earlier in the day, with two old high school friends, I ate with chopsticks for the first time at Sam Wo's rickety, four-floored Chinatown restaurant. I had come to San Francisco from Tucson to study abstract expressionism, and to inform my poetry with its action philosophy....

MM: At San Francisco State College I went through the catalogue and found a course in creative writing and poetry taught by a man named Robert Duncan. Other members of the class were Jack Gilbert, later a Yale Younger Poet, Helen Adam, the great ballad-writer known as the "Fairy Poet" in her Scottish childhood, Lawrence Fixel, who's still publishing today, and other variously gifted writers. Once in a while, Stan Brakhage, who became a major experimental filmmaker, came to class just to observe. Except for Brakhage, the students were older than me. I became friends with Robert and his lover, Jess. By then, I was living with my first wife Joanna. We thought of Robert and Jess as uncles or aunts—in a family situation. I'm speaking of our feeling about them and the poverty-defying elegance of their home and the hermetic quality of their life.

JF: Robert Duncan was born in 1919; you were born in 1932. How did Duncan react to your poetry, how did you react to his?

MM: First thing I brought in was a Petrarchan sonnet in the style of John Milton:

> Dead drugs, dead dogs have split my neighing head
> In colloquies of bitter light and shade
> That blazed and flecked my tympanum and flayed
> My horseshoe skull and hooving arms with dread. . . .

Something like that. It was a poem I'd written earlier, when I was teaching myself forms. I taught myself the villanelle, the sonnet, the sestina, and so forth. . . .

JF: That's something people used to do. Under the influence of creative writing workshops, they no longer seem to be doing it. I'm younger than you but not *that* much younger than you. For me, if you wanted to be a poet, you found out about metrics and forms. Certainly lots of poems had been written in these forms. It doesn't mean that you're gonna write in forms forever, but it's something to learn. A lot of people who have taken creative writing courses have grown up not knowing what the forms are at all—or believing that they should discount them.

MM: It's important to know the forms at some point and to be able to write them and to be able to write in basic meters. We should enjoy them, even glory in them—because they're not of much use anymore! That was why my sonnet distressed Robert Duncan. Maybe, unconsciously, I showed him this work to bug him, because I could see where he was at. At first he was bothered by my formal poems. He didn't know what to make of this intelligent young man, well put together, and trying hard—

JF: Good looking—

MM: [*Laughing*] Good looking, and who liked him so much, bringing in those poems. I backed down and showed him what I was writing currently and he liked that. An audible sigh of relief exuded from Robert, and then we began to be friends. His poetry is luminous, extraordinary. He was writing what became his book *Letters* (written 1953–56). He was essentially experimenting with what Charles Olson called "projective verse," although he didn't tell us that. Duncan promoted projective verse heavily to us. He did not explain that what *he* was doing was projective verse. Later, I came to understand that he was utilizing the enormous capabilities of which he was master in order to stretch and shape a field for himself in which he would write projective verse that had entirely the stamp of his face, his mind, his hands, his ear.

JF: Yes, Charles Olson's essay, "Projective Verse," had appeared in 1950. That word "field," which you used, is an important part of Olson's conception. For Olson, the page is not neutral: the page is something to be worked with. Robert Duncan recognized the importance of Olson's work very early on and was a close friend of his. Later (1960), Duncan published a wonderful book, *The Opening of the Field*.

MM: Too many people believe that Charles Olson was preaching a "doctrine" of projective verse. He was saying, "Hey, man, look what I can do this way." Telling you how he did it. Robert was one of the people who understood that.

JF: You took peyote in 1957. Your "Peyote Poem" was published in 1958. That same year, you showed art at the Spatsa Gallery.

MM: That was my show of visionary banners and wands. They were paintings of black blots based on Gérard de Nerval's poem, "El Desdichado"—the *soleil noir* [black sun]. The wands were based on shapes of Saint Patrick's cane, which Antonin Artaud had in his possession at one time.

JF: When did you come upon Artaud? He was an enormous influence, and I'm sure one of the things that moved you towards the theater.

MM: Shortly after my arrival in San Francisco, I met the young surrealist poet Philip Lamantia. Lamantia first took me to Kenneth Rexroth's soirees. Philip helped me to find translations of Artaud. I was not able to read French; if it was bilingual it was best because I could study it. One fortunate thing that happened was that I was given the manuscript of Artaud's 1947 radio play, *Pour finir avec le jugement de dieu* [*To Have Done with the Judgement of God*]. It was a translation that was never published by Guy Wernham, a writer living in North Beach. He had translated Lautréamont's *Les Chants de Maldoror*, the nineteenth-century book much loved by the surrealists. *To Have Done with the Judgement of God* is one of the most powerful visionary political works of our times. It begins with an insanely lucid picture of the military madness of the Cold War.

JF: You wrote about it in your first book of essays, *Meat Science Essays* (1963). You called it "the most intelligent book of recent times" and described Artaud's message as the assertion that "we are physiologically being crushed and exploded by our own organs, and by insane aspects of society. . . ." There's a marvelous, untitled poem of yours from your first book, *Hymns to St. Geryon* (1959): "I wanted to turn to electricity." It strikes me as so much like Artaud. The book also contains your "Peyote Poem." Had you read about Artaud's experience with peyote?

MM: Oh, yeah. Here's the poem you're speaking of: [*Reads poem*]. That's sweeter than the late Artaud would have been, though not his early poems.

JF: It's a poem about a relationship, a poem about marriage. [*Reads from poem.*] One senses some of the same wildness and violent contradiction in the work of Philip Lamantia.

MM: I happened to take out an old notebook of mine, at random. I took it from 1958. Stapled in the 1958 notebook was a letter from Philip Lamantia, who was in New York. It's Christmastime, and he's coming back to stay with his mother, and he'll see us on Christmas day or the day after. (His mother lived at a far end of town, which was hard to get to in those days.) He'd been reading his own poetry with the jazz artist, David Amram. (Amram is a mahatma!) Philip had been moving around in Greenwich Village, where Jack Kerouac was reading poetry at the Village Vanguard.

JF: So here's this whole fermenting pot of stuff which you walk right into—Artaud, Philip Lamantia, peyote, painting. The artist Jay DeFeo was a neighbor of yours at this point, wasn't she?

MM: A year or two later.

JF: She began doing her monumental painting, *The Rose*, which was a focal center of the Whitney's Beat show, in 1958.

MM: The second time Joanna and I moved we rented a huge studio apartment which couldn't exist today—it would be turned into two or three apartments. It rented for a price that was so trifling even we could pay it. It was right above Jay DeFeo's studio apartment. It was in a no-man's land between the African American district of the Fillmore and plushy Pacific Heights. Those days were before what Amiri Baraka calls "negro removal" and which the government called "Urban Renewal," so there was little hostility between Pacific Heights and the Fillmore. You had the vitality of the Fillmore District, with Jimbo's Bop City and great places to buy food—wonderful grocery stores down the street, ten blocks. It was cheap there. A lot of people began to live in that neighborhood with us. Kirby Doyle moved in. Then Bruce Conner showed up from Nebraska. Robert LaVigne, the biographical painter of the Beats, showed up in the neighborhood, and Wallace Berman and family moved up from Los Angeles. All of these people moved to an area within four blocks of us, and not more than five or six blocks away, was the East/West House, a collective commune of young Zen scholars. In our flat we lived above Jay DeFeo and Wallace Hedrick, and we lived next door to some fine New York artists. Below us was the early

"Beat" painter, Joan Brown, who has become well known since her death in 1990. We were all young folks. My flat was a meeting place for a lot of poets and for people like William Jahrmarkt, "Billy Batman." Billy opened the Batman Gallery a block away in 1960. The DeFeo flat was a meeting place both for the abstract expressionist painters of the area and the new figurative painters who emerged out of the abstract expressionists: David Parks, Elmer Bischoff. Even Willem de Kooning came there. I met de Kooning when he was drunk in the hallway and looking for Joan Brown. I didn't have any idea that it was de Kooning. I took him in and made him a cup of coffee and he showed my little girl Jane how to make clay animals! [*Laughing*]

JF: It sounds wonderful. It sounds like an idyllic situation. "This is all alchemy...."

MM: We were poor. It didn't take much to survive because we didn't have anything. Somebody *gave* you a car. Nobody sold their old car if they had a friend. In the community you gave it away. If the car door didn't work, you tied the door with a rope. And everybody gave you their furniture when they moved. Somebody went to Majorca: "You want my furniture?" "Yeah." "You want the paintings too?" "Yeah." If you weren't careful, you could have more furniture and more cars than you wanted. And of course they were all worthless. By today's standards, I suppose they're antiques, and they had the beauty of being selected by artists and lived with and loved.

JF: The paintings were not so "worthless"—but not at the time.

MM: They were valuable at the time because of who did them. I lived in a bare style of empty room. Just a brass bed, and a baby crib in another room, and fireplaces with open gas jets and a table in the kitchen. I used much of the space for hanging art—by Bruce Conner, by George Herms, by Wallace Berman. In one big room I did nothing but exhibit Bruce Conner or George Herms.

JF: A shrine. How does one live? You live with Beauty. Your "place" is not neutral; your place is going to affect your spirit.

MM: That's it! We were also the centers of suspicion. We were the only revolutionaries around—we knew our phones were tapped. We were sneered or jeered on the streets because we looked like free spirits. That didn't happen in North Beach—which was like a reservation. In North Beach one could get away with being a sappy beatnik wearing funny-looking sandals and a beret and pounding on a drum and getting bagel crumbs in your beard. They were the poseurs putting on a show for the town buses and giving the media the image. Nature, of course, was important to us. Kenneth Rexroth, with his knowledge and attitudes, encouraged us to go into nature. Kenneth was a naturalist and an outdoorsman—as well as an engine head. One day we had a conversation as he lay under his car repairing the transmission.

JF: He was an autodidact in all senses!

MM: He also told us that on the Pacific coast we were more related to Asia than we were to New York or Paris. My friends from high school were here studying Alan Watts. Watts not only expounded on Asian religion and thought; he also wrote about the environment in the most prescient way. The things he said about the environment in the 1950s are still at the cutting edge. However, the hero of the ecology movement is Sterling Bunnell. Sterling gave many ideas to every one of us, including Alan Watts. He turned Alan Watts on! [See Alan Watts's autobiography, *In My Own Way* (1972). Bunnell and his associate Michael Agron were psychiatrists at the Langley-Porter Clinic in San Francisco. It was through their efforts that Watts first took LSD—Ed.] Sterling is the most remarkable man I've ever known in my life. I met him in 1957, shortly after I'd taken peyote; we started talking about peyote experiences. Then, he and I started going together, with our families, looking at nature from Iceland to Africa to Death Valley.

JF: You went with Sterling Bunnell to Mexico in 1962 and met the shamaness Maria Sabina.

MM: Yeah. I was working for Dr. Frank Barron of the Institute of Personality Assessment and Research (IPAR) at the University of California. Frank is now teaching at UC Santa Cruz, he was the primary authority on twins and also on creativity in writers. At the time he was publishing in *Scientific American.* He was the person who turned Timothy Leary on to psilocybin; that is before Leary had had acid. Barron was using the last of his Rockefeller grant to study creativity in writers to fund, basically, *me* taking films of people high on psilocybin. The film was shown at the American Psychological Association. We ran out of psilocybin. The Argyle Laboratories in Toronto informed us that they couldn't furnish any psilocybin. They had sold all they could make for the next six months to the United States Army! This was at a time when I no longer wanted to take psychedelic drugs myself; I'd had enough experiences and had been through what I believe was a dark night of the soul. But still, this was an interesting pursuit and Frank was a large-minded man. So it devolved upon Sterling Bunnell and myself to go to the mountains of Mexico and Oaxaca into the cloud forest country and bring back living cultures of psilocybe mushroom—which we in fact did. In the middle of the rainy season! The story in itself would be a book. We went to Maria Sabina's mushroom ritual. Outside it was not only rain: it was crashing, booming, thundering rain, in the peaks and cliffs. The roads were impassible with downpour and rock and mud slides.

JF: What was Maria Sabina like?

MM: I felt her "Saints, Christs, Mushrooms" cult was not the way to give psilocybin. Her followers were dejected and alienated. I might also have been a little superstitious and scared because of the lightning and the beating rain on the tent while we gathered mushroom samples. (By the way, we brought back five species of psychedelic mushrooms and a previously unrecorded *salvia divinorum* which was psychedelic.) We also visited *curandero* Isauro Nave, a native Indian shaman who introduced us to salvia divinorum, which he called "Leaves of the Good Shepherdess."

JF: Were you yourself knowledgeable about these mushrooms or was it Sterling?

MM: Sterling. My knowledge of nature has been largely gained through "field work" with people like Sterling and Richard Felger, a botanist, and ornithologist Hans Peeters. They set me on my own studies. I would be obsessed and fascinated by something they'd show me so I would go into it myself. But it starts with being on hikes, field work, with them: or even with late night talk sessions at the kitchen table. This has resulted in trips to East Africa, Mexico, and South India.

JF: You said at one point that the poem which first gave you a proper sense of yourself was the one you read at the Six Gallery in 1955: "For the Death of 100 Whales."

MM: The poem was my anger against an Icelandic NATO airbase's G.I.'s machine gunning whales from powerboats. It lifted me from concern that the poem should be a ballad into its being projective verse—and that may have had a lot to do with who I am artistically. Certainly I was enraged and projective verse outlined the energy of the anger.

JF: There's a point, I think, in which nature becomes extremely important in your work—even down to the cell.

MM: But it's earlier than you're thinking, Jack. It goes back to my being six years old. I was reading "little green books." They were small, dense children's books about three inches high, about five inches long, and handsomely designed. Type big enough for kids. They were about the nature of the earth, about the nature of plant life, about fossils, about mammals. I dwelled on those books and they were the other side of my looking into hollow logs and lying on my stomach looking at the life in a spring pool. My grandfather was a man who was committed to nature. He admired it and did not believe in destroying it in any way. He walked regularly and I walked with him sometimes. There were forests in that part of North Seattle in those days. Later in Seattle, when I was about ten, I lived next to an eighty-acre nature preserve, right behind my stepfather's house. It was a Boy Scout training camp. The trees were mostly first or second growth—as it had always been in Seattle—right in the heart of West Seattle, on the hill. Our yard ended and the camp started and there was to be no trespassing: but I took it all as my yard! I was so hard to keep out that I finally made friends with Clark Schurman, the director of the camp. He taught me much about nature and a bit about mountain climbing. He also took me other places in the Seattle area to go canoeing and things like that. He had been the chief guide on Mount Rainier.

JF: The way in which you bring nature into your poetry—as structure, as myth—seems to me extraordinary. One can recognize a McClure poem at a distance of ten feet at least partly because of that understanding of nature. That biological basis of the poetry—seeing poetry as an exploration of biology. That seems to me really new and visionary on your part.

MM: It would be if I felt responsible for it! When I was interviewed about my "Poisoned Wheat" poem (see *Huge Dreams*, Penguin, 1999), the interviewer asked me, "How did you know in 1964 what was going to happen in the world?" I make a number of statements in the poem which absolutely came true, so it looked like a visionary poem. Maybe that is what a visionary poem is. It was like I was standing at the foot of a mountain, and there were avalanches starting on the mountain. I'd say, Look, *that* avalanche is going to hit that area over there and cover it, and that's going to set that area loose there, and that other avalanche is going to fall onto the glacier and much of it is going to slide and cover this area of habitation. You can just see it. One "avalanche" was overwhelming overpopulation; another was the dissolving of biological knowledge into "politicalisms" like capitalism, communism, socialism, colonialism, and racism. And another was the bloody crisis in Israel and Palestine. Stirred by the treason of American politicos, the poem laid itself out. Robert Duncan and I were talking about rat overpopulation experiments that we read about in biology journals as we walked down 17th Street in San Francisco in 1962. It's not amazing to me, but it's amazing to people today. I don't see how I could *not* have been keenly interested in biology and finding a new view. This preceded what's now called Deep Ecology.

JF: But to understand biology as a basis of your poetry goes beyond that. Almost nobody else has done it in the way you do it. There's a kind of deep connection between the syllable and the cell. In your poetry you don't see people as "just individuals" but as entities related to something larger than they are. But the thing that's larger than they are isn't God—which is the usual way in which that perception is presented. You bring poems way back to the Big Bang.

MM: I think it comes from early readings in alchemy and Jacob Boehme, in Swedenborg—not to mention William Blake, who was my main man. Then the great turn-of-the-century biologist Ernst Haeckel. And philosopher Alfred North Whitehead. And *The Divine Love and Wisdom* by Ashvagosha from the first century: I always took it that when Ashvagosha said "Tathagata" ["He who has fully arrived," i.e., the Perfect One. A title of the Buddha—ed.], he was speaking of the universe, as Whitehead would. A naive reading of it, but not as naive as the reading of it by people early on who thought it was a crypto-Christian document and believed Ashvagosha was talking about Jesus!

JF: There's always been a religious element to your work.

MM: I believe in the religious experience. It's one of the primary experiences. I *don't* believe that one needs God in order to have religious experience. Meister Eckhart said that belief in God negates the ability to experience God. I don't want to *know*. I want *the situation to manifest itself in me*. From all the realms.

JF: You mentioned at one point that you thought of the poems in *Hymns to St. Geryon* (1959) as being *political* poetry.

MM: I thought my first book, *Hymns to St. Geryon* was a revolutionary document. I thought it was revolutionary to poetry and therefore it was revolutionary to politics. A little naive! I was young.

JF: "Dallas Poem" is certainly a political poem.

MM: I wrote "Dallas Poem" for photographer/artist Wallace Berman. Wallace showed me a photograph he had doctored. Wallace took the news photograph of Jack Ruby shooting Lee Harvey Oswald, who was theoretically the assassin of President Kennedy, and he altered it so that the man in the white suit and white hat holding Oswald as they escort him out of the jail is duplicated—made into twins. In Berman's version there's one man in a white suit on *each side* of Oswald as Jack Ruby is literally in the act of shooting Oswald. It was the ultimate statement of everyone's feelings about the assassination of Oswald: it was fishy! It creeped everyone—even more than the murder of Kennedy.

JF: Those one hundred whales were shot, too. "Dallas Poem" was published in the final issue of Wallace Berman's magazine, *Semina* in 1964 and then in your book, *Star* (1970) and then reprinted in *Huge Dreams* (Penguin, 1999).

[Reads poem.]
I think there's a deep connection between the shots that murder the whales in "For the Death of 100 Whales" and the shots that kill Oswald. "BANG!" "What are souls...?"

MM: Souls are luxuries that we, who are rich in energy emotions and goods, give to ourselves and our friends. They are useless and have no value. They give us pleasure and cause envy. Souls don't outlive us but while they are with us we see and feel more deeply.

Part II

JF: Michael, I'm about to go to a conference dealing with the teaching of poetry. I found myself thinking about your work. It occurred to me that you could be a conference! You're a poet whose work extends in so many directions that if somebody wanted to put together a McClure conference, it could be done. There would be courses in poetry, of course, but also in ecology, in art, in biology, in being a Californian, with its sense of place....

MM: Theater would be a section of it. I was rereading the fifth-century BC Greek poet Aristophanes's play, *The Frogs*, a great piece of comic theater, and I realized what a source it had been for me in writing *Gargoyle Cartoons*, a collection of eleven short comedies. And in *Gorf*, a full-length comedy. I realized that some of the personae in *Gorf* had been inspired by the bare-faced ribaldness of Aristophanes's forthright plays. Also how much inspiration had come from Lorca's plays and puppet plays. Neither Bernard Shaw nor Eugene O'Neill did it for me. My sources were John Webster, Shakespeare, Marlowe, Lorca, Yeats, and J. M. Synge to some extent. My favorite playwright at a fairly early age was Jean Genet. All of this is avoiding the subject of Artaud, which is an entire subject in itself! I heard the broadcast of Artaud's censored radio play, *Pour en finir avec le jugement de dieu* in 1968, when Jean-Jacques Lebel liberated the tape from Radiodiffusion francaise and sent it back to Allen Ginsberg, LeRoi Jones (Amiri Baraka) and myself. It's the great visionary statement on the Cold War. I felt close in time to Artaud but very distant in language since I didn't read French well. He seemed like an older brother. His French seems to me like that of the troubadours: it has crazy rhyming birdsong patterns![1]

JF: Had you read Artaud's *Concerning a Journey to the Land of the Tarahumaras*?

MM: Yes. I read it in my next to last year of college at the University of Arizona.

JF: For a course?

MM: Oh, no. I was haunting the library for information on the subject of peyote. Artaud's text might even have been in an anthropological journal, since it dealt with the peyote rite.

JF: Artaud is redefining theater. How does Artaud affect your sense of theater?

MM: My first play, *The Blossom* (1960) was even more Artaud-like than most people realized since I had imagined it being done with holographic figures floating in space—above the stage. I also saw it as a dynamiting of American theater and even of French Absurdism. I have Billy the Kid quoting Chekhov's play, *The Seagull*, in a moment of extreme homicidal madness. Probably the strangest aspect of the play was that it was the original persons, the characters of the actual, historical Lincoln County Range War, but they were all dead and they had no memories of one another. Consequently they did not know what their relationships were to the other people in the play. These relationships were being shaped out with projective verse, which I was writing for the first time.

JF: What kind of reception did your play receive?

MM: The first performance was in my kitchen, shortly after it was written. Kirby Doyle (one of the Beats who is forgotten and who deserves great attention!) came by with the people who now run the theater troupe, Mabu Mines: Lee and Ruth Brewer. I wanted to see the play performed. They performed it for me. The play was written in a dream state. I went through a period of hypnotic suggestion, which I worked out with Sterling Bunnell. We had thought out a method which was a cross between hypnosis and auto-hypnosis, which he administered to me on some occasions previous to writing *The Blossom*. This was to plant the seed from which the play could grow—though I didn't write the play in a state of hypnosis. But it was while I was in a state that I saw the play being given birth to in my unconscious, where it formed as a stalactite—like a transparent stalactite of ice with the play inside of it. And the stalactite fell onto a pink, moving floor and moved towards my consciousness! I wrote the play without changes—after sitting down to write a few days later.

JF: "I wanted to turn to electricity...."

MM: "I wanted to turn to electricity." I was also tremendously moved by *Danton's Death*, the first play written by Georg Büchner (1813–37). I was just talking with Carlos Murillo, a young Chicago playwright, about that, and he agrees with me that it is probably the greatest first play written in the nineteenth century. That was another model. Carlos is in the process now of retranslating Büchner's *Woyzeck*. Those, along with Elizabethan playwright John Webster, were my sources—along with a large amount of study about Billy the Kid and the Lincoln County Range War. But you asked me what my first experience of the play was. It was an experience of electric excitement: I remember my hair standing on end and being *electrified* by the first kiss on the brow of Dionysus. It's a rich, powerful and energizing thing to become the vehicle for a theater piece and to see your own spirit and meat enacted on a stage. The next performance was at the University of Wisconsin in Madison. It was directed by Robert Cordier, a Belgian director and filmmaker.

JF: This was something the public could come to.

MM: It was being done at the University of Wisconsin at Madison as a student project in the drama department. Drama department officials came in and saw what we were doing and they forbade the play. But the students refused to drop the play, and Cordier, who was a professor, also refused to drop the play. So the drama department said, "If you do that play, we will kick the students out of the university." And, believe me, in February or March in Madison, Wisconsin, the snow is very deep! I didn't feel like getting those kids kicked out, so I said, "OK, I'll withdraw it." They said, "If you'll withdraw it, we'll let you do one performance, but there must be no audience invited—just whoever happens to walk in." Cordier was not the only person who threatened to quit if the play was canceled; so did Morgan Gibson, a poet and biographer of Kenneth Rexroth, who was teaching there at the time. The compromise was that there would be only one performance: nobody would be told about it, but anybody who dropped in could see it. Well, you can imagine that everybody heard about it. It was a beautiful production. Cordier had one role played by two different women. Meantime Cordier tried to fly in his film crew to film it, but there was a hitch at the airport.

JF: This was long before Luis Buñuel used the device of one role played by two women in *That Obscure Object of Desire* (1977).

MM: I wanted to talk Julian Beck and Judith Malina at the Living Theater into doing my play, *The Beard*. They were of course deeply influenced by Artaud. I wanted them to use a dozen Billy the Kid's and a dozen Jean Harlow's and I wanted them all to be naked except for blond wigs and cowboy hats and boots. Guns and mirrors and rolling around on the floor.

Standing up and speaking in choruses to each other and then acting out other parts. I was never able to get Julian to do that—which kind of surprised me! I thought Julian would go for *that*! [*Laughing*] Julian Beck was the first person I ever gave *The Blossom* to. He lost it in a taxi cab after I gave it to him! A few years ago in New York Judith Malina directed the Living Theater in a mind-shaking and extraordinary production of my play *VKTMS*. An important event for me!

JF: The Living Theater was very politically charged. We mentioned your distinction between "revolt" and "revolution." You say in *Scratching the Beat Surface* (1982), "Blake was the revolt of one man. He was not a revolutionary but a man in revolt. A creature in *revolt* can conceive that there is NO solution and that there will be unending construction and destruction. REVOLT perceives the continuance of action and energy from multiple sources." Your understanding of theater, it seems to me, was one enormous revolt—but it was not meant to be a revolution. You were not trying to gain power.

MM: The Living Theater was doing that. I have never met a more perfect anarchist spirit than either Julian Beck or Judith Malina. The longer I knew them, the more I realized how clearly that was the case. I spent time with the Living Theater people in San Francisco. By 1963 or 1964, our concern was not so much with "the revolution" so much as it was with stopping the Vietnam War. I think that took precedence over everything. We seemed much of the time to be actively involved in "revolution" or "revolt." Probably the *discussion* of it went on more after we got to the hippy era in the Haight-Ashbury, where there seemed to be a younger group of people looking for discourse. Looking back, my feeling is that we were involved in environmental causes, we were involved in activity against the war, in protesting censorship of what we were about and what we were saying—and we were kept busy with that. I don't think we had a lot of time to discuss it. We were deliberately living a gypsy revolutionary lifestyle. Drugs were part of it—not just taking them but taking them to deepen our consciousness, which we felt was a liberational act.

JF: It's hard to conceive now of the situation in the sixties. The war wasn't a "subject" among other "subjects." It was like this enormous cloud that covered everything. People would write an ordinary movie review and end it by saying, "And the war is bad." The war was commented on in places where you didn't expect it to be commented on.

MM: The war was *everyday life*. Where I lived in San Francisco was beneath a flight pattern for the transport planes carrying materiel to Asia, so we were reminded of it many times a day.

JF: One might almost call the war a "mini" series—not so "mini." It was on TV, it was in the newspapers on a daily basis. It was a constant, evil presence that people were feeling.

MM: Anyone wanting to get a sense of that should look at Robert Duncan's "Passages" in *Bending the Bow* (published 1968). But amazing things were happening. In 1965 or 1966, the Communications Company of the Diggers[2] asked me for a poem. I wrote an antiwar poem, and within three days I was reading it on Walter Cronkite's television news program. *The Walter Cronkite Show* dropped in to get the Haight-Ashbury viewpoint on the war, and I was pushed forward to read it. I remember how the poem started: "War is decor in my cavern cave. . . ." That is, in the "cave," the apartment or dwelling I have—"war is decor" there. It's so much around us, it's like the paintings on our walls or the clothes on our wives.

JF: What kind of response did you get from that appearance on *The Walter Cronkite Show*?

MM: Nobody mentioned it to me! I was presented quite well, but nobody ever mentioned it. This was at a time when people would stop you on the street and tell you that you had your name in Herb Caen's column in the *San Francisco Chronicle*. I don't know whether it was because my appearance on the Cronkite show spoke for so many people or because the poem was so obscure nobody knew what it was about! But I thought it was quite a clear poem!

JF: Your play, *The Beard*, appeared in 1965. Here is a description of some of the history of that play from the 1967 Coyote Press edition:

> *The Beard* was presented four times before direct police intervention. First by the Actor's Workshop of San Francisco, where it proved to be too much for that organization: despite the efforts of the director, the author and the actors, the Workshop establishment impeded in every possible way a performance of the play—including forbidding the presence of newspaper reviewers. Despite this censorship, Michael Grieg's review (heralding the play as the "most effectively upsetting and creatively stimulating work by a local writer that the Workshop has ever presented") slipped into the *San Francisco Chronicle*. *The Beard* was next presented at the huge Rock and Roll Fillmore Auditorium to a wildly enthusiastic capacity crowd, where it was accompanied by Anthony Martin's light projections and a sound system utilizing rock music. The third and fourth performances . . . took place at San Francisco's North Beach theater night club, *The Committee*. These two performances were surreptitiously tape recorded by the San Francisco

Police Department, and at the fifth presentation, again at *The Committee*, police interrupted the ending of the play by filming it with whirring cameras, and then hurried backstage to arrest Mr. Bright (*Billy the Kid*) and Miss Dixon (*Harlow*). Alternately, the actors were charged with "obscenity," then "conspiracy to commit a felony" and finally with "lewd and dissolute conduct in a public place."

Twelve days later, *The Beard*, now represented by the American Civil Liberties Union (after an offer of help from [lawyer] Melvin Belli), was presented in Berkeley by Rare Angel Productions to a capacity crowd, which included more than one hundred expert witnesses. These witnesses, invited by Rare Angel Productions, included Lawrence Ferlinghetti, Alan Watts, members of the academic community, members of the clergy, and photographers and tape-recording crews whose function was to record the police filming and taping of the performance. Seven members of the Berkeley Police and District Attorney's department arrived two hours before the performance, and began harassment of the actors, the author, and the stage crew. Malcom Burnstein of the ACLU and the author forbade any taping or filming of the performance, a directive ignored by the police and DA's office. The evening turned into a "happening," with the audience wildly cheering and applauding the attorneys, the author, the actors, and denouncing the civil authorities. After the performance there were speeches by invited celebrities, and the police left quietly. It was not until five days later that Berkeley also brought charges of "lewd and dissolute conduct in a public place."

After five months of litigation, Marshall Krause, of the ACLU persuaded the San Francisco Superior Court that the charges were inappropriate, and the case was dropped from court—an important legal precedent having been set. Following the San Francisco court action, the Berkeley court withdrew its charges.

In Los Angeles *The Beard* was shut down—"busted," you say—by the police for fourteen consecutive nights. The California State Senate tried to pass a law against obscene plays, naming *The Beard* specifically; the measure lost in the Criminal Committee by one vote. Later, a production of the play in New York City won two Obie Awards. Two things strike me about your work in the theater. The first is that you had an *audience*. People were very clearly supporting your work. At the same time, your plays were being reviewed in the newspapers, and so on. What was the relationship between the audience support you experienced and the official "reviews"?

MM: After *The Beard* had gone through all its legal turmoil and received rave reviews in London, I removed myself from the theater for a couple of years. I was a success, I had won all the cases; the play had received two

Obies; we'd beaten the endless arrests in Los Angeles—which was the last set of busts we had. I just said, "I don't think I've got time for this! I'll write a novel or something." I was pulled—jerked—back into the theater by seeing John Lion's Magic Theatre production of Alfred Jarry's *Ubu Roi*. It was done in the front of a barroom, cabaret style. I saw the actors turning into furniture, turning into other beings, swirling around the stage madly. I saw the utter insanity of Father Ubu in his denunciations. It was an exciting direction! I was invited to see the play by a mutual friend of mine and John Lion's—a man named Richard Ogar. He was a theater reviewer for one of the counterculture papers, the *Berkeley Barb*, I believe. He had been one of the journalists who stuck up for *The Beard*. The counterculture papers, which were strong at the time, supported *The Beard* unanimously. The *San Francisco Chronicle* never reviewed it until the day it left town for New York. The *Chronicle* had a gentleman old granny as a reviewer who pulled his nightgown over his head and shrieked if anything had naughty words in it. He persuaded himself to go see the last performance in San Francisco as it left for New York production. He said it wasn't really dirty after all! It had been promoted as a dirty play. *The Beard* had also been strongly supported by *Newsweek* and attacked by *Time* magazine, so it was a national and international scandal. When I began working with John Lion, and the Magic Theatre began producing plays of mine called *Gargoyle Cartoons*, the audience was not the usual theater audience—which I've never liked: upper middle-class people who are going to theater for cultural reasons and to improve themselves. That has little to do with spirit and a lot to do with pretensions that I don't care for. Instead, there was a free-floating audience in the Bay Area moving from Oakland to Berkeley to San Francisco to Marin—to wherever. They were free-floating in that they were as much a rock 'n' roll audience as they were a cabaret audience as they were a theater audience as they were a dance audience as they were a poetry audience. They simply wanted a high-spirit level and a penetrating level of experience from their entertainment. These were remarkable people. They were the same people you'd see at the Fillmore one day and see another day at your play, sitting there in the little cabaret theater. (This was before the Magic Theatre got huge!) In general, we were pretty much in an ongoing war with the two big local newspapers, *The Chronicle* and *The Examiner*. But they were playing a game with us. As long as John and I could say completely outrageous things or *nearly* unprintable (but still printable) things, they would print almost anything we said. They'd have interviews with us and then go and review the plays and tell everybody they were just terrible, mindless things. In the meantime, we'd gotten what's called "puff" publicity—which is advance publicity—so that by then we had our audience come in and see the plays. After that it was word of mouth. It was a real audience, tremendous support. It was not a grand-scale audience; it was an audience big enough for several theaters and a couple of rock 'n' roll halls.

JF: "Fit audience find, though few," as Milton said.

MM: They were wonderful. And the actors were the same way. Some of the actors were from the University of California Theater Department; some of them were professors there—amazing as it sounds! Some were Business Administration majors. Some were anarchist-socialist hangers-on around the fringes of things. Some were young people who would become inspired by the art of acting and became an absolutely amazing actor for a year or two of their lives, simply as a part of their own spiritual development. The Magic Theatre wasn't the only troupe like that. There was also the Blake Street Hawk Eyes. Five or six years later it centered largely on an actor named Bob Ernst and a fine playwright, John O'Keefe. In the Hawk Eyes you had future stars like Whoopie Goldberg developing themselves. They were doing spontaneous theater games—before such things were public venue items. This was the secret, special, high art background of Berkeley! There was also the ongoing Mime Troupe of San Francisco, which was an old Stalinist, political, Brecht-oriented group that played in the parks—free, with donations. They also played in schools and traveled from city to city. Often they produced plays of such irony that people would flock to them—brilliant flashes of anger and humor in these Mime Troupe productions. Out of the Mime Troupe theater came Peter Coyote, along with Peter Berg and Emmett Grogan, all of whom moved over to Haight-Ashbury and formed the Diggers. The Diggers were the anarchist group set on liberating the flower children of that time—1966, 1967, 1968—from their backgrounds. Later Peter Coyote became head of the California Arts Council: Peter was the motorcyclist and junky head of the California Arts Council under Governor Jerry Brown, who was a good man to have there after Ronald Reagan! After a period of five or six years, the Magic Theatre moved to San Francisco and became big industry: John Lion was running the second largest theater in San Francisco. The Magic Theatre did productions of my plays on a regular basis—eleven or twelve productions. One of the last ones they did, during the 1978–79 season, was *The Red Snake*—my revisioning of a revenge tragedy by James Shirley from the 1600s. It starred Peter Coyote, who came back into theater to do that and then went on to his film work that we see now. [Information about the Magic Theatre is available at its web site: http://www.magictheatre.org/—ed.]

JF: When Peter was on my show, he told me how much he envied you when he was a young man.

MM: Really!

JF: Your talent, your good looks—also the fact that you were a poet. He *tried* to be a poet. He had great difficulty in a course he took with Robert Duncan—probably at your suggestion.

MM: Well, we're close friends! We were a little bit at arms' distance back in those days. But I think that his admiration was more than matched by my admiration of him. What I remember is him telling people what a fool I looked like riding my Harley! [*Laughing*] Peter slips onto a motorcycle and it becomes part of him. Not so with me! I got my motorcycle because I'd written Freewheelin Frank's autobiography [*Freewheelin Frank, Secretary of the Angels, as Told to Michael McClure* by Frank Reynolds (1967)—ed.][3] Frank and I split the advance. I took that money and asked the president of the San Francisco chapter of the Hells Angels to build me a bike that was a dupe of Freewheelin Frank's bike except Frank's was purple and mine was yellow. I wanted the experience of doing that, of having that life, even of going to meetings and to places with the Angels. But I didn't have long-range plans; I wasn't anybody who wanted to ride a bike from here to Los Angeles. Peter Coyote was a real cowboy out on his motorcycle.

JF: There's a wonderful photograph, taken in 1968 by Rhyder McClure, of you with Richard Brautigan on Haight Street in San Francisco—and you're on your motorcycle. Tell me more about your connection with the Hells Angels. *Freewheelin Frank, Secretary of the Angels* is listed "as told to" Michael McClure.

MM: I *typed* the book; I didn't write it. It's not cowritten at all. Every word in it is by Frank Reynolds, except for two names that I changed to keep him out of jail. Donald Allen, who did the final editing, might have made some changes, but I didn't notice any. It's safe to say that every word in there is Frank's. I met Freewheelin Frank at a Bob Dylan concert. It was 1965, at the Masonic Auditorium. Dylan had asked Allen Ginsberg to invite poets, Hells Angels, and other interesting people. We all sat in the front row with Joan Baez. This was right after Bob had gone electric. I was sitting next to Joan Baez, and Allen Ginsberg was sitting behind me, and on the other side of me was Terry the Tramp, an interesting Hells Angel. Freewheelin Frank was a couple of seats away. At the intermission we went into the men's room and they were smoking a joint and they handed it to me.

JF: Was this when Larry Keenan's photo of you with Allen Ginsberg and Bob Dylan and Robbie Robertson at City Lights was taken?

MM: Yes, that was about a week later. Terry the Tramp and Freewheelin Frank both really caught my attention as gifted speakers—really interesting people with a twang in their voices you couldn't hear anywhere else. I mean a "twang" of spirit, not a "twang" of accent. I think Terry had been an actor, and Frank had been from the Ozarks. He spoke in a kind of Biblical way underneath it all. Frank and I hit it off and became good friends. I said, "You ought to write your autobiography, Frank, because you tell stories so well." He said, "I don't know how to read or write—I can't do that. Would you write it down?" Well, I liked Frank, but I knew how dependable the Angels were and weren't. I said, "I'll tell you what, Frank. We'll *start* it. If you're here Wednesday at 9 a.m., we'll start it." And he was there Wednesday at 9 a.m. knocking on the door. This was a surprise to me because at the time Frank was doing speed—"geezing amphetamine," as he put it. After that first session, he asked whether we could continue. I said, "Yes, but if you miss, we'll have to stop." He never missed. We became close friends, brothers. We wrote every day for a number of hours. I did make a contribution to the book—primarily in two ways: I would ask him questions and I would insist that he describe things concretely. I would just stop typing if the description became abstract. I also said, "If I ever think you're lying, I won't type." That never happened. Frank just doesn't know how to lie! So my contribution is mainly invisible: it's questions that I asked—which I didn't type—and I insisted on the language being concrete. He'd say, "Then I took out my gun." I'd say, "Wait a minute, Frank. I'm stopping typing. You gotta describe the gun. What kind of a gun was it? Where did you get it? Whatever is salient about the gun to you is what you gotta say right now. Just keep saying it, I'll keep typing." Also, if he started talking about religious stuff, I stopped. Because by that time, he'd begun reading again. He'd left notes on my door that said, "I'll be back at noon." I said, "Frank, if you're illiterate, how can you write, 'I'll be back at noon'?" He said, "Wellllll, I can read a little bit." I said, "I think you can read as much as you want to, maybe." So I loaned him Dante's *Inferno*, with the illustrations by Doré. He was *fascinated*. It was translated into the most beautiful and understandable blank verse by White. He read one page a day—a page would take him maybe an hour or two to read. Then he started reading the Bible. Then for a while things got *very* hairy. He'd start spouting Biblical quotations and making prophecies and things. I said, "Frank, I can't type this!" That's the only part where I acted as a real editor. That was not for me! This book was *literally* "as told to": it's Frank's words. Then Donald Allen dovetailed it all together in fitting ways.

JF: You had an extraordinary experience once the book appeared.

MM: Frank had "author's paranoia." This is an ordinary thing for someone to have—but it's not a good thing for your Hells Angel brother and partner to have! He came to me and said, "You gotta stop the book." I said, "I can't do it, Frank, I can't. We've signed a contract, it's under way." Then Pete Knell, the president of the Hells Angels, and a couple of brothers came over and they said, "Michael, you've got to stop this book. It's upsetting Frank. And if it's upsetting Frank, it's gonna tip the apple cart all the way through the club, and things are not gonna be happy." I said, "I can't stop it because it's being set up in type now. And you know what: I wouldn't stop it if I could, because I think it's a great book." Which happened to be the right thing to say. At that point, Pete said, "Well, if it is, it'll all be OK. And if it isn't—god help you!" [*Laughing*] These were decent guys. You might worry about getting yourself knocked to pieces, but they wouldn't hurt your family or your house or anything. They were not like the Oakland chapter, this was the 'Frisco chapter. When the book came out all was well, my bike was built and I'd ride it. Sometimes I'd go around on the Angel bus with them, go to the movies with them. I went to a couple of meetings.

JF: What was Frank's final reaction to the book?

MM: Frank likes the book a lot! I hope that someday the book will be seen in somewhat the way *Black Elk Speaks* is seen—as a singular piece of history but of an outlaw warrior cult of the mid-twentieth century. There were some good reviews, but the book frightened wimpy reviewers. It's out of print. I wanted to print it again and then print his letters to me from the time he left the Angels until now—a selection of a hundred or two hundred letters. We've been writing continuously. He was in jail for six years for arson, and he wrote me from jail. In jail he became initiated into zazen practice and Buddhism. Now he's a nature hermit in northern California, living in the country in a trailer ten miles from anything except trees and a waterfall and his major concerns are environmental and visionary.

JF: You told me once that he's fine while he's in nature, but he gets into trouble when he comes into the city.

MM: It's easy for him to get into a stew when he comes into the city. It's easy for him to get oversocialized. I have a similar problem myself, so I know just where he's at.

JF: You called yourself a "hermit" earlier today.

MM: On the other hand, Frank was just down here about a year ago. It was the same day that I was reading at the book fair, down in the Embarcadero. I took Frank along and gave him part of my time to read, so he read some of his poems. He loved it, and people loved it! The ideal thing would be to start with Freewheelin Frank's book, go to my archive at the University of British Columbia, and take out the letters he wrote to me and add them to the book. It would be his whole life—which is what I want someone to do! It would be *Freewheelin Frank, Secretary of the Angels, and Letters from Jail and Forest.*

JF: Michael, you mentioned a reading you did with the Hells Angels in attendance.

MM: It was at a Hells Angels meeting. After my play, *The Beard* had been cleared of most of its trials, I guess I was feeling ebullient. The second play I ever wrote, *!The Feast!*, was written in Beast Language, like my *Ghost Tantras*. It has thirteen people seated at a long table. It looks like a Last Supper. The person in the middle has lion paws, the people on each end are Black people, and they're all dressed in many-colored robes. And they speak back and forth and sing in Beast Language—*Sprechstimme*.[3] They enact an elaborate and beautiful ritual. It's a play about consciousness. I think it's one of the most beautiful things I've written. *!The Feast!* has been done only once—in the Batman Gallery in 1960. William Jahrmarkt of the Batman Gallery, Kirby Doyle, Morton Subotnick, Robert LaVigne, Philip Whalen, Joanna McClure, and David Meltzer were all in it.

JF: There are some wonderful photographs taken by James O. Mitchell of you watching that production.

MM: We did it in a collage style. We didn't go in much for costumes beyond huge paper beards. A friend made some lion paws for Kirby Doyle, who was the Christ figure, the lion figure, in the center. Years later, I thought, I could rent the largest theater in San Francisco for one night. *!The Feast!* was never meant to be memorized. It would be difficult to memorize. It's meant to be read off of scrolls. I thought the Hells Angels could do it in their outfits—they're all bearded—and all we'd need is a pair of lion's paws for the one in the middle. For the women we could use a couple of "mamas" from the Club. We could just do it! Maybe one rehearsal for tech and lights. And we could pack that place for one night. The Hells Angels were a big thing in San Francisco at the time. They were "radical chic"! It would be easy for George Montana, Freewheelin Frank and me to play the music—although I wanted Frank to be in the play. We were playing as a group at the time. We were called Freewheelin McClure Montana. It would be easy to get musicians to play along with us. So I asked Frank, "What do you think the Hells Angels would think of renting the Orpheum Theater and presenting this play for sixteen hundred people?" So Frank talked to Pete Knell. The question was put on the agenda of one of their meetings. I went to the meeting, and I'd been warned in advance that if only one member blackballed the proposal, they wouldn't do it. So it had to be 100 percent agreement. I was playing it hard: I really wanted to do this. The meetings were rough—people got knocked down. Somebody starts to sit down and somebody else pulls the stool away from him. Kid stuff—only these are bruisers, strong guys! Some of them are smart, and some of them aren't so smart, and they're all temperamental. At the beginning of the meeting, Pete introduced me and gave them an idea of what I wanted to do. I gave them details, and I read the play to them—in Beast Language. There I was standing in front of a basement full of Hells Angels, some of them drunk—some of them high on other things. The first thing is that the play's thirteen characters say their names aloud, loud and firmly:

> YEORG!!
> NARGATH!
> RETORP!
> SHARACK!
> VALETH!
> SHEREB!
> THANTAR!
> AYNAK!
> RAYTAR!
> OHTAKE!
> THAYTOW!
> BOONDOO!
> DOOBOON!

Then there's a speech by Yeorg, after which the whole thing turns pretty much into Beast Language. So I was reading it to the Club—and they were restless. After a while they were standing up, yelling. This was not the usual meeting! Now, when you're there, a guest at a Hells Angels meeting, you're under the protection of the Brotherhood. Nobody will lay a finger on you. You're protected. Until you get out the door at least! [*Laughing*] So I knew nobody was going to do anything. They'd have to answer to Pete for it, and he was sitting behind me at a table. I was halfway through the play, and these Brothers started yelling, "Shut up!," "Shut the fuck up!" Just a few of them, but vociferously. Nothing subtle about it! So I read *louder*. And louder. And louder. Finally, one guy said, "Read *faster*, man!" Pete was making them stop. There were only a few guys doing it. The rest were well mannered, according to their sense of manners. I realized that if I skipped a word, a single syllable of it, these guys are very sensitive in their own way, and they'd know it, and I'd lose face. I had to read the *whole thing* from beginning to end! I couldn't speed it up; I had to slow it down a little, if anything. I read through the whole play. At the end I was shown out. And the decision was not to do it. I did hear from Frank that I just barely lost: they *were* interested. It would have been an ideal thing for them. I presented the idea as an image. I think what was wrong was that it hadn't been written by an Angel. My feeling is that's what kept it from being done. If Frank had written it, it would have been on stage, I'm sure. I thought we'd make money from it. We would have charged a lot to see it—probably five dollars a head in sixties' dollars! [*Laughs*]

JF: You got mail from ASCAP, the American Society of Composers, Authors and Publishers, in today's mail. That's a connection with Freewheelin Frank, too.

MM: Yes, it is. It's about my song, "Mercedes Benz." I wrote "Mercedes Benz"—my version of it—when Freewheelin Frank and I were playing music together. This was after we worked on his autobiography in the morning or afternoon. He'd stay, we'd have dinner, and after dinner we'd smoke and drink and play music together. He played tambourine and harmonica. I played autoharp, and we were joined by electronic composer George Montana, who played *anything* from Sarangi and violin to autoharp. We played a few gigs and we sounded somewhere between drunken cowboy music and Shiva hymns. We were "Freewheelin McClure Montana."

JF: That autoharp was a "Zimmerman," right? And it was given to you by Bob Dylan.

MM: I don't remember that it was a Zimmerman, but it was given to me by a Zimmerman! Bob Dylan did give me that autoharp. Another connection was that for a while Freewheelin Frank was the boyfriend of Janis Joplin. Not an exclusive position—she had a few boyfriends! But he was there for a pretty long time.

JF: When she made the record of "Mercedes Benz," which is on her last album, *Pearl* (1971), you had to phone her up, didn't you?

MM: No, she phoned *me* up. She was concerned about it. She'd been singing "Mercedes Benz." She'd picked it up in New York City from Rip Torn and Emmett Grogan of the Diggers, who were singing it as they remembered it while they were shooting pool with Janis. Then Emmett got disturbed that she was singing it. Emmett phoned me several times about it and said, "You've gotta talk to Janis, she's singing your song." I said, "That's all right with me! Good!" I didn't realize he was talking about money, about recording. I suppose I didn't think that anybody but Bob Dylan, the Beatles, or the Rolling Stones made anything on their albums! So I never got around to calling her. But she called me. It was fairly late in the evening. I remember standing on the stairs in that flat we had on the third floor in the Haight-Ashbury. She said, "I'm singing this song you wrote—my version. Is that all right?" I said, "Yeah. Would you sing me your version?" And she sang me her version over the phone. And I said, "Well, I prefer my version." She said, "Let's hear it," so I got down my autoharp and I played it. She said, "I prefer *my* version!" [*Laughing*] It seemed like immediately afterwards—it must have been a few weeks, in later 1970—she was dead. She'd overdosed. When I think about it now, I realize that she had already recorded the song when she called me. My name was printed on the record—not on the sleeve of the album but on the record itself. I recently heard a story: she was recording the songs on *Pearl*, and they got tired and turned off the recording equipment. She said, "Turn it back on," and spontaneously sang "Mercedes Benz" a cappella. I guess everybody was blown away. When that happened, she must have thought, "Oh, oh. Emmett's been telling Michael." He was telling me to get ahold of her, so he must have been telling her to get ahold of me.

JF: Michael, we've talked a little about friends like Peter Coyote and Bruce Conner. I'd like to mention Diane di Prima. She writes about you in her excellent memoir, *Recollections of My Life as a Woman: The New York Years*. She says that you were a kind of soul brother—someone who understood her.

MM: First time I met Diane was about 1960. I was traveling back to the East Coast. I'd been given a handful of cocaine crystals from a junky's drugstore robbery. Apparently these crystals had been in the back of a safe for ages—since cocaine was legal. In 1960, cocaine was rather exotic. Nobody cared or knew anything about it. I never thought—before crack—that it was addicting. In New York City I met Diane for the first time in her apartment in the—was it the Hotel Albert? I felt that I met my sister. We stayed up all night talking about Keats and Shelley and the Romantic poets. It felt like we had always known each other. Then we went out walking with her lover of the time, Peter Hartman, who was there also—went out walking on the New York docks early in the morning. I thought I was looking at the New Albion. I believed New York was an ancient New Albion shining brightly in the morning light after a night of talking about Shelley and

Godwin and Traherne. I've always been close to Diane. It's an ongoing, platonic relationship.

JF: Alchemical as well, I'm sure.

MM: Alchemical as well. Diane's poem, "Rant," which contains the line, "THE ONLY WAR THAT MATTERS IS THE WAR AGAINST THE IMAGINATION," is my favorite contemporary poem. In the cover notes I'm writing right now for a CD of Ray Manzarek and me playing at the Noe Valley Ministry in San Francisco, *There's A Word*, I've quoted that line. The only other line quoted is William Blake's "The tygers of wrath are wiser than the horses of instruction" from "The Proverbs of Hell" in *The Marriage of Heaven and Hell*. I think everyone also owes a lot to Jerome Rothenberg, along with Diane. Not only for his poetry and great anthologies like *Technicians of the Sacred*, but for his rewriting of the Dada odes. We already knew these poems, but I don't think it occurred to us how much *use* they could be for our own poetry until Jerome made that evident. I see an impetus for Diane's poem in Rothenberg's Dada odes in the same way that I see it in some of my own most vivid poetry. Diane is a nonconformist and ongoing revolutionary of the spirit from her dancingly bright theater to the luminosity of *Loba*. She's a friend with whom you never step into the river twice.

JF: With the Dada odes you are also getting something of the milieu which produced Antonin Artaud, about whom we've spoken extensively. One of the extraordinary things about Jerome Rothenberg is that if you name any single important poetry movement of the twentieth century, he's part of it. Ethnic poetry. Avant-garde poetry. Performance poetry. Just name it, and he's right there.

MM: His two-volume anthology, *Poems for the Millennium*, is everywhere. It's a big lighthouse for thinkers. A similar thing has been done by Karl Young, who has created a vast, subterranean Carlsbad Cavern of archives from Lettriste documents and poetry to the works of d.a. levy, a Buddhist poet from Cleveland who died under mysterious circumstances at the age of twenty-six in 1968. Karl's web site is: *Light and Dust Poets*: http://www.thing.net/~grist/l&d/lighthom.htm.

It's a vast anthology. Now that Jerome is no longer subterranean, we still have a subterranean cavern going.

JF: Thank you, Michael.

MM: Thanks, Jack. Jack, if a reader wants to know more about Wichita days or the San Francisco fifties, my novel *The Mad Cub* sheds some direct light. Also my second novel, *The Adept* is full of sights, thoughts and sounds of the sixties. Did you know Novalis said, "Man is a sun and his senses are planets."

Notes

1. In 1947 the French Radio Service commissioned Antonin Artaud to write a radio poem. He responded with *Pour en finir avec le jugement de dieu* (*To End God's Judgement*), which was to be broadcast in February 1948 as part of the series, *The Voices of the Poets*. The day before the scheduled broadcast, Vladimir Porché, director of the RDF, canceled the program. A recording was made of the play, which featured Paule Thévenin, Maria Casarès, Roger Blin, and Artaud himself, but it was not broadcast until many years later.
2. From *The Diggers Archive* (http://www.diggers.org/overview):

The Diggers were one of the legendary groups in San Francisco's Haight-Ashbury, one of the world-wide epicenters of the Sixties Counterculture which fundamentally changed American and world culture. Shrouded in a mystique of anonymity, the Diggers took their name from the original English Diggers (1649–50) who had promulgated a vision of society free from private property, and all forms of buying and selling. The San Francisco Diggers evolved out of two Radical traditions that thrived in the SF Bay Area in the mid-1960s: the bohemian/underground art/theater scene, and the New Left/civil rights/peace movement.

The Diggers combined street theater, anarcho-direct action, and art happenings in their social agenda of creating a Free City. Their most famous activities revolved around distributing Free Food every day in the Park and distributing "surplus energy" at a series of Free Stores (where everything was free for the taking.) The Diggers coined various slogans that worked their way into the counterculture and even into the larger society—"Do your own thing" and "Today is the first day of the rest of your life" being the most recognizable. The Diggers, at the nexus of the emerging underground, were the progenitors of many new (or newly discovered) ideas such as baking whole wheat bread (made famous through the popular Free Digger Bread that was baked in one- and two-pound coffee cans at the Free Bakery); the first Free Medical Clinic, which inspired the founding of the Haight-Ashbury Free Medical Clinic; tye-dyed clothing; and, communal celebrations of natural planetary events, such as the Solstices and Equinoxes.

First and foremost, the Diggers were actors (in Trip Without A Ticket, the term "life actors" was used.) Their stage was the streets and parks of the Haight-Ashbury, and later the whole city of San Francisco. The Diggers had evolved out of the radicalizing maelstrom that was the San Francisco Mime Troupe which R.G. Davis, the actor, writer, director and founder of the Troupe had created over the previous decade. The Diggers represented a natural evolution in the course of the Troupe's history, as they had first moved from an indoor milieu into the parks of the City, giving Free performances on stages thrown up the day of the show. The Digger energy took the action off the constructed platform and jumped right into the most happening stage yet — the streets of the Haight where a new youth culture was recreating itself, at least temporarily, out of the glaring eye of news reporters. The Diggers, as actors, created a series of street events that marked the evolution of the hippie phenomenon from a homegrown face-to-face community to the mass-media circus that splashed its face across the world's front pages and TV screens: the Death of Money Parade, Intersection Game, Invisible Circus, Death of Hippie/Birth of Free.

The Diggers broadcast these events, as well as their editorial comments of the day, pronouncements to the larger Hip Community, manifestos and miscellaneous communications, through broadsides and leaflets distributed by hand on Haight Street.

3. *Sprechstimme* = "speech song": a type of half-singing and half-speaking introduced by Arnold Schönberg in his *Pierre lunaire* and *Glückliche Hand* (also used by Alban Berg in *Wozzeck* and *Lulu*).

Realm Buster: Stan Brakhage

Steve Anker / 2001

From the *Chicago Review* 47, no. 4 and 48, no. 1 (Winter 2001/Spring 2002): 171–80.
Reprinted by permission.

Michael McClure: Stan is a realm buster, and I use "realm" as the word is used in Biology and Zen. Stan uses his energy and it's almost like moving his shoulders powerfully to break the walls between realms. Some of these realms are the concept of painting, the idea of poetry, the meaning of music, what portrait is, what personal physiology is; other realms that Stan opens up are human and other biology, also the nervous system, ideation—how things are conceived; and then there's the separation between hearing and seeing, sound and silence, and music and sound, which are all explored and more or less brought into one shape in his work. When enough realms are opened, the walls between them torn down or ignored away, then consciousness and concrete experience become one sizeless event in the sizeless event of the Taoist uncarved block which is either the universe or the body, as you see it.

Stan likes to say that he was frustrated in his early desire to be a poet, and that his hundreds of hours of film are closer to music than to poetry. I can appreciate that, especially in terms of Messiaen or Vivaldi. I also hear his delight in Madrigals, as much as other music. But Stan derives some of the organicity of his huge body of work from the style and thoughts of some liberated poets of today. I'm thinking of the works of Robert Duncan, as they branch like rivers and streams, one from another, lighting the dark of the night or lighting the dark of the body and mind. There's also the sizeless willingness of Charles Olson's spirit in Stan's films—Olson's willingness to let things break, to let things fall down and go boom, and to trust that they will all land on all fours. Further, there's the sheer trusting experimentality of Gertrude Stein in Stan's work and there's Stan's love of the wry, aesthetic wit and intellective delicacy of Louis Zukofsky.

I first met Stan in 1954, at which point he has described himself as being "the houseboy of Robert Duncan and Jess Collins," meaning by that that he helped them fix meals, do dishes, and slept in the flat below their place. I had just begun to know Robert Duncan and Jess Collins through Robert's first poetry workshop at San Francisco State, which included myself and Helen Adam, a balladeer of the strange and haunted, who was in her girlhood in Scotland called the Fairy Poet. On what was perhaps my first visit of Robert and Jess's San Francisco flat in 1954, Stan came upstairs to visit. My impression was that Stan was inhabiting the floor below Robert and Jess, which was the housing, as I understood it, for the Centaur Press of Kermit Sheets and James Broughton. Stan is the same age as I am, within a few months, and also as I am, Kansas-born. When I saw his huge head with dark, tousled hair and intense eyes that were simultaneously focused and staring, I recognized a kindred spirit.

I saw Stan visiting Duncan's lectures at the workshop he was teaching on a number of occasions. Stan was absorbing the energetic principles of the concept of field from Olson via Duncan, and he was taking in the intensely biological shaping-ideas of Robert Duncan and the beautiful, unique concepts of collage of Jess Collins. Stan was a young man who was *sui generis* and coming up as a member of an artist foster family of *sui generis* individuals. Stan's myriad-mindedness is both on the surface and below the surface. Surface-wise, Stan is myriad minded in the art of film, and so busy freeing realms from walls between them, that it's impossible to keep up with him. On the less visible field he is tirelessly investigating not only the arts and history with a voracious love for them, but he's also digging through realms of science—particularly the biology of seeing and the neurochemical anatomy of the nervous system. Stan agrees with Thoreau that, "One must stand up to live before one sits down to write," or to edit film for that matter. And Stan stands up not only with his travels and his varied adventures and family mountain life and film, but also with the large scale of his passions, his happinesses, his pleasures, his modesties. He's fought a battle with the arts just to be the genius that he is and to create his own art of the film. His wars have *not* made him cruel or small-minded, but allowed his full generosity to come to scale and to empower him to love and help friends.

Steve Anker: I find your idea about Stan being a realm buster very exciting and actually very pointed. Since you mentioned that he feels his art is closest to music, I'm wondering if you think his constant return to poetry—both in terms of specific works of the poets you alluded to, but also in how he uses poetry and central ideas of modern poetry aesthetically in his own work—has a direct correlation to a world of words embodying impulses and ideas as distinct from the world of images?

MM: What I mean to say was that Stan attributes a greater resemblance of his work to music than to poetry. I honor the fact that his work is deeply akin to music, but I feel that it has its roots in, among others, Robert Duncan's poetry, wherein for instance the long serial poem Robert wrote called "Passages" shifts over and becomes another poem and then returns to the streambed of its poemness, and then disappears while he's writing other poems, and then these other poems connect with other poems, creating what people have compared to a tree or a stream, but in fact it's more like the mycelium, the unseen part of the mushroom that brings fort the fruiting body that we think of as the mushroom. It's a tangled, big, unseen, vital presence going on underneath the creativity, which we then see as the flowers of individual *series* or *circuits* of films or as *films themselves*. And then also, one of the things I didn't mention, but you had spoken of earlier, is Stan's relationship to Creeley as an inspiration for some of his vision. Stan speaks well of Creeley's work himself, but I would add that he sees Creeley's *improvisation*. I don't think Stan follows jazz and Creeley has followed jazz, and through Creeley, Stan is inheriting a sense of jazz improvisation which neatly accompanies his sense of Pollock-like improvisation. Also, with Creeley in many of the short, early poems and parts of the larger, longer poems, there is an almost hypnogogic imagery following the poem. I know Stan sees that as much as I do when I read Creeley.

SA: One of the aspects of Stan's work which has had the greatest impact, especially in the world of film, is its relation to the dailiness of his own life and how he's able to make use of this through film images. That was radical especially in the beginning but remains so—in fact may be even more radical now than it was thirty years ago.

MM: I agree completely. I see it as still more radical now. He has gone through what could on one hand be perceived as the ordinariness of life in the home, and then on the other hand, to my way of seeing it, is seeing life in the home, in the family, in the body, with one's pets, with the floor, with the window, as being free of realm—not fitting into the idea of, itis a tree, it is a floor, it is a pet, it is a wife. It is a life and it becomes more extraordinary at a time when ways of perceiving in the sciences, as well as in art, are being carved smaller and smaller. I agree with you: it's more extraordinary now. People may have tried to do what Stan is doing, but good luck to them. I hope more of them can. Stan stands there looking more extraordinary as he continues his work, and even more unique.

SA: Stan's art is really about allowing the viewer to have a sense of discovery of even the most mundane elements in life, that there really is a uniqueness to everything, at least as manifested in his film visually.

MM: What I get from Stan is the sizelessness of myself. He views himself in a sizeless way. He sees these things as not having size. By not having size, I mean not having scale. I suppose one could say he sees everything monumentally, but that's not true either, because he also sees some things microscopically. But microscopically and monumentally are beside the point if there isn't any sense of scale. And if there isn't any sense of scale, if there's no proportion, if there is sizelessness, we're free in it. We're free for the first time.

SA: We're especially free from the ordinary and conventional ways of making sense with our eyes.

MM: Stan is *against* making conventional sense with the eyes. He is committed to it. But it may be because he can't. I mean, this is Stan. This is part of the wonderful thing about it—we're seeing his physiology. He may have made a manifesto out of this, but we're seeing what he does. We're seeing the critter. We're seeing the man there doing what he does.

SA: We're also being given a direct way to experience his kinesthetic sense of moving through the world. I think in addition to the dailiness of his art, which has been so radical going back to the beginning, one of his great achievements is how his work embodies his own particular kinesthetic energy. This is brought out through the rhythms—in a sense, the music—of the flow of his energy. I think that direct comparisons to poetry have to do with repetition, rhythmic gestures, or particular phrasings within each film. I think what's been so remarkable in his work, is his ability to free images—the way that he's able to record elements in his world, fee them as images and position them within the flow of his own kinesthetic energy. That's something we're much more used to, recognizing in the worlds of poetry, music, and other time-based art forms.

MM: Unfortunately we don't see it in a lot of poetry. Maybe that's why Stan likes to ally himself with music. Maybe we can see more of it in music. We see it intensely when we see it in poetry, but this is not what we're finding in the recent generation of free-verse poets. Free verse died and there's nothing left that's constructive. There are people doing it, but . . . well, Stan and I come from the same direction. That's what interests me. He mentions in an interview somewhere finding that article on Jackson Pollock in *Life* magazine in 1948, and what it did to his life, what it did to his worldview. There's also what it did to mine. It's different, but we're both coming from the same direction, and my reaction to seeing Pollock in *Life* magazine, was there's something really exciting going on out there. I want out there! I was prepared to the extent that, although I was pretty young, I had seen and was familiar with the surrealist painters—Dalí and Picasso for instance—but Pollock was big news! Soon after that I was becoming initiated into jazz by going to late-night jam sessions. It was in the same manner of experience, although it was different experience. You do get the thought sometimes that all moments are the same moment—the content of them is just different for different people. I felt sometimes like Stan and I were having the same moment. He was having his Jackson Pollock moment; I was having my jazz moment; he was having his Messiaen moment. But also, we were both headed out of Kansas. We had both been born in the year that was the height of the Dust Bowl and in which soil electrolytes had been stirred to such disturbances, it probably was rare even in the state of Kansas. There was literally energy in the air and energy in the seasons which maintained themselves like that for a couple of decades afterwards, and we were taking that out with us when we left. We had crazy Kansas eyes and crazy Kansas ways of seeing the violence of things that we did see there, as well as the sensitive human crudeness of things. I remember seeing, as I'm sure Stan does, reapers reaping by hand, not by mower. And then I remember seeing people reaping with horse-drawn reapers, and then later the tractor began to come in.

SA: It's fascinating to me that so many remarkable people have come out of Kansas. Do you think that coming from the Midwest, which is relatively flat, by comparison with the mountains of Colorado and the East and West Coasts, has made you guys more sensitive to and responsive to upheavals, including as manifested in art?

MM: I do think that the violence of the weather that we saw in our childhood, which I believe was probably more extreme than it is today, extremes of heat and snow and wind, and in the violence in the people of Kansas, whether it was manifested as bar fights or tent revivals, which we saw a fair amount of in those days, probably quickened sensitivity to emotional whirlings as much as to seeing the mountains or the oceans. In Stan's case he went to the mountains; my case, I went to the ocean.

SA: Could I ask you something about the world of myth, which has always been very central to Stan? Many of the titles of his films reference the worlds of classic mythology, classical thinking and learning, and of course classical art. This has become an increasingly hermetic practice over the last thirty years, and I think at this point in time only rare specialists and poets are actively engaged in the world of myth and the vast numbers of cultures that have added to and referenced this world over the centuries. It's always been interesting to me how much Stan, more than any other filmmaker, recognizes the importance of this, and how much it informs his world. I'm curious how you've thought about that over the years, especially since the world of myth is so much more central to the domain of poetry.

MM: Myth is death, which makes it completely useable for the romantic poets. For instance, take a sonnet of Keats where he braids up a vision out of Dante and the myth of Zeus changing his mistress into a heifer, so that she can escape from the watchful eyes of the hundred-eyed peacock god, Argos. That Keats would take Dante and classic Greco-Roman mythology and mix Dante's vision with that mythology and turn it into an incredibly beautiful and delicate sonnet of his own, shows just how dead myth was in the pre-Victorian Romantic period where myth was being used heavily. You see Blake reinventing myth from ground zero. We see Stan using a myth, but what Stan produces doesn't really have anything to do with the myth, it has to do with what Stan is living when he thinks of that myth.

SA: In one of his earliest writings, Stan says that he is learning to be a transformer. He's learning the magic of transformation and calls himself "a magician."

MM: I think you mentioned that Stan spoke about spells. And when I hear the world "spell," I think of two things: I think of the spells by the old kindred, the pre-Celtic people, the Cruithins of the British Isles, and I also think of the Asian tradition of the spell. One of the forms of the spell is the tantra—pre-Buddhist, and shifting into Buddhism in its early stages there's a period where tantra pours into the infrastructure of Buddhism. Tantra originally meant a ceremony or set of actions or imaginings to change the shape of the universe. I would think of that as being the closest I can think of to a spell, in my life. Over the phone I read Stan the very last of my "Ghost Tantras" as I was writing them. There were spontaneously written, a book of ninety-nine poems in what I call "Beast Language." I'd been writing them for about three or four months and Stan gave me a call—this was in 1962 or 1963. Stan called me up from wherever he was. I was back in San Francisco after a trip to Mexico and I said, "Wait just a minute, Stan," and I finished the last tantra. He waited for a moment and I said, "Here it is, Stanley!" He didn't have any idea what it was or what the "grahhhhrs" were about. Nobody knew I was writing these, and I read him the ninety-ninth tantra in Beast Language. It was the first one to be heard by another person. I'd been hermetic and secretive in the writing.

SA: One of the ways Stan understands his task is that he is making the act of cinema sacred—both in the making, but then of course in the experiencing. And I think what you're describing is the process of a sacred act; it really allows the person a chance for transformation and to recreate their universe.

MM: You're absolutely right. I think that's a beautiful definition of what his work does. To further verify that, I think of the next to the last time I saw a work of his at the Pacific Film Archive, and they had blacked out the exit signs so that it would be as black as the inside of a skull. It was a high-level experience and something almost knightly or grail-questy about it—particularly for me since they were films I hadn't seen before, and were particularly gorgeous films—the one with the title about the cat and the green worm. . . .

SA: I'd like to ask something concrete: Stan's been making films for about fifty years, and you've been watching films no doubt for most of your life, also well over fifty years. These are same years in which there's essentially been a revolution in understanding film—not just in the more poetic realms of film, but even in terms of narrative, commercial film. In these years we've had French and many other new waves; we've had a new understanding and redefinition of narrative films, including within the terms of American cinema. I'm curious how your sense of Stan's work has developed alongside and in relation to other forms of film, and how you have continued to see the value of film in the course of your own life over these last fifty years?

MM: Stan is a true alchemist in the sense that I honor and is a true visionary in the sense that I honor a visionary. I cannot even place his films on the same ground with anything that comes out of Hollywood. I can't make the comparison. Stan and a few other enormously gifted persons ranging from Jack Smith to Bruce Conner to Bruce Baillie to Kenneth Anger created a new art, and I can't see mixing it up, with the narrative film, much less the Hollywood film. My recent experience is seeing *The Cat of the Worm's Green Realm* was one of the deepest—and of course the film was set in a nest of other films of Stan's. It was set in a nest of hand-painted films, which were stimulating, like looking at the paintings inside of a Paleolithic cave, except abstract, also slightly reminiscent of the eye visions that you get on hearing Stockhausen's music. But then, to come up with this *Cat of the Worm's Green Realm*! That's wonderful. I felt like when a caterpillar makes its pupa and the being of this maggotlike, wormlike eater of leaves, lovely little thing in itself, melts into a primal substance, in an alchemical process where it is conjoining and introducing mercury and sulfur, and creates a butterfly as a final result. I have seen this process where the pupa has been opened and a glass wall has been inserted in the cocoon. The transformation takes place so that you can see it through glass. I felt as if the same transformation was taking place inside of me, particularly in that film, that I had been melted inside into mercury and that I was transforming and I wasn't going to be the same again afterwards, and I didn't want to be. And it wasn't going to be the biggest thing that ever happened in my life, but it was going to be part of my life. It wasn't going to be a movie that I went to and walked out of, and ho-hum I can't even remember what happened.

SA: One of the things that comes to mind as you speak about this is that Stan's recent films, pretty much all of his hand-colored ones, can seem so slight and can seem in comparison, to melt or blend into one another. But they are in fact so delicate—in the end so very distinct from one another—and I think they can be so easily misunderstood because of their simplicity and their delicacy, that they can be taken for granted. I think as you speak about the caterpillar and the butterfly, you're talking about common insects which seem so second-nature to us all, and yet they are so miraculous. The process of transformation which you describe is also so miraculous, and when this is understood with a renewed appreciation one realizes that it is one of the great aspects of living. But it can be so easily overlooked. I think that's part of the lesson of his later films: that they can seem to be only scratchings, to be only crude, basic, elementary kinds of expressions. But they really demand and in the end offer a unique piece of yourself to have any value. If you allow them to enter yourself, they take up a very special place which I don't think is occupied by anything else of this kind. So it's special—in other words, as simple as they may seem and as seemingly crude as they may seem, they become incredibly precious parts of our beings.

MM: I don't think it could be said better than that. I would like to say, it's wonderful to be able to observe a truly great artist in a new art form working, as perhaps Monet, worked in his old age, and what an enormous pleasure it is, and what an enormous pleasure it is for us to have this conversation.

Artists on the Cutting Edge: Michael McClure Delivers a Passion for Poetry

George Varga / 2001

From the *San Diego Union Tribune*, March 5, 2001. Reprinted by permission.

[*Lines from Michael McClure, "Peyote Poem" (1958)*]

Seeking the unexpected is almost as important as the quest for meaning to Michael McClure, the pioneering Beat Generation poet who served as a mentor to Doors' singer Jim Morrison and wrote "Mercedes Benz," one of Janis Joplin's most endearingly quirky songs.

"It's very important to surprise myself," said McClure, who performs Thursday night at Sherwood Auditorium in La Jolla at the opening program of this year's Artists on the Cutting Edge series.

"I'm one of those artists who say: 'Well, if I knew what it was before I do it, I wouldn't sit down to do it,'" he continued. "I do it to find out what it is."

For this veteran writer and erstwhile cultural revolutionary, "it" can—and does—take many forms.

Now sixty-six, he is an insightful novelist and essayist, an Obie-winning playwright and an esteemed poet. He's now recording two albums with pioneering minimalist composer Terry Riley, who contributed the music to a just-concluded Bay Area production of McClure's play, *Josephine the Mouse Singer*.

McClure is also a longtime partner of former Doors' keyboardist Ray Manzarek, with whom he has performed poetry-meets-music shows since joining forces in 1988. The two are featured in *The Third Mind*, a sixty-minute video released last year by Mystic Fire (www.mysticfire.com). It showcases their work together, along with cameos by such kindred spirits as Lawrence Ferlinghetti, Anne Waldman and the Fugs' cofounder Ed Sanders.

But it is poetry that remains McClure's first and greatest passion, and his most vital outlet for creative expression.

"I would say you either are a poet—and there is nothing you can do about it—or you're not," he said, speaking from his Oakland Hills home.

"And the only thing that teaches poetry to you is your own experience. It's not a profession, it's an art."

Recalling his days as a fledgling young writer in the early 1950s, McClure said: "I never had any interest in poetry as a profession. No poet or painter I knew back then had any indication they would publish a book or sell a painting. You did it because you were driven. Now, it's a different world."

Heartland Roots

It was McClure's zeal for poetry that brought him to San Francisco from his native Kansas nearly half a century ago.

Like other seekers before and since, he sensed that California's fabled city by the bay offered limitless possibilities. And the possibilities for American poets were limited in the late 1940s and early 1950s, when McClure decided to pursue the power of words and their ability to convey the richness of human existence.

"Even when I got to San Francisco there couldn't have been more than maybe twenty people who had the nerve to stand up (in public) and read a poem," he recalled.

"The country was in such a depressed and enraged state of Cold War thinking then that there was no tolerance for such a thing as poetry out there. And maybe the only tolerance in San Francisco was in North Beach. Because as (fellow Beat poet) Ken Rexroth said: "North Beach is to poets as Barcelona was to Spanish anarchists." It was a place where you could go be, although you couldn't declare: 'I am a poet,' because you'd get yelled at—and maybe even hit—if you did.

"I didn't worry about that. But people were violently opposed to anything that went against conformity. And poetry in this country was on its dying toes."

But not for long.

On October 7, 1955, McClure joined with several other maverick poets, most notably Allen Ginsberg (who appeared at McClure's invitation), for a public reading at San Francisco's Six Gallery.

It was then that Ginsberg debuted his epic poem, "Howl." And it was then that the Beat Generation took root, driven by the mind-expanding imagery and full-throttle passion for living of Ginsberg, McClure and such cohorts as Ferlinghetti, Gary Snyder, and Jack Kerouac. With liberating force, their work galvanized many in a white-bread, button-down generation of young Americans eager for an alternative to the pervasive conservatism of the day.

The Beats' emphasis on freedom, spirituality, sexuality and protoenvironmentalism was visionary. Ditto their sometimes zany, Dada-inspired sense of humor, especially in an era in which almost any deviation from the norm or expression of individuality was regarded with suspicion and hostility.

"I'd seen one poetry reading before the Six Gallery reading, but it was a 'good-time reading.' At this one, the veil of silence was broken," McClure proudly recalled.

"I don't know whether anything comparable is happening today or not. I figure, if it's happening now, how would I know?" And he added with a laugh, "Why would they want me to know?"

Interview with Michael McClure

Sergio Cohn / 2004

From *Café Review* 16 (Winter 2005): 5–12. Originally published in *Azougue* (Brazil), 2004.
Reprinted by permission.

Sergio Cohn: Charles Olson once said, that, "poetry is breath," which one could relate to Greek "pneuma." He also said that poetry is energy transported to paper to be freed by the reader. You say energy defines poetry. What relationship do you find between Charles Olson's conception of poetry and your attempt at building a systemless system?

Michael McClure: Breath is always a tool in creativity and Charles Olson made me especially aware of it. I read Charles's work early in my life and spent some time with Charles in San Francisco and visited him in Gloucester, where we walked in a forest which had been the site of Dog Town, a setting of one of the *Maximus Poems*. Charles, who was a physically huge man, sat down on a stump in the forest and mimed writing a projective poem, flourishing a branch in his hand as if it were a pen. One day reading his essay "Projective Verse" aloud to friends, its intelligence hit me like a light turning on. Soon after, I wrote my first play *The Blossom* in projective verse. A few years later in 1961, I used a quote from Allen Ginsberg on the back of my book, *The Book/A Book of Torture*. I was pleased with Allen saying, "McClure's poetry is a blob of protoplasmic energy." But I was beginning to realize that energy, though it's often protoplasmic, is never a blob when it is active. In fact, some of the best active structurings of energy I have made are in the shape of poetry in that book. I read recently that Noam Chomsky believes that Language is most important as a tool for thinking and as a means for structuring thought. Chomsky believes that communication "in general" is a relatively minor aspect of language. I agree with those ideas of Chomsky's as much as with Mallarmé's statement: "Poetry is the language of a state of crisis." One reason we love poetry is because we discover the inspirations of poets; these prove that we can recognize our own inspirations and not bluntly or quietly allow them to pass. Biology and biological aspects of nature fascinate me for similar reasons. Certainly Nature/Life is a state of crisis and the shiftings of the migratory paths of wildebeest that I have seen in Tanzania are a state of constant mammal discovery. As the herd passes, one can feel they are enflamed by the route they are choosing—it is one with their muscles and hormones, and it is shifting as they rediscover it century after century. Our interiors are like that—the black meat of our insides is constantly shifting in directions and times.

As artists we are hungry to use the instruments of our art to deepen, broaden, and enrich self-experience. We don't attempt to build a systemless system but we discover that we are a systemless system. With the invention of projective verse, Charles Olson proposed a means of seeing and experiencing the field of our energies and senses more deeply. As a projective poet I do this for my pleasure—I believe this is the way D. H. Lawrence rejoiced in his poetry. It is something like what I find in the great Dada poets and in William Blake and the visionary Japanese Dōgen and in the mystic Jacob Boehme. It is what I hear in the piano music of Thelonious Monk—and done with great mammal elegance. This is the way that I experience Jackson Pollock's paintings.

William Blake said, "Energy is eternal delight."

Sergio: In *Ghost Tantras*, you use nonsemanticized sounds in a way we only had seen before in Artaud, Michaux, but these two authors seem to play on variations with the human language. In your book you do not seem to make a distinction between the sounds of man and other mammals. Instead of creating an exotic effect, your use of language in this case seems to expand the boundaries of what we would normally consider a human being. Wouldn't this be a poetic illustration of the position you put forth in YOHRRRRRRR essay "Wolf Net": "When a man does not admit he is an animal, he is less than an animal. Not more but less."

McClure: Yes, and unless we realize that an animal is much more than what we think of as a social man, then we do not have any conception of the boundlessness we can explore. Someone asked how I would transcend language. I said that language is an instrument of creation and consciousness. I have no desire to transcend it—it is our means, not a barrier, to understand what is out there, and in there. The word *divine* is out of fashion or I'd say that language is one divine possibility. And it is the one I choose; poetry is my art. I deeply enjoy the invented language of Henri Michaux, Hugo Ball, Kurt Schwitters, and many others but they were caught up in the linguistic discourse of European thought, even as they free themselves. There's no immediate relationship between those works and the Beast Language poems in *Ghost Tantras*.

Artaud is another case—Artaud's screams are intensely moving at gut level, they can be heard on the banned recording of *To Have Done with the Judgment of God*. My book of ninety-nine poems in Beast Language, *Ghost Tantras*, comes from a religious and physiological experience—and they exalt the Goddess Kundalini, coming as they do from the inspiration of a ball of silence in which I could hear the whirlings and roarings and growlings of the sounds of the ninety-nine poems. I was surprised when the first tantra came out in "baby talk" but as I continued to write they grew into hierophantic speech. The Romantic Percy Bysshe Shelley had written about the possibility of a nonmimetic poetry—one that didn't mime the world but existed as itself. In writing *Ghost Tantras* I was taking the dictation of their own active presence, but no word in English was disallowed, no image from daily life was kept out, no secret or apparent manifestation of inspiration was disavowed. They are body poems that I believe exist in more dimensions of experience and self-experience than most poetry that I know of. I gave a reading of one of them to four lions in the lion house of the zoo and a tape of the four lions roaring with the poem. Later, I was asked to do this again for a documentary film, and again the lions roared with the poem. The poems have been used by psychiatrists in jails to give some ease to prisoners. Sometimes, before the poems were in a book, we passed the manuscript around the table and everyone read one—it gave a lot of pleasure. Everyone pronounces them their own way but all the ways are right. These poems come from the areas of meat-muscle and synapse and spaces that you create when you read or sing them. And Sergio, you're right, there's a strong connection between this and my belief that when a man does not admit he is an animal, he is less than a man.

Sergio: Your poetry clearly reflects an interest in biology, which does not appear as a mere tool for describing the natural world. On the contrary, in your case, language is blended into the landscape as if it were itself an organism. Biology appears here as a systematic science along the lines proposed by Gregory Bateson. At the same time this vision of language is compatible with the Zen tradition as well as the Native American philosophies also present in your work. In "99 Theses" you state, "meat is thought." Do you consider that the concrete world is where we actually find the spirit?

McClure: The concrete world is no different from any world, and it is the exact isomorph of nothingness. Nothingness is called *sunyata* in Zen and in Zen's sister discipline *Hua-yen Buddhism*. But *sunyata* is not absence of something, it is nonpresence, even nonpresence of nothingness—an infinitely changing thing and nonthing. We think of ourselves as explorers of a concrete world, and our instruments are the traditional five senses—sight, sound, taste, touch, smell. To them, add "affective perception," which includes sense organs such as the nodes on the mesentery of the guts that inform the unconscious nervous system regarding the degree of tension in their area. To these can be added proprioceptivity, the enormous and miniscule—essentially sizeless, or size shifting—perceptions of the interior states of passion, emotion, physicality, and imagination. In the mid-sixties an article in *Scientific American* spoke of eleven senses that the authors identified, I imagine one of them was the pheromonal sense which is separate in its brain pathway from conscious perception of odor. (Pheromonal experience is atrophied in humans but it is functioning). We admire and love what we see in the world and we sense it with the perceptions of our five, or our eleven senses. But imagine a thousand senses, or a trillion senses. What would we be aware of? Our sensorium of a thousand, or a trillion senses, would define and create a concrete world. In "To Glean the Livingness of Worlds," which is a reply to Rilke's eighth "Duino Elegy," I say, [*reads poem*].

Friedrich Schlegel, a nature philosopher from the time of Goethe said, "All art should become science and all science art: poetry and philosophy should be made one." Right now science is often real alchemy and is endlessly opening. I am thrilled by the beauty of what happens day by day in biology—even in the teeth of omnipresent mindless reductionism. At the same time I'm staggered by real Hells being created in sinks of human overpopulation.

I am more convinced of the need for art. I believe art must be inspired.

Sergio: Ezra Pound divided poetry into three categories: Phanopoeia, Melopoeia, and Logopoeia. When you say that "poetry is a muscular principle," wouldn't you be, besides blurring the lines between the categories, going beyond this tradition since you are using the whole body as a poetic instrument?

McClure: At first Pound was a lighthouse shedding rays in new directions. Then I realized what a limited guide he is, and also that he is a brilliant and entertaining designer of limitations. I love much of his *Cantos*, and the doorways he opens in them, and his *Confucian Odes* translations seem ever new. If you become involved with Pound, (who is an industry in the academies), you will never hear from Pound about Shelley, D. H. Lawrence, Mayakovsky, Lorca, Blake, and hosts of Pound's visionary contemporaries of the Transition movement. Artaud, ethnic poetry, or the visionary language acts of Herman Melville, such as his novel *Pierre*. Pound is a man on the ecotone of great breakthroughs in art and science, and there is some real pleasure in the Troubadours, and his revisits to the Roman classics, and the wonderfulness of his playing in history, like a baby, in what he called the "Tale of the Tribe." Much beauty. He's a great example for beginners to gain some freedom. On the other hand, he could never know what we need to know to go past the Ballet Mechanique and listen to our inner energies aroar. He claimed Walt Whitman as a father, but he never knew that Whitman said, "A MOUSE IS MIRACLE ENOUGH TO STAGGER SEX-TILLIONS OF INFIDELS." Or that Whitman's *Song of Myself* is one of the most detailed records we have of a religious experience.

Sergio: Some ecologists hold that the balance of an ecosystem may be judged by the presence of great predators, as they are at the top of the food chain. Taking this into account, how can one draw a parallel between poets and great predators?

McClure: Sergio, the thrust of your question has an antipolitical aspect that is too complex and too important to answer in brief. My generation: Amiri Baraka, Diane di Prima, Robert Creeley, Jack Kerouac, Allen Ginsberg, Gary Snyder, Joanne Kyger, Philip Whalen, and others, have with outspokenness, in the ongoing universal biocidal war against nature, been an ongoing source of social sanity and reason. The effects of this are not measurable in a political or societal way. The willingness to out-speak with their own bodies in public places is more antipolitical than political. We have spoken out endlessly for what Herbert Marcuse called the "Negative." It is an outspokenness and a living example of disdain for "one dimensionality." For Marcuse one dimensionality is the absorption into the inner life of the rules of social commerce, propaganda, and urban insanity, until there is only one dimension and there is no difference left between what was once our inner life and commercials for tennis shoes, obliteration of Nature, and factory farming of living animals. As a poet I make my statements against the "American Way." What we depend on are the great examples of inspiration and imagination whether it is in the late Goya-like painting agonies of artist Philip Guston (which shook me yesterday in the museum—so much so that I had to stop and be thankful that Guston presented these horrors). Where am I without Jack Kerouac's great *Mexico City Blues*, the Sung Dynasty Buddhism of Su Tung-po, and the love sonnets of Neruda; where without the thirteenth-century Japanese Dōgen (founder of Soto

Zen), Amiri Baraka's raging reestablishment of Blackness against the sea of White, Robert Creeley's dynamic jewels of fresh news of our passionate condition, or Diane di Prima's epic *Loba* and her *Revolutionary Letters*? Where without many such other brilliancies of poetry? Without them we would all have lost far too much.

I'll finish with a poem. [*Reads from Shelley's "Political Greatness."*]

A Fierce God and a Fierce War: An Interview with Michael McClure

Rod Phillips / 2007

From *A Fierce God and a Fierce War: An Interview with Michael McClure* (Coventry: Beat Scene Press, 2007). Reprinted by permission.

For more than four decades, what Lawrence Ferlinghetti once called Michael McClure's "lush green ideas" have been a highly visible and controversial topic of American literary discourse. The author of more than forty volumes of poetry, fiction, essays, and plays, McClure is one of the most prolific and enduring figures to emerge from the Beat movement. Since his first appearance at the Six Gallery reading in 1955, McClure's poetics have established him as one of the preeminent voices of American environmental consciousness. His poems and essays, steeped in the language of biology and ecology, have relentlessly and beautifully reminded us of the intricate web of the natural world, and our place within it.

Much of the recent critical attention given to McClure's writing has focused on his persistent message that humans must strive to regain our biological identity as mammals. But there is also a strong and relatively unnoticed political component to McClure's poetry evidenced by his 1965 anti–Vietnam War poem, "Poisoned Wheat." For McClure, politics and ecology are tightly bound together, and any discussion of the poet's political views—such as his opposition to the war in Vietnam or to the current Iraq war—is firmly grounded in his ecological worldview. As "Poisoned Wheat" demonstrates, McClure's mammalian poetics has a radical biopolitical component that seeks nothing short of abandoning political structures as we know them and replacing them with a new culture based on biological realities.

In early 1965, McClure began to learn of the alarming potential for the use of biological weapons such as defoliants and crop poisons in the Vietnam conflict. News of such policies moved McClure to respond with a long poem he titled "Poisoned Wheat." Published as a fourteen-page chapbook, and bearing a striking hand-cancelled portrait of outlaw Billy the Kid on its cover, the poem first entered the American consciousness as an antiwar tract, mailed directly to hundreds of influential readers.

"Poisoned Wheat" is a poetic manifesto that would foreshadow much of McClure's writing for the next three decades, as it attempts to look for solutions to the world's catastrophic problems outside the normal channels of politics and ideology. McClure's poem attacks each of the world's prevailing political systems—capitalism, communism and fascism—systems which he sees as "a preprescribed pattern of guilt leading to escapism and cynicism" for their failure to effectively address the problems of life on the planet.

McClure's demand that humanity—"come out of the closet— / OUT OF THE CLOSET OF POLITICS / And into the light of their flesh and bodies!" remains a constant in his message as the poet enters his seventies. For McClure, the only means of survival is the rejection of political solutions, and the embrace of a new, biologically informed worldview. Acknowledging the "biological self" and embracing humankind's mammalian "wisdom of the gut" are the means of McClure's revolt against the political forces of war and environmental destruction in the twenty-first century.

Rod Phillips: Some critics and historians have viewed the Beat circle as apolitical or, at times, politically naïve. Your reaction? Do you recall much discussion about Cold War foreign policy among Beat writers during the late fifties and early sixties?

Michael McClure: The reading that's often called the initial reading of the Beat Generation in San Francisco in 1955 at the Six Gallery was the first time Allen Ginsberg read the poem "Howl," Gary Snyder read "A Berry Feast" which is radically environmental. "Howl" at the time was outrageously outspoken and was certainly political. I read poems which today would be called environmental, but actually were antibiocidal poems: "For the Death of 100 Whales" and another mystical poem about Point Lobos, one of the most beautiful places in the world. Philip Whalen's poetry was already deeply embedded—up to its waist—in Zen and the beginning of deep Zen insights and into the politics of the environment. He'd just come back from fire-watching and was moved in very much the same kind of ways that Gary Snyder was moved. Philip Lamantia read the poems of his deceased friend John Hoffman, who had died in Mexico. Philip's radicalism did not come out in that reading, because he was reading extraordinary prose poems by John Hoffman, and had availed himself of the reading to memorialize his friend. But Philip Lamantia was a gifted surrealist who was the only American surrealist who was recognized by Breton at the age of fifteen. And I believe everybody is aware of the radical political stance of the surrealists.

At that time I would have still called myself an anarchist in the manner of Kropotkin. Gary Snyder was a Buddhist anarchist, with direct emotional, political, and personal descent from the Wobbly tradition in Seattle. Allen Ginsberg's politics were coming directly out of socialism in New York. He'd grown up as a kid at socialist meetings, deeply committed to social issues. Our master of ceremonies was Kenneth Rexroth, an anarchist, pacifist, poet, and philosopher—as well as a gifted naturalist.

We were probably about as radical a group as you're liable to pull out of history as a group of five young men having their first poetry reading together. I don't think you're going to find anybody more radical politically, and I don't think you're going to find anybody speaking out in times more unconfirming, more ugly, and more demanding of reducing one's self into the typical social situation and its paths. We were outcasts; we were looked at like misplaced cannon fodder during those early Cold War attacks that the US was making on the Asian mainland. And we were also—every one of us—up for the draft.

These critics and historians who have viewed the Beat Generation as apolitical, or at times, politically naïve are strange. They must be coming from a primitive place regarding politics, or just a complete misunderstanding of the times—or likely they're right wing. I really don't understand. There could be one possibility, and that would be that maybe some critics and historians who look to the Beat Generation as being only the years before 1955 and the Six Gallery reading; in that case "Beat" is more of a New York phenomenon, and more literary and philosophical.

But what happened in 1955 was, of course, Kerouac was in the audience. He heard Snyder read. He heard all of us, and it was like something major happened—something that I don't believe could have happened in New York. Soon he wrote *Dharma Bums*. A lot of people on the East Coast think that America stops at the banks of the Hudson River. And I know some academic critics carve out a very small space to work in—say 1945 to 1955 in New York—and then just deny anything else because that was a very researchable area. And the research to be done from 1955 to 2005 is beckoning to people who are interested in what really happened, and in knowing what the United States was really like beyond New York City.

Phillips: I think a lot of the critics I'm referring to here are from the right wing—people like Norman Podhoretz.

McClure: Yes, I imagine that these critics are right-wingers—like Norman Podhoretz. They seem sort of Pickwickian and museum-bound. It's a way of attempting to disarm or detoxify the fact that some of the Beats were the initiators of an Asian-tinged environmental awareness, which has already been taken into the main fabric of American culture and has done real good.

Phillips: Among the major Beat writers, the most difficult one to make sense of, in regard to the Vietnam War, is Jack Kerouac. He's often seen as almost totally apolitical, and then later increasingly conservative as he ages and becomes more reclusive. I'm wondering if you have any insight into Kerouac's political thoughts?

McClure: Yes, I think I do. I cared much for Jack. He was a part of what I would call the earlier New York Beat scene, which was not political. It was more literary, with guys hugging guys, and ideas being born about literature and art. It was kind of wonderful. He was much rooted in that background.

But in 1954 or 1955, when Allen was showing me letters he was getting from Jack Kerouac at the time Jack was writing *Mexico City Blues*, it was clear that there was a huge transformation going on in this man. *Mexico City Blues* is, to my mind, the great religious poem of the twentieth century. Since then we've seen *Some of the Dharma*, which was published recently by Penguin; these are Jack's Buddhist notebooks, and you get a further sense of his transformation. I don't know where all this depth of insight comes from. I can't even imagine what some of the sources for it are—because I'm intensively studying some of the same sources that he must have mastered then. Jack was open with a very grand Mahayana view when he walked into the Six Gallery reading. I keep bringing up the Six Gallery reading because that is where we all met. And Jack walked into the Six Gallery, and he heard Allen read "Howl," and he was yelling "Go, go, go!" But "A Berry Feast" by Snyder may have had the largest effect on Jack, because it was after that that he writes *Dharma Bums* which is about nature.

And it's after that that he goes down to Big Sur, which is a terrible bleak vision of nature. But Big Sur itself can be pretty bleak sometimes, and the novel is extremely accurate, especially given that he may possibly have had the D.T.'s at the time. I'm in *Big Sur*; Jack calls me Pat McLear. I was with him part of that time, and I suspect he had the D.T.'s, or was edging to it. And I think that an alcoholic crisis is a crisis which can drive somebody inwards and force them to back away from an overextension of themselves. Jack talked about this; he was frightened by the effect that he was having on people. It scared him, and I think that made him drink even more.

Arthur Rimbaud was one of the great French poets of the nineteenth century. But he quit at seventeen, went to Africa, became a gunrunner—and some people say, a slave trader—and the only writing he did after that was pieces for geographical or scientific magazines. Salvador Dalí was a great, great painter of the imagination, but at some point something happened, and he started, essentially, doing perfume ads, and signing his name to the bottom of them. Philip Guston was one of the most delicate of the abstract expressionist painters, and then he went through a great change and became a heroic social critic. It took Guston a few years, and we really don't know what happened, but he ended up doing these huge canvases; simple cartoon paintings of people in Ku Klux Klan outfits driving trucks filled with human feet. That is a radical change for Guston—and Kerouac had a radical change, the way many artists have radical changes. In Guston's case, I dig it. In Rimbaud's, it's interesting. In Jack's, I regret it. But this doesn't change who he was or what he was. He was there, he did it, and he's terrific.

Phillips: How did your political views, and those of others in the Beat circle, manifest themselves?

McClure: Part of the answer to that question is in the *Journal for the Protection of All Beings: A Visionary and Revolutionary Review*, volume 1, published in 1961 by City Lights, and edited by myself, Lawrence Ferlinghetti, and David Meltzer. In 1960 we began sending out letters. We offered a place for anyone with thoughts against the damning conformity in America to present their readings, their feelings, their ideas: thoughts that could not be published elsewhere. We contacted nearly everyone we could think of, from Harpo Marx to Linus Pauling who was responsible for the discovery of the nature of the chemical bond and got the Nobel Prize for that, as well as a second Nobel for Peace. We contacted as many people as we could.

We published Thomas Merton's beautifully ghastly "Chant to be Used in Processions around a Site with Furnaces," about the burning of the Jews. We published a statement by Bertrand Russell. We published Gary Snyder's "Buddhist Anarchism," for a political position of Buddhism. We published part of what I think is the most visionary political document of the mid-twentieth century: the opening fragment of "To Have Done with the Judgement of God," by Antonin Artaud, which is truly a profound statement about the Cold War, and what preceded it. Also an interview with Allen Ginsberg and Gregory Corso which is a zany take on politics. At that time Allen and Gregory had decided on zaniness as a tool, in much the same way that I decided to make myself a kind of literary enzyme by leaning on the world "mammal" and drawing people's attention to the fact that we are mammals. I first used "mammal" and it drew so much attention that I realized, "Ohhh, people don't realize that they're animals; they don't realize that they're a mammal." So I used it often after that; I realized it was kind of a tool.

We had a statement in the *Journal for the Protection of All Beings* by Camus: "The Artist as Symbol of Freedom." We had my radical antisociety essay "Revolt" which also appeared in my *Meat Science Essays* a few years later. We had David Meltzer's benign and lovely "Journal of the Birth." We had an interview with William Burroughs who had some advanced political ideas which sounded wacky at the time, but which seem to have a core of truth to them today. Robert Duncan's "Properties and Our Real Estate" was a very meaningful part of the collection. There's Herb Gold's piece on "Picturesque Haiti" about the filthy colonialism and postcolonialism in Haiti, which was still being sold for tourist entertainment. Norman Mailer's "An Open Letter to John F. Kennedy and Castro" was in there. And then there were several documents at the back of the journal: "The Surrender Speech of Chief Joseph of the Nez Perce Indians." "A Declaration of Rights" by Percy Bysshe Shelley—I don't think you can get more politically radical than that any time or any place. We took a small quote from Hermann Hesse, and we had a photograph of a giant panda, calling attention to the threat on their being and their beauty.

[*Laughs*] This is not exactly an apolitical statement, and *The Journal for the Protection of All Beings*, as it spread, was having a pretty enormous effect on those who were hip enough to realize they were right. They realized there were other people thinking the way they were; this was a confirmation of it, and we were not shutting down, but instead we just might be opening up. Remember, *The Journal for the Protection of All Beings* was first published in 1961.

I had occasion recently to consider editing a Beat Generation nature anthology, and I got it all together in my mind. I had trouble with no one except Gregory Corso. I thought "What on earth could I use of Gregory's?" I couldn't use "Don't Shoot the Warthog" or "Requiem for the American Indian"; they're not nature poems. And then I remembered "Bomb" which is a great four-hundred-line poem by Gregory which was published as a broadside by City Lights and sold for a nickel or a dime. It's a limitless statement about what the bomb is capable of doing to the earth, to civilization, to nature, to the movies, to us, to penguins—and the whole thing is done with a fearless lack of guilt. I think that it is the quality of guiltlessness about the bomb that makes it a truly great poem, and it is certainly a great nature poem. Recently at Gregory's memorial I called attention to this poem and read a few lines from it. It is enormously funny, and it is enormously truthful, and it is enormously frightening, and it is enormously effective politically and psychically.

That was written in 1959, if I'm dating it right [actually 1958—Ed.]. I want to go back, for the sack of these critics and historians that you're speaking of, and point out that "Howl" itself is pretty damned political. We poets on the stage were about as radical as anybody I know. I was familiar with anarchist working men's circles meeting around San Francisco at the time—not that I was part of them, but I was aware of them. I want to point out that one of Allen's poems after "Howl" is a poem called "America." It is one of the loveliest, and most good-natured, and effective put-downs of middle-class, cold-war conformism and hatred that I've seen. I heard it read for the first time at the second Six Gallery reading. I refer naïve critics to "America." I also refer them to some poems in *Kaddish*, which go back to 1961.

I recommend that they go back and take a look at when my "For the Death of 100 Whales" poem was first published in 1956. I'm pointing out what should be well known. That would be a place for people to start if they're researchers, critics, and historians—rather than starting on the Atlantic side of Hoboken.

Phillips: In the first few years of the 1960s antiwar dissent had yet to really emerge in mainstream America. How and when did you first become aware of American involvement in Vietnam?

McClure: I became aware of the ongoing wars in Asia, and their hidden purposes, in the early fifties, maybe even the late forties, when I registered for the draft, and I hated it, I hated it. Now when did I first become aware of the American involvement in Vietnam? Although I was in my early twenties and had a daughter and was writing poetry and essays—a lot of it fairly radical politically—I managed to go with the stream of information about our involvement in Vietnam. It wasn't until I read about the poisoning of wheat in Cambodia that it triggered real, active, resistance—in the written form.

Phillips: How did you first become aware of the use of crop poisons as a weapon in southeast Asia? It seems that as in your poem "For the Death of 100 Whales," a news story becomes a catalyst for a much broader poetic discussion of a planetary issue.

McClure: I became aware of the use of crop poisons, particularly in Cambodia, by means of several standard news sources, but mostly from our beloved Pacifica station KPFA. I was intensely angered. I was writing in my journal about it, and poet Josephine Miles called me; she's an interesting poet and was a professor at the University of California, and she asked me to come and read poetry to her class. I said, "Josephine I'd like to do that, but at this time I'm pretty angry, and obsessed about what the US is doing in southeast Asia." She said, "Well then, come on over and say whatever it is you want to say." So I wrote a lengthy blast about what was happening in southeast Asia, and went over to her class at the University of California in Berkeley and read it. I can't tell you the effect it had, but I think it certainly got through to everybody. It was after that, I looked at the pages and said: "Aha—what I have here is really a projective poem." I write projective verse, which is a form of verse originated by Charles Olson, and used by Robert Creeley, Denise Levertov, Robert Duncan, as well as Ed Sanders and Diane di Prima. I felt that there was really a projectivist poem in this blast. So it was a matter of finding the projective presentation—freeing the structure to the breath of the voice, and inspiration. That would have been in 1964, and I believe "Poisoned Wheat" came out early in the year in 1965.

Phillips: Who was the publisher?

McClure: It was published by Robert Hawley's Oyez Press, which had published a number of broadsides by everyone from me to Charles Olson, Joanne Kyger, and Robert Duncan. Hawley is one of the unsung heroes of this; Robert Hawley's name should go down printed in gold. He was an expert in Americana and he had a handsome well-known Americana bookstore. He devoted enormous amounts of time and funding to his Oyez Press books—it was the first press in the US to take the great American poet Larry Eigner seriously. He was one of the first people to publish Ann Charters's important critical work, like her early work on Olson. Robert Hawley was so much a part of the times and published many books—and a lot of them were politically conscious. I'd worked with Hawley before; he'd published the first classic posters for *The Beard*, before *The Beard* was even written—when *The Beard* was an imaginary performance event.

He phoned me about publishing something as an anti-Vietnam War broadside, and I said "I think I've got it for you."

I believe we mailed out six hundred copies of it. We mailed them out to everybody that we could think of—of all political stripes, of all backgrounds. What we hoped was that it would give them assurance that there was somebody else out there seriously beginning to oppose the war. The effect of such would be to notify the right, reassure the left, and hopefully shift the center to a better direction, because what was going on was just an argument between the left and the right about how much and how often to bomb—not about stopping, but just how much was right. It was crazy. The war was already at that state. We sent it to every journalist that we could think of, very anchorman that we knew of, all the poets, novelists, political workers. It was quite a thing mailing it out.

Later it was published in the *San Francisco Oracle*, which was the influential and visionary magazine of the Haight Street community in San Francisco, which of course went out all over the country. The first eight lines of the poem were also published in Ed Sanders's journal *Fuck You: A Magazine of the Arts*.

Phillips: Do you remember what kind of reaction you received from the people you sent it to?

McClure: Not much—that is, other than from people I knew. I don't think we expected to hear back from people. We didn't invite them to write us back; it was more of a throw of the dice. Probably we didn't think there was much to say in response—except to say that "We're with you." I felt that many people were with us, and I knew that a lot of people were enraged, and that we were forcing that particularly ugly incident as a subject of discourse.

I gave it to Bob Dylan and he sat there and read it carefully—line by line, word for word—as he reads things. He was interested but he didn't show approval or disapproval; he's careful. Then he handed it back to me with a "That's cool, man." I took this as good, because as intense as Dylan was becoming, it showed him that the other poets—on the page—were out there too. He was beginning to kick out his own jams at that time.

Phillips: Can I ask about the cover design? Why the cancelled portrait of Billy the Kid on the cover?

McClure: In *The Beard* and in *The Blossom*, two early plays of mine, murder is glamorized as an act beyond daily nature, under certain circumstances. In *The Blossom*, an early play which is particularly important to me, all the characters in the Lincoln County range-war, including Billy the Kid, are in eternity swirling together, and they don't remember their previous lives, or who they are in relation to each other. It's a play that's killing obsessed—murder obsessed—whether to be murdered, or to murder. I felt that Billy the Kid was like Arthur Rimbaud and was visible from our side of the century as a pioneer of his age, and that what he had done in avenging his employer Tunstall was a virtuous act in eternity—although a confused one in any eternity. In "Poisoned Wheat" I felt: "This is enough of glamorizing Billy the Kid for that." It was Hawley who had published first the poster and then the first private copies of *The Beard* which used that photo of the Kid, so it seemed appropriate to me to take those photos out of the file and use them for the cover of another production. And I said "I'm canceling him; I'm canceling what I said about the Kid earlier. I don't love Billy the Kid any less, but I'm canceling what I said earlier."

Phillips: The poem declares that "POLITICS IS DEAD AND BIOLOGY IS HERE," and offers what Allen Van Newkirk would call a "biocultural" worldview—one in which the false and decaying rule of politics is replaced by biological realities. How did you come to this concept?

McClure: By means of so many routes that unwinding the vines of them, one from another, would be quite a thing to do. I came to it through Sterling Bunnell, one of my oldest friends, and the most brilliant biologist I've ever known, and the most brilliant naturalist I've ever had the opportunity to do field studies with. I believe I was reading Marcuse that early. It was also coming to some extent through Gary Snyder. I was a big reader of *Science Magazine* and of *Scientific American*, and was reading a lot about biological research being done at the time, like Calhoun's research into overpopulation in rats; Robert Duncan and I were discussing those experiments at length, while we took long walks. It was clear that the discourse of politics was, as Chomsky so clearly pointed out, just the settling and decision for a very cruel middle ground from the two extremes. That kind of discourse continues things as they are and had to be kicked aside—in the same way that the radical Dadaists at the end of the First World War decided to kick things aside. Some of them were doctors, and they said, "This is enough: if World War I is Western civilization, then let's have Dada." That idea accounts for some of the zaniness of the ideas that are still there in 1959—the way Allen Ginsberg or Gregory Corso present things. It took bravery to present them.

Phillips: At times, "Poisoned Wheat" verges on the prophetic, with warnings of a future of unchecked human population growth, genocide, and mass starvation (not to mention the collapse of Communism). Any comment on the accuracy of the poem's predictions, given thirty-five years of elapsed time?

McClure: I would say that they were dead-sure things that I predicted. It's as if you're standing at the bottom of a mountain, and you see up at the top a huge avalanche breaking off the side of the mountain; you can safely say it's going to hit bottom. You can pretty definitely say that it's going to come down. There's that ridge of boulders over there which is overpopulation, and there's that ridge of boulders over there which is the petroleum addiction of western civilization. Mass starvation was going on already; genocide was going on already. I said what was there, and what was indisputable to be the future, and it was clear. I was reading as much biology as I was philosophy, such as the work of the German mystic Jacob Boehme, and I was talking with biologists and mammalogists, and ornithologists, and social friends as much as I was talking with Robert Duncan and others.

It was clear in 1964 that communism would fail as would capitalism, and that the greatest threat was from overpopulation, and that genocide could only become worse because that's an adjunct of overpopulation. And mass starvation was certainly at hand, because they'd already started the "Green Revolution" which is going to make it worse and worse—and which the public is still buying wholesale. So except for being a little embarrassed by writing the opening of the poem in Beast Language and really not getting it down, because I thought that maybe this was going to be a great poem like Antonin Artaud's, I was sure about what I was saying.

Phillips: A related question: Do you feel that humans have moved closer to a "biocultural" worldview in the decades since "Poisoned Wheat" was published?

McClure: A lot of people in the Western world who have had the chance to do so, have done so. But they are so monstrously and so evilly opposed, by everything from the pharmaceutical multinationals to the chicken feed industry, by companies like Archer Daniels Midland, by what we used to call "the seven sisters"—the oil companies—that it becomes very difficult. It was the same situation during the Vietnam War, but it's bigger now, with the governmental kleptocracies of the Third World, and the greed, rage, and hatred of the First World joining against human mammals. But I'm sure that there are more of us aware now than ever before, and I think that the Beats had their share to do with that, and I'm proud of it. It all has to be seen through.

Phillips: Do you still see this move away from politics and towards biology as inevitable?

McClure: I believe that it's inevitable that people become saner. As the situation progresses, there will be individuals who, being sane, will follow Alfred North Whitehead's concept of reason, and who will think in terms other than the truly insane discourse of politics that continues now. If I look for a sister civilization to ours, in which there's so much general delusion about who the deities are, I would look to the Aztecs. Spengler saw civilizations as being like organisms; I would think that the closest organism to ours would be the Aztec civilization, where at the inauguration of the Temple of Huitzilopochtli in about 1600, it is claimed that nearly forty thousand captives had their hearts cut out in sacrifice to the hummingbird god—the god of war. We seem much like that—but only at the kleptocratic and totally mad top levels of retrograde government. I'm sure en masse we have more and more people knowing what's going on, and maybe fewer and fewer people believing in Huitzilopochtli, the hummingbird god, but not knowing what to do about it. Our politicians call the hummingbird war god "The Market" and the war is on the environment and people of color. It's a fierce god and a fierce war.

Beat Poet Michael McClure on Jim Morrison, the Doors, Allen Ginsberg, and Jack Kerouac

Anis Shivani / 2011

From the *Huffington Post*, March 3, 2011. Reprinted by permission.

There are few poets as underappreciated today as Michael McClure. For close to six decades now, he has been writing visionary poetry, lauded by many of the most original American minds of the second half of the twentieth century—figures such as Robert Duncan, Robert Creeley, and Allen Ginsberg. McClure seems to have been at the center of many of the most important artistic developments of the last fifty years. His new selected poems, *Of Indigo and Saffron*, is just out from the University of California Press. This seemed a good time to tach up with him for a wide-ranging discussion about his own poetic, his major influences, poetry and science, and poetry and biology, not to mention his formative associations with leading poets, artists, and musicians.

Anis Shivani: Leslie Scalapino, a San Francisco language poet, picked the poems for *Of Indigo and Saffron*, just issued by the University of California Press. How do these selections differ from your earlier selected poems? Was there a particular emphasis for Scalapino? Did you collaborate in the selection?

Michael McClure: Leslie Scalapino writes in her introduction: "This is not a traditional selected poems. It does not seek to represent the body of work of a poet by encapsulating the books in excerpts . . . my choice of poems was based on tracing certain gestures as related to vital elements in Michael McClure's poetry: particularly, a struggle evident in his work for apprehension of being and language of poetry—as that language is enactment of being."

If I had edited this selected, I would have *known* what belonged in it, and used my set pieces and pieces that were bravado with my conscious and established ends. That is what we do when we edit our own works. Instead, I receive exhilaration from Leslie's selection, which shows a me who is freed of the surface, and the armoring of self-image. We know we are many. Leslie presents one of my many, which is close to me and allows me the feeling of freedom—not to be dragging around a dinosaur tail of self-image. On seeing one of her earliest drafts I was delighted and stepped back. As her editing continued, she presented more groups of poems and my pleasure grew at her finding another shape of my poetry that is so deeply representative of all that I am. Once or twice she asked for advice—as in her selection of my Beast Language poems, *Ghost Tantras*. Also, I made sure that the entirety of my biopolitical poem, "Poisoned Wheat," is in *Of Indigo and Saffron*.

Shivani: You have remained consistent with your from over fifty-five years of writing poetry: the poem centered on the page, with some lines in capitals interspersed throughout. Once you got this form down, did you ever feel like experimenting with other forms? Why has this form been so productive for you?

McClure: Let me call what I do "shape" and not "form," but more of that later. I have never gotten shape "down"—shape remains open, not fillable nor unfillable nor closeable. When I wrote my verse play, *Josephine the Mouse Singer*, the poetry became narrow, supple, intense, and soft like the lives and voices of mice. In another drama, *The Blossom*, my poetry is long-lined, disruptive, angry, fierce. In new writing in this selected, "Swirls in Asphalt," there is a newborn shape, and shapes I have never confronted before, and they slip in and out of the sizelessness of moments, and from the being in one moment to another without linear chronology. Writing my biomorphic, centered verse is protean for me. Also, I enjoy many traditional forms and use their standard requirements, especially the sonnet, which can be the perfect instrument of poetry in the hands of Shelley or Keats.

Shivani: Do you see a danger, as you limit the line to the breath, of the lines flowing almost too smoothly, too rapidly? Can this form lead to piling on phrases upon phrases, instead of forcing one to pause and check the interrelationship of ideas, as might be more true of a line not correlated with the breath?

McClure: My poetry at its truest is an extension of my physical person. It isn't my nature to extend constructions until they begin to pile up and overlap or cataract themselves away. Strange as my poems might appear on the page to some readers, and as unlikely as some might guess it to be, a goal in my life and poetry is the maintenance of equipoise. However, equipoise is as likely to be understood as the concept Reason. For an understanding of Reason I would look to Alfred North Whitehead's understanding, an apprehension and action, not intellectual apparatus.

Shivani: In your essay "Breakthrough," you write that "Robert Creeley reminded me of Olson's maxim that form is the extension of content," but also that you "could not use this [Olson's] concept of *form*" in your work. What was the contradiction there, and how did you solve it?

McClure: My poem, "Rant Block," published in *The New Book/A Book of Torture*, written in what I believe to have been a dark night of the soul, begins, "THERE IS NO FORM BUT SHAPE! NO LOGIC BUT/SEQUENCE." These lines answered for me my youthful quarrel with the concept of form. "Form" became invalid after the freedom I found in the work of Jackson Pollock and Bop.

Shivani: In your essay "The Beat Surface" in the book *Scratching the Beat Surface*, you write, in connection with Francis Crick's use of your lines from *Peyote Poem*, about the "reaching out from science to poetry and from poetry to science that was part of the Beat movement." What do you mean by this? Similarly, in the introduction to your recent collection *Mysteriosos and Other Poems*, you write: "Like Crick, I believe that flesh and consciousness are one thing—and I see there is no wall between biology and poetry."

McClure: Schlegel the German Romantic wrote, "All art should become science and all science art; poetry and philosophy should be made one." When I gave my first poetry reading in 1955, it was the time to go beyond existentialism. Reductionism had reached its peak in the sciences and in art. Inspiration and imagination were there to be freed and reflect their presence in nature. One hundred fifty years earlier Shelley saw Nature being there—to erase huge codes of fraud and woe. The fifties were marked by fraud and woe, but Francis Crick performed a luminous deed in his elucidation of the DNA molecule. He, like the new poetry, began shaking free from mechanistic ideas of biology—from pinpoint reductionisms to an understanding of all life to be a single molecule. It was surprising to be on the stage reciting a poem "For the Death of 100 Whales" and to hear Allen Ginsberg recite "Howl" while Kerouac shouted "Go!," and to understand that we were not speaking to but *for* the audience.

Shivani: You also write in the same essay, "Much of what the Beat Generation is about is nature." Do we have too freighted a conception of Beat poetry as being urban?

McClure: Following the publication of *On the Road* some academic critics leapt on the Ginsberg/Cassady/Kerouac romance, which gave them much to write about and answered some of their problems regarding the new American writing. After 1955 we became, intentionally or not, the first literary wing of the environmental movement. (Please note: Jack Kerouac went from an East coast kid driving Route 66, looking at cows with awe, to climbing Desolation Peak, a fire lookout in the North Cascades, with Gary Snyder in *Dharma Bums*. He later experienced his depths in the vastness of nature in *Big Sur*. A new critic could write about the effect of coastal California, Mexico City, and Jack's free-form but deeply experienced Buddhism and give a wider view of what happened.)

Shivani: You always make a distinction between the intellectual and the intellective. What does intellective mean to you?

McClure: Intellective is use of the intellect with fresh circumstances without being freighted down with societal mental structures. Intellectual is the performance of thinking with preestablished customs and viewpoints, good and bad.

Shivani: Was Allen Ginsberg intellectual or intellective?

McClure: When I first met Allen, he was a young socialist, bohemian, artist intellectual living in San Francisco's North Beach, and even then his sparks of imagination kept him high above intellectualism. Allen grew from intellectual to what I would call "Mahatma," as in Mahatma Gandhi. Mahatma meaning "Big Soul."

Shivani: The Six Gallery reading where Ginsberg first read "Howl" and you read some of your youthful poems—the inaugural moment for the Beat Generation—seems impossible to conceptualize today. Did Ginsberg ever tell you that he had become jaded over time, particularly after the sixties, that such a renaissance of innocence was more difficult to imagine in postmodern culture, where irony and surface are everything?

McClure: It was not Allen's nature to be jaded, but being swept in the samsaric undertow of media, overpopulation, censorship, and the attempt to disparage or hide what we accomplished, all of us have had troubled moments. Possibly at the Six Gallery we were innocent, but all of us were serious. We felt a new seriousness. We were variously socialist, Buddhist-anarchist, anarchist, surrealist-visionary, and Zen. The reading's master-of-ceremonies Kenneth Rexroth, in the sharpness and acuity of his person, lacked any innocence that I'm aware of. Postmodern irony and surface that you speak of, were in 1955 entropic, militaristic, and dreary—as they remain today.

Shivani: You have often talked about the "biological basis of poetry," as you do in your essay "Hammering It Out." About Olson you say, "I believed that the spring of poetry must be more physical, more genetic, more based in flesh, and have less relationship to culture." How do your thoughts differ from Duncan and Olson? Is your view more mystical than theirs? You've also referred to Artaud as a key influence, as someone who showed you the "open space of verse" and the "physicality of thought."

McClure: Robert Duncan introduced me to Charles Olson's essay on projective verse, with which I wrestled long and hard for an understanding of an absolutely new poetics, grounded in one's physique, perceptions, and inspiration. It is about prehension—apprehension by the senses. Stirring in the body is the heart and joining with the breath, expressing itself outwardly, energetically onto the field. The field might be the sheet of paper or the screen or the vocal air. Robert Duncan called his personal projective verse, "composition by field." His punning meaning was that he dealt with the "feeled," as in his earliest projective work, *The Opening of the Field*.

Artaud's solid and daunting denials of lies and politics, as in the opening of *Pour en finir avec le jugement de dieu* [*To Have Done with the Judgment of God*], and his horrific explorations, like flaying of the psyche and Manichean screams were there to be read, heard, and imagined. An inspiration to be straight with oneself. I see that we seek out inspiration, not just for its beauty and thrill, but because the existence of the inspiration proves to one the reality of their own inspiration.

Shivani: Is Olson the major figure in American poetry after Pound?

McClure: I do not like seeing poetry as literature rather than art and I'm not happy with the separation of poetry and the sister arts. I prefer to see Art as Art. I perceive that a major figure after Pound would be Jackson Pollock, and instead of looking at "American" Poetry as William Carlos Williams exhorted all to do, I would look worldwide at the poetry of D. H. Lawrence, Federico García Lorca, Vladimir Mayakovsky, and of course Charles Olson, and all.

Shivani: Can you please talk about the set of poems called "Fields" in *Simple Eyes*, where you take off in multiple directions from a boyhood photograph? This seems to be one of your most successful experiments.

McClure: *Simple Eyes: Fields* came winging to me with the news that it wanted to seek shapes on the page and hover around a boyhood snapshot of myself wearing a sweater vest from the neighborhood of YMCA in Seattle. In the major earth-moving reconstruction of the enclosed basement of the YMCA, gangs of boys had mock wars, hurling clods of clay at each other and shouting. In the hilly and forested neighborhood of the YMCA, I delivered newspapers from an oversized canvas pouch around my neck. And walking through a marshy area in the morning on my way to school, I'd like down at the edge of the vernal pound and look at fairy shrimp, large fresh water crustaceans, swimming on their backs; water beetles; pollywogs swimming around and others wriggling out of the jelly mass of the egg cluster. This moment was an opal-a universe of living stuff. What I call "the spiritual autobiography" of *Fields* lifts out of those experiences, which sometimes take the shapes of much more recent experiences connected to them.

Shivani: Can you please discuss your relationship with Robert Duncan? Was he the poet who most gave you a sense of vocation?

McClure: Robert Duncan and Jess Collins, in their household filled with sculptures, collages, paintings, sounds of Webern and Lou Harrison, and their attention to the arts and biological sciences made an example for me of one of the ways in which life might be lived. Another example was Wallace Berman, photographer and collage artist, and his family who led an equally complex and rich life.

Shivani: In "Hail Thee Who Play!" you write: [*quotes from poem*].

McClure: "Hail Thee Who Play!" is dedicated to James Douglas Morrison. Jim Morrison and I met because of his interest in my play *The Beard*, an erotic *success de scandale*, a confrontation between Billy the Kid and Jean Harlow in a blue velvet eternity. It was arranged for us to meet at an Irish bar. We disliked each other at first sight—both with long hair and leather pants—and began sullenly drinking Johnny Walker, which quickly turned to talk about poetry and Elizabethan theater and actors. The simpatico we arrived at so quickly seems like a triumph of meat. Usually when I say "meat" in my poetry, and it's a word I often use, I mean flesh. But "flesh" is too good, so clean, so contrived—far away from the experience of actually touching the stuff or eating the stuff. I take it as my mammal duty to remind others that the flesh we love and touch is *meat*, which is the same thing as and inseparable from *spirit*. To continue our lives we devour spirit as well as make love to it. It's mammalian MEAT.

Shivani: "Meat" appears in your play *The Beard* as well, in the confrontation between Jean Harlow and Billy the Kid.

McClure: In *The Beard*, when Harlow or the Kid speak of "meat," they use the word in at least five different ways; from sarcasm to contempt to admiration to love, that's what we all do. We use the word all those ways.

Shivani: Also in your essay, "The Beat Surface," you write: "We hated the war and the inhumanity and the coldness. The country had the feeling of martial law.... We saw that the art of poetry was essentially dead—killed by war, by academies, by neglect, by lack of love, and by disinterest. We knew we could bring it back to life." You did bring it back to life. Do you see an analogy today, as we fight another perpetual war? Is poetry again dead? If it is dead, why is it so? Who or what can bring it back to life?

McClure: In spite of the smothering effort by many in the academy and by the ignorant, poetry is alive. It is often hard to find, because it is dodging the samsaric breakers and one-dimensional undertow, or it is in plain hearing in the art of Bob Dylan, or kept a little out of the way from readers in the dimness of misinformation about poetry. There is no finer poet than Diane di Prima who, like Joanne Kyger, does not broadcast or flaunt her rich creation. Amiri Baraka seems to be in the midst of a personal renaissance of commitment and clarity. Jerome Rothenberg continues bringing me news of poetry that I never imagined. Clayton Eshleman is exploring the Paleolithic galleries of his person. Philip Lamantia's almost lost poetry will be published soon, in a Collected Poems by a major university press. Poets of modesty, brevity, and intense genius like David Gitin can be found in small press editions. Online sites contain shimmering ongoing streams of poetry by younger people who do not press for public recognition—they have to be sought out.

Shivani: *Three Poems* brings together your longer poems, "Dolphin Skull," "Rare Angel," and "Dark Brown." You seem to have a particular affection for these three poems. Did they teach you things you hadn't known in your shorter poems?

McClure: "Dark Brown" is my first breakthrough in searching out the possibilities of projective verse and the freedom that I saw in the paintings of Jackson Pollock and Clyfford Still, and in the music I was listening to, whether Jazz or Scarlatti. The poem "Dark Brown" remains as the best statement I could make at that time of freeing myself from what Marcuse calls one-dimensionality. Moshe Feldenkrais describes it as the family and social structures binding up one's motor nervous system. Reich saw it his way. This struggle for liberation is inherent in "Dark Brown" and it remains dear and important to me. "Rare Angel" is a huge patch, or series of patches, of deepening and expansion of my voice, feelings, and thinking—not only into what I was learning while travelling and doing field study with biologists, but what the assembling of these experiences/actions into a poem actually created under my fingers and in front of my eyes and ears. "Rare Angel" dips into Paleolithic hunting scenes and the near unbelievabilities of childhood. "Dark Brown" is a future-modern work that could only come out of the 1950s but now I see many other resemblances: to Haida tribal art and Tang Dynasty Chinese amalgams of Zen, and to what we could call "primitive" thinking. On the other hand, "Rare Angel" seems to me to be like a big personal huggable bear. "Dolphin Skull" the third long poem, began with studying the psychoanalytic sketches of Jackson Pollock and using their field as the jumping off point for my own self-trust. Writing it was one of the most enjoyable experiences of my life.

Shivani: Your book that seems to me most relevant to the state of the world today is *The New Book/A Book of Torture*, reissued as part of *Huge Dreams*, with an introduction by Creeley. In "Mad Sonnet 11," you write: [quotes poem]. You are countering war and madness with love. Is such a position possible today?

McClure: *The New Book/A Book of Torture*, from 1959, was scrawled and typed out when I believe I was having a dark night of the soul. I agree that *The New Book/A Book of Torture* might be the most relevant to this immediate present in the USA. Rimbaud was searching for, and living in, what he called "an arranged derangement of the senses." He knew a derangement of sight, sound, taste, touch, smell, and all of the other senses brings about a condition of what might be called "voyancy." This is not anomie, deracination, vertigo, schizyness, depersonalization, or something resembling those. In fact, today it is the condition of overpopulation insanity, media obsession, gluttony, druggedness, genetic feedback [as Konrad Lorenz wrote of], and drinking from rivers polluted not only by pathogens, but as importantly, with synthetic hormones. Of course, there's climate disruption and worldwide food shortages everywhere except in the developed countries. That hardly covers it, but Calhoun's studies of overpopulation and social sinks, as well as Artaud's vision of post–World War II USA, were things that I spoke of with Robert Duncan and Philip Lamantia. We're living it now. Looking around we can feel the stressed and scrambled shapes and combinations in cars, airplanes, and burger shops.

Shivani: You took Jim Morrison very seriously as a poet. And you have had a rich collaboration with Ray Manzarek of the Doors. Tell us about these relationships.

McClure: When Jim and I were in London, in the late 1960s, working together on a screenplay from my novel *The Adept*, he showed me the manuscript of his first poems, *The New Creatures*. It is hard to believe that there was a better poet than Jim, at his age. The manuscript was perfectly edited by his wife, Pam. I urged Jim to publish it and when he demurred because of his concern that it would be read as rock-star poetry, I persuaded him to do a private publication, and helped him distribute it. Jim and I were close friends and we drank a lot. Often he visited San Francisco and stayed with my family and me, sometimes I stayed with Jim and Pam when I was in LA. Strange and it sounds, Jim had a fear of reading his poetry to an audience without a band backing him. We gave poetry readings together, hung out, drank, took drugs, and even performed with the Living Theater. When I wrote a hallucinatory comedy about our escapades, he flew up from LA to see the play. After their ovation, the actors came out and applauded us!

In 1986, Ray Manzarek and I began a collaboration of piano and voice, improvising in the manner of jazz. We have given at least 170 performances. My goal was to continue what we had started at the Six Gallery with a new audience; through poetry to speak of nature, politics, and freedom. Ray wanted to continue what he had done early on with the Doors, to bring meaningful spiritual experience to people. We performed in coffee houses, beer bars, museums, colleges, rock clubs, the Rock & Roll Hall of Fame, jazz clubs, dance halls, night clubs—any place that would have us. Ray and I have two albums and are about to edit a double album, "Live from San Francisco," and there is a documentary about our work together, "Third Mind." Our next gig will be in Poland, when we fly to Krakow to perform in honor of Milosz at his centennial. Besides the States, we have performed together in Japan, Canada, and Mexico.

Shivani: Can we say that the fundamental problem with poetry today is that it is quotidian and pedestrian, rather than visionary in nature? Do you see any visionaries around? Are there many paths to the visionary? Is it possible that the most visionary is that which at first appears the least visionary?

McClure: There are many "visionaries" around but few William Blakes, or Meister Eckharts or Eihei Dogens. It is probably that much of the visionary begins with what appears to be ordinary. Haikus are like that too.

Shivani: Can the visionary become commoditized?

McClure: It is ceaselessly commoditized—both the true thing which is not harmed by commoditization, and the military-industrial "visionary" which becomes small wars and proud public scandals and entertainment devices to be held in one's hand.

Interview with Poet Michael McClure

Jonah Raskin / 2013

From *SF Gate*, November 15, 2013. Reprinted by permission.

Michael McClure, eighty-one, might be the most photogenic of all the Beat Generation writers, and may be the most beautiful of the young male poets who stormed North Beach when City Lights was a bookstore no bigger than the proverbial hole-in-the-wall. Moreover, more than any other Beat poet, he's been wild about wild beasts, both real and imaginary, as in his illustrated book for children, *The Boobus and the Bunnyduck* and in "For the Death of 100 Whales," a kind of funeral dirge that he read at the historic Six Gallery poetry jamboree in 1955 that launched the San Francisco Poetry Renaissance.

This month, City Lights is republishing his 1964 classic, *Ghost Tantras* (ninety-nine pages; $13.95), a collection of ninety-nine poems in which he pushes language to the outer edge of human expression. Written in conversational English and in a guttural "Beast Language" that he created, *Ghost Tantras* begins rambunctiously and ends on a note of tranquility. The new edition includes a spirited introduction by McClure in which he takes readers behind the scenes and describes the process of spontaneous creativity that gave birth to the poems. "I have no idea what I'm doing—just writing," he explains.

All in all, there's no other book of poetry like *Ghost Tantras* in the annals of Beat literature. Fifty years after he self-published his experiments with language, the world of publishing has finally caught up with the book and the author, now in the midst of a revival as a spirited performer of the spoken word.

With bass player Rob Wasserman and drummer Jay Lane, McClure plays to audiences on college campuses and at venues such as Sweetwater Music Hall in Mill Valley. Janis Joplin, with whom he cowrote the hit song "Mercedes Benz," would not be surprised by the youthful energy that he still exudes as though just arrived fresh from Kansas, an American Shelley ready to shift the shape of reality itself.

When he showed up in San Francisco in 1954, McClure enrolled at San Francisco State and took literature classes. Then he met the bad boys who were remaking American literature: Allen Ginsberg, Jack Kerouac, Gary Snyder, and Lawrence Ferlinghetti. Ever since the Six Gallery reading, he's fused the spoken word to live music. In the 1960s, he caroused with Bob Dylan. Years later, McClure and keyboardist Ray Manzarek of the Doors took their rock-Beat act across the country and recorded several CDs.

During a morning conversation in the Oakland hills, where he lives with his wife of twenty-seven years, the sculptor Amy Evans-McClure, he talked about his love for the verses of Percy Bysshe Shelley and recited lines from some of his most beloved poets—William Blake, John Keats, Walt Whitman— and his contemporary, Diane di Prima.

Question: Why is City Lights republishing the book after all these years?

Answer: Of all my works, it's the one I most wanted to be republished. It draws together everything in my own personal experience from that time in the early 1960s. It also opened doors to the possibilities that followed: my novel, the years as a resident playwright at the Magic Theatre; the work with musicians such as Ray Manzarek of the Doors, who died in May; and all the way to the present day, performing at the Sweetwater with Rob Wasserman and Jay Lane.

Q: You read from *Ghost Tantras* to animals at the San Francisco Zoo.

A: Bruce Conner and I went there to record roosters. We ran into the lion keeper, who was also a poet, and he invited us to see the lions. I read and they roared. We roared together. You can Google it. I also read Chaucer to kangaroos that waved their heads back and forth and to seals that were barking.

Q: I've been staring at the cover of the new edition that shows a very wild-looking caveman. What's the story?

A: That's me with a lot of makeup on my face—and a lot of hair—that the artist Robert Lavigne applied.

Q: In the best-known photo of you, you're elbow-to-elbow with Allen Ginsberg and Bob Dylan.

A: Allen, Bob, and I hung out together in San Francisco, went to parties and shared ideas. One day, Dylan said, "Let's take a picture of the three of us." Larry Keenan shot us behind City Lights; it's Jack Kerouac Alley now. Lawrence Ferlinghetti has done a great job renaming so many of the alleys.

He has also done more than anyone else around to create the audience that we have for poetry. His *Coney Island of the Mind* has sold more copies than any other book of contemporary poetry except Pablo Neruda, plus he's published nearly everybody at City Lights.

Q: With the exception of Ferlinghetti and Gary Snyder, you may be the last major poet standing from that generation of poets who first published in the 1950s.

A: Don't forget Diane di Prima, who's still alive and still in San Francisco. She might be the greatest living American poet. I like everything Diane has written.

Q: On the back cover of the new edition, there's a quote from the actor and director Dennis Hopper—"Without McClure's roar there would have been no sixties." What does that mean to you?

A: That's praise from a real genius as an actor, director and photographer. We hit it off from the start; we were very close for years; like me, Dennis was from Kansas.

Q: Have you ever thought who you'd be now if you hadn't left Kansas?

A: That thought has never entered my mind. Everyone I knew wanted to get out of Kansas; most of the people in my circle left. I have hardly ever gone back.

Q: The poems in *Ghost Tantras* seem to me to be love poems.

A: Love is humanity's greatest invention.

Q: In the new introduction to the book, you write about your "shyness." Hard to believe.

A: I thought I was the shyest person around until Allen Ginsberg brought Jack Kerouac to my house in San Francisco. Jack had a deep-down shyness—way more than me. I overcame my own shyness when I read at the Six Gallery in 1955 with Ginsberg, Gary Snyder, and Philip Lamantia—when we all put our toes to the line in the sand. That was a pivotal moment in a life punctured by pivotal moments.

Q: You've always emphasized the political nature of the Beats, especially in your book *Scratching the Beat Surface*, one of the best books about you and your fellow poets.

A: We were definitely not uprooted from politics. We were environmentalists, though there were times when we talked about the environment and audiences booed us.

Q: Why did you write the poems? Do you remember?

A: I wanted to change the shape of the known universe.

Q: Do you remember the city when you arrived on December 31, 1954, and ate with chopsticks for the first time in Chinatown?

A: I remember shacks and goats on Twin Peaks. I remember falling in love with the wildflowers, the beauty of the ocean and Mount Tam, and I remember growing to hate all the wars. Roads were narrower then; traffic was lighter; the natural world seemed so close. Then houses crawled up all the hills, and there were more and more people, more cars, more everything. I belong to a generation that wasn't trained by the computer. I read a lot of books. I still do.

Break on Through

Garrett Caples / 2013

From the *San Francisco Bay Guardian*, November 12, 2013. Reprinted by permission.

I drive up into the East Oakland hills, past nineteenth century "Poet of the Sierras" Joaquin Miller's odd little cabin, to visit Michael McClure. Based on his youthful good looks, you'd never guess he was a few days shy of eighty-one, but the trail McClure has blazed through literary history testifies by length, stretching back to 1955 when—alongside Philip Lamantia, Philip Whalen, and Gary Snyder—he was the youngest participant in the famous Six Gallery reading at which Allen Ginsberg debuted "Howl." It was a seminal moment in postwar American poetry. "We all put our toes to the line that night and broke out," he says. "And we all went our own directions."

Beginning with his first book of poems, *Passage* (1956), McClure would find himself going in many directions, writing novels, essays, journalism, and even Obie-award-winning plays like *The Beard* (1965). As a countercultural figure, he could roll with the times, reading at the Human Be-In in 1967 in Golden Gate Park; associating with high-profile rock acts like Bob Dylan, the Doors, and Janis Joplin (for whom he cowrote the 1970 classic, "Mercedes Benz"); and appearing in movies like Peter Fonda's *The Hired Hand* (1971) and Martin Scorsese's *The Last Waltz* (1975). In the mid-1980s, he even began performing with the Doors' Ray Manzarek on piano, releasing such CDS as last year's *The Piano Poems* (Oglio Records). And though I've come to discuss *Ghost Tantras*, his 1964 self-published book of "Beast Language" reissued this month by City Lights, we inevitably touch on the recently deceased keyboardist with whom McClure played over two hundred gigs.

"Ray died at a very wonderful time," McClure says. "He's seventy-four and at the height of his powers. People say, 'You must feel broken up about Ray,' but I'm actually happy to know someone who stepped out in his own glory. The last time I saw him was [last] November. We had just done a performance at the Sweetwater in Mill Valley. That night Bobby Weir sat in. It was like the Doors and the Grateful Dead embraced."

The Language of the Beast

But *Ghost Tantras* predates most of these famous exploits. The origins of what McClure calls its "Beast Language" can be traced back to his early play *!The Feast!*, performed in 1960 at SF's Batman Gallery.

"The walls had Jay DeFeos and Bruce Conners on them," he recalls. "The actors were dressed in Indian blankets and torn white tissue paper beards, seated before a long table that carried black plums and white bread, black wine. Thirteen of them performed a Last Supper-like rite and spoke in Beast Language and English of the melding of opposites and the proportion of all beings, from the incredibly tiny to the cosmic."

"Beast Language" might be described as a roaring deformation of language into something less oriented toward signification and more toward the physicality of the body, poetry as "a muscular principle," as he writes in the original introduction, rather than as a mimetic text conveying images and ideas. Take, for example, these lines from tantra 46: "NOWTH / DROON DOOOOOOOOR AGH ! / Nardroor yeyb now thowtak drahrr ooh me thet noh / large faint rain dreeps oopon the frale tha toor / glooing gaharr ayaiieooo." Signification isn't the prime motivation here, nor is it entirely absent, as snippets of sense emerge and dissolve amid a sea of syllables. Such moments almost suggest reading Chaucer or *Finnegans Wake*, texts in some distant version of our own tongue, but they just as quickly vanish into phrases that resist intelligibility ("gaharr ayaiieooo").

Yet despite this resistance, the writing of *Ghost Tantras* was also bound up in visionary experience. McClure began *Ghost Tantras* in 1962 while working for the Institute for Personality Assessment and Research, for the University of California.

"My role with IPAR was to give psilocybin to artists and to film them in that timeless state of high," he says. "I was probably the ideal person because I had given up the use of psychedelic drugs myself. Already, after a lot of experimentation in psychedelics and several essays that had been published by City Lights in *Meat Science Essays* (1963), I wanted to write a deep exploration of these highs after reading Henri Michaux's gorgeous *Miserable Miracle* (1956), which was his—I felt personally—inaccurate description of the mescaline high. That inspired me to want to write clearly about this experience. Meanwhile, I had begun practicing Kundalini yoga, which is a chakra-centric yoga, and I was beginning to have powerful experiences."

"Art with No Edges"

This desire to convey visionary experience might seem at odds with *Ghost Tantras*' frequent resistance to signification, yet the apparent paradox might be resolved through abstract expressionism, which McClure insists was "one of my most profound sources, the art with no edges, the art with no limits." Viewed thusly, *Ghost Tantras* aspires to the degree of autonomy accorded to nonrepresentational art by not referring to experience but rather offering it.

"Allen Ginsberg had introduced me to Mark Rothko, and I got Rothko's phone number," McClure recalls. "I had *Ghost Tantras* and I wanted to show them to him but in the meantime I lost his number, as you did in those days. I always thought Rothko would be the right person to see the fields of letters in *Ghost Tantras*, as you see in one of his field paintings. If you look at *Ghost Tantras* in a different way, you see that each one is a field, a work of visual substance. Or nonsubstance.

"I knew I was tangoing with my own personal ridiculousness when I wrote these. I don't mind that, because in my writing when it's at its most intensely serious it's also at its most comic. And I call to mind what I think are some of the most important poems of the twentieth century, Federico García Lorca's "Gacela of Unforeseen Love," which is among the most intense love poetry I've every experienced. It's also kinda comic. My own poetry, when I believe in it the most, also has an edge to it that is not serious, or it's *serious*, all right, but real seriousness has an edge that breaks on through to the other side.

"It was part of the massive and inspired creativity that was rushing around me," he concludes. "That's probably the best clue I can give to anyone who wants to understand the sources behind *Ghost Tantras*, as part of the huge energy that was amassing itself and pouring through California at the time."

Poetry Questions: Michael McClure

Rebecca Foresman / 2013

From the *New Yorker*, January 14, 2013.

Michael McClure began his career as a Beat poet in the midst of the San Francisco renaissance. In 1955, he took part in the legendary six Gallery reading, along with Allen Ginsberg, Gary Snyder, Philip Lamantia, and Philip Whalen. McClure went on to become a central voice in the countercultural movement, collaborating prolifically with rock musicians and political activists. In addition to his poetry, McClure writes as a journalist, documentary filmmaker, playwright, novelist, and lyricist.

McClure's poem "Mephisto 20" is featured in this week's issue. I spoke with him about the striking interplay between Thoreauvian transcendentalism and Old Testament fatalism in the poem.

Rebecca Foresman: Before we get to some of the juicy Biblical questions, I want to share a passage taken from Thoreau's *Walden*: "Time is but the stream I go a-fishing in. I drink at it; but while I drink I see the sandy bottom and detect how shallow it is. Its thin current slides away, but eternity remains. I would drink deeper, fish in the sky, whose bottom is pebbly with stars. I cannot count one."

When I read the lines of your poem, "all probable / stream bottoms / finding stars," I thought of the quotation above. I'm curious: did you have *Walden* in mind as you were writing?

Michael McClure: Thanks, Rebecca, for the lovely quote from Thoreau. A phrase of Thoreau's close to my heart is "revel in the contradictions of love and pain and deep thought." No, I did not have *Walden* in mind as I was writing "Mephisto 20." Another phrase from another writer close to that time and close to the transcendentalists often pops into my mind: "A mouse is miracle enough," as Walt Whitman said, "to stagger sextillions of infidels." And I would be happy, atheist that I am, to think that my poems stagger an occasional infidel.

Foresman: In a certain light, "Mephisto 20" seems to narrate the experience of sitting on the floor and delving into deep meditation. Does meditative practice figure into the poem? Has it shaped your life as a writer?

McClure: Yes. Though transcendentalism is one of the deep breaths of a young, still-healthy America, my poetry, especially my late poems, are born, in part, from sitting on the floor in meditation. I practiced tantra yoga in my early life, and now practice Zen to Hua-Yen, or Flower Garden Buddhism. This has provided an aerial platform for my writing for several decades, and there is much in my poems from Hua-Yen Buddhism, a practice intended to elucidate the actual moment of Buddha's enlightenment. It deals with—it endlessly unwinds in greater and greater shapes—the sizelessness and uncountable myriadnesses of imagination and sense made one.

Foresman: In another light, the poem reads as a reflection or banishment from Eden, perhaps from the perspective of a postlapsarian man, or even the devil. I'm thinking of the line "The garden does not sleep at night," and the title, which seems to refer to Mephistopheles, the tempter and corrupter. Would you talk about the title?

McClure: In Goethe's play, Mephistopheles (he who hates matter and the light that clings to it) has many more aspects than are easily noted by the quick reader. He is not only the tempter, but he is the "inspirer-er" who brings back sleepy, discouraged Faust into worlds of imagination, inspiration, and swirls of consciousness. When seen in that character, the daemon is much wiser, more Puck-like and fascinating, than in the usual interpretation. Mephisto carries these aspects for me. The names Mephisto and Mephistopheles both have complex etymologies and faux etymologies. Another Mephisto is an angel who helps God in the construction of the universe, and in the creation of orcas (killer whales) and giant sea mammals, creatures dear to me since my Puget Sound childhood.

Foresman: Yes, I'm remembering your poem "For the Death of 100 Whales." In "Whales," as in much of your poetry, you study animal instinct with reverence In fact, the raw energy of "Mephsto 20" seems to be driven by the example that animals set for us in the world. You begin with an image of toes gripping the floor "PRIMATE STYLE," and the human brain is compared to a butterfly sensing "blotches of color, and pulses of organs."

McClure: Since the *New Yorker* accepted my poem, I've often thought of "Mephisto 20"'s butterfly as the butterfly that often appears on the cover of your magazine. If the topmost layer of our most highly active and thinking material membrane, right beneath the skull, was peeled away from the rest of brain and flattened out on a sheet, it would have the shape of a winged butterfly about to fly into "blotches of odor and pulses of organs." Butterfly in ancient Greek is "psyche," which, given the insights of William Blake, Francis Crick, the thirteenth-century Japanese visionary Dōgen, and our own biology, has the potentiality to take us anywhere and into any moment. I'm particularly interested in the final parallel drawn between the human speaker and game animals: [*quotes poem*].

Foresman: If "Mephisto 20" is indeed speaking about the state of fallen man, how does animal instinct come into play? Are these final stanzas hinting that we should do as Thoreau insists and "simplify" our approach to life, as the animals do?

McClure: When walking, in 1973, at the edge of Ngorongoro Crater in East Africa, I was alarmed by the twitch of a zebra's haunch as the herd walked tightly around me. "Mephisto 20" is dancing with the idea that we may be even more alive than we understand.

Beat Poet Michael McClure Tries New Style at Eighty-Three

Sam Whiting / 2015

From the *San Francisco Chronicle*, November 10, 2015. Reprinted by permission.

In the sixty years since the famed Six Gallery reading that introduced the Beat Poets, Michael McClure has read his words in any number of forms and settings.

But he'd never done anything close to what he was doing Saturday, November 7, which was to walk around a room reading his words as they hung on a wall. McClure, eighty-three, had put poetry to twenty-four abstract horse monoprints by his wife, Amy Evans McClure, sixty. The words and the image merge on the same print. But McClure's words on paper don't have the impact of McClure's words on paper as read aloud by McClure.

"Ripple. Grullo. Thicket," he reads from one painting in a voice that is as commanding as Richard Burton reading Shakespeare. "Houyhnhnm," he neighs, as proof that he is now also fluent in the horse dialect.

"You have to understand that Michael is the most amazing trickster of a man," says Jack Foley, who came from Oakland down to Palo Alto for the event. "He's so connected to words and to language that he can pull off something like this and make it quite beautiful."

The show, titled "Sculpture & Monotypes by Amy Evans McClure Words by Michael McClure," is at Smith Andersen Editions through November 25, but McClure was only there to open the show on Saturday. He has no other Bay Area readings scheduled, and if this turns out to be his last, it will have been the right setting. Smith Andersen is in a converted auto garage, and so was his first public reading.

That was on October 7, 1955. McClure was twenty-two and fresh out of San Francisco State, living at Scott and Haight streets and coming over the hill to Six Gallery, which had sculptures hanging from the rafters and a plank stage on floor, on Fillmore at Greenwich.

McClure had met Allen Ginsberg at a party, where they bonded over mutual admiration for William Blake. McClure and Ginsberg used to meet for coffee in North Beach. "He'd read me Jack Kerouac's letters which were fascinating to me."

Beats Beginning

During one of these meetings, McClure told Ginsberg he'd been asked to organize a poetry reading at Six Gallery but he didn't have the time, because his then-wife was expecting.

"Allen said, 'Do you want me to put together the reading?' and I said, 'Absolutely, man, that would be good.'"

And so began an event that was neither recorded nor filmed but is generally considered to be the moment that sparked the Beat Generation. On the bill that Friday night were Ginsberg, McClure, Gary Snyder, Philip Whalen, and Philip Lamantia, with Kenneth Rexroth as emcee. A historic plaque marking the spot notes that Kerouac was also on the bill, but he did not read. What Kerouac did was drink from a jug of garage wine and freeform his own poetry by yelling out words like "Dig it" and "Go, go" during the readings.

McClure read "For the Death of 100 Whales," which presaged the Greenpeace Save the Whales movement by about twenty years, but that was all but forgotten in the wake of "Howl," which Ginsberg introduced that night.

"As we spoke, we realized from the results that we were speaking for the people," McClure says. "We were saying what they needed and wanted to hear, and that encouraged us. We drew a line in the sand and decided not to back off that line."

Now they are all dead and gone except for Snyder, who is a practicing Buddhist in the Sierra foothills, and McClure, who is a practicing Buddhist in the Oakland hills. He likes to start his day with meditation and a hike in the forest behind his house, which is what he was doing under the redwoods last March when he took a step on slick footing and his legs went out from under him.

"I was temporarily suspended in the air like Wile E. Coyote and then dropped."

Hip Surgery, Rehab

He cracked a bone and had to have hip surgery. He spent three days in the hospital and ten in a rehab facility, and nine months later, the early morning hours he once devoted to meditation are devoted to working out in a gym to get his leg back under him.

He has been walking with a cane, and the surgery left him with a tremor that makes it impossible for him to read his own handwriting.

But he's not complaining. "Until I was twenty-seven, I thought I was going to die before I was twenty-eight," he says. But he's now been married for twenty-nine years and decided the time was right for his first-ever collaboration with Evans McClure, an accomplished artist in her own right.

For fifteen years, Evans McClure has been making sculptures of horses, which she can hear from her studio window, facing Butters Canyon. Her horses can be seen outside the Orinda Public Library and inside the McClure home. One such horse, an Appaloosa, sits in the living room, and the three of them—McClure, McClure Evans, and the horse head—were sitting together when McClure had a revelation.

"I said I love the spots that are painted on there because they remind me of gestural art, like Pollock or Clyfford Still," he recalls while sitting outside before his reading. "Maybe we could do a series of paintings of spots like you paint on the horses."

Paula Kirkeby, who owns Smith Andersen and represented the late Bruce Conner, invited the McClures to do a joint print project, and suddenly they had their theme.

"We were totally serious about it," he says, "and devoted to the idea."

Evans McClure put the spots and patterns of an Appaloosa onto paper, in ink and watercolor. To fix them with the right words, McClure got a series of note cards and on each card wrote two words.

"I wanted to put the consciousness and the perceptions of a wild horse, not a domesticated horse, into a deck of cards that I could flip through," he says.

The words and images were combined in the print shop at Smith Andersen. As each of twenty-four unique images rolled off the press, McClure went through the cards to find the words to go with it. It was performance art with no one there to witness it.

Once the prints had their words, the McClures decided to do it again in reverse order, this time applying a print to each of the cards. This forms a series called "Appaloosa Deck." There are four decks of thirty-two cards.

The prints and the cards moved from the shop to the gallery on the other side of a wall. Also in the show are Evans McClure's horse sculptures greeting people as they walk in the door.

As the crowd built on Saturday, McClure rested in a side room. Then he came out, without the aid of his cane, and leaned against a display case.

"Am I clear?" he asked at the start, warming up his voice. He introduced the artwork, then left the safety of the display case and walked around the room, looking at each of the twenty-four prints and reading the words behind glass.

It was all over too soon. Nobody wanted to stop hearing his verse applied to verse. The audience stood there awaiting a poetry encore. McClure thought he had left his anthology, *Of Indigo and Saffron*, at home, but a copy magically turned up.

He read several haikus, and a poem that fit the theme of the "Appaloosa Deck." "Horse heads swirling in rainbows," it began.

The audience still wanted more, so he reached for a second book, *Ghost Tantras*, just reprinted by City Lights in a fiftieth-anniversary edition. His hands were so shaky they could barely turn the page, but they found their way to page thirty-nine.

"This poem comes from 1962," he announced: "MARILYN MONROE, TODAY THOU HAST PASSED THE DARK BARRIER" [*reads the first stanza of poem*]. That was just the first stanza, and the audience was entranced.

Index

ACLU, 29, 84, 86, 131
Actor's Workshop, 84–85, 130
Adam, Helen, 77, 117, 145
Allen, Donald, 81, 134, 135
"America" (Ginsberg), 167
Ark (magazine), 38, 52, 77, 78
Ark II/Moby I (magazine), 81, 94
Artaud, Antonin, 15, 48, 73, 74, 88, 99, 104, 107, 119–20, 126–27, 128, 141, 142n1, 156–57, 159, 171, 177, 180
Ashbery, John, 32, 91
Auerhahn Press, 37, 38, 41–42, 46, 82

Baez, Joan, 21, 35, 134
Ball, Hugo, 73, 74, 156
Baraka, Amiri, xii, 82, 87, 87, 94, 99, 104, 109, 120, 126, 159, 160, 179
Barron, Frank, 122
Bashō, Matsuo, 14
Beck, Julian, 128, 129
Berman, Walter, xii, 55–56, 92, 120, 121, 125–26, 178
"Berry Feast, A" (Snyder), 162, 164
Billy the Kid (character), 4, 13–14, 17–18, 24–27, 28, 45, 63, 72, 85, 112–13, 127, 128–29, 131, 162, 169–70, 178
Black Mountain, 39, 60, 69–70, 78, 81, 94

Blake, William, xiii, xvii, 15, 18, 34, 47, 48, 86, 89, 96–97, 104, 106, 125, 129, 133, 141, 149, 156, 158, 181, 183, 191, 193
Blake Street Hawk Eyes, 133
Blau, Herb, 84–85
"Bomb" (Corso), 166–67
Bomb Culture (Nuttall), 17
Brakhage, Stan, xii, xvi, 20, 57, 115, 117, 145–51
Bunnell, Sterling, xii, xv, xvii, 43, 122, 170
Burroughs, William, xxx, 20, 41, 69, 72, 78, 82, 103, 114, 166

Cardenal, Ernesto, 108–9, 110
Charters, Ann, 168
Chomsky, Noam, 155, 170
Circle (magazine), 38
City Lights, 37, 41, 72, 87, 117, 134, 165, 166, 182, 183–84, 186, 187, 195
Clemente, Francesco, xi–xii, 88, 92, 107
Collins, Jess, 52, 117, 145, 178
Connor, Bruce, xii, xiii, 8, 46, 53–55, 57, 59, 76, 92, 107, 111, 116, 120, 121, 140, 150, 183, 187, 194
Cordier, Robert, 128
Corman, Cid, 94–95
Corso, Gregory, 10, 69, 78, 103, 165, 166–67, 170
Coyote, Peter, 133–34, 140

197

Creeley, Bob, 15, 32, 33, 38, 39, 54, 69, 73, 81, 94–95, 104, 109, 146, 159, 160, 168, 173, 175, 180
Crick, Francis, xv, 9, 32, 55, 175, 191

Dalí, Salvador, xiii, 92, 148, 165
Danton's Death (Büchner), 127–28
de Born, Bertrand, 32
de Kooning, Willem, 8, 23, 55, 92, 121
DeFeo, Jay, 51, 52, 55, 75, 120–21, 187
di Prima, Diane, xii, 41, 57, 87, 94, 104, 140, 159, 160, 168, 179, 183, 184
Dickinson, Emily, 96, 97
Diggers, 133, 142–43n2
Dōgen, 114, 156, 159–60, 191
Duncan, Robert, xi, xii, 9, 15, 28, 38, 39, 40, 43, 52, 53, 60, 69, 73, 76, 77–78, 81, 88, 92, 103–4, 110, 117, 18, 119, 124, 130, 134, 144, 145, 146, 166, 168, 170, 171, 173, 177, 178, 180
Dylan, Bob, 21, 46, 134–35, 139, 140, 169, 179, 183, 186

Eigner, Larry, 95, 168
Evergreen Review (magazine), 80–83, 86, 87
Everson, William, 9, 38, 76, 81

Felger, Richard, xv, 123
Ferlinghetti, Lawrence, 37, 43, 81–82, 85, 87, 131, 153, 154, 161, 165, 183–84
Floating Bear (newsletter), 87, 94
Four Seasons Press, 41

García Lorca, Frederico, 48, 54, 56, 81, 93–94, 126, 158, 177, 188
Genet, Jean, 126
Ginsberg, Allen, xii, xiii, 10, 32, 37, 40, 42, 51–52, 53, 64, 69, 71, 72, 73, 75–76, 78, 80, 90, 99, 109, 105–6, 115, 126, 134–35, 153, 155, 159, 162, 163, 164, 165, 167, 170, 173, 175, 176, 183, 184, 186, 188, 189, 193
Gitin, David, 179
Grove Press, 22, 41–42, 72, 81
Guston, Philip, 92, 109, 159, 165

Haeckel, Ernst, xiv, xv, 47, 48, 50, 125
Harlow, Jean (character), 4, 14, 18, 24–26, 27, 28, 45, 63, 72, 85, 113, 128–29, 178
Haselwood, Dave, 37, 38–39, 41–42, 82
Hawley, Robert, 5, 168, 169
Herms, George, xii, 55–56, 57–59, 92, 121
Hoffman, John, 162–63
Hopper, Dennis, xii, 8, 115, 184
Hoyem, Andrew, 41
Human Universe, The (Olson), 41

Indian Journals (Ginsberg), 41

Jargon Press, 37, 38
Jarry, Alfred, 10, 132
Johnson, Ray, 4
Johnston, Ellis (grandfather), xi
Johnston, Marian Dixie (mother), xi
Jones, LeRoi. See Baraka, Amiri
Joplin, Janis, 139–40, 152, 182, 186
Journal for the Protection of All Beings (magazine), 81–82, 165–66

Keats, John, xvi–xvii, 183
Kerouac, Jack, 8, 10, 27, 43, 69, 70, 72, 76, 80–81, 100, 103, 113–14, 120, 154, 159–60, 163, 164–65, 173, 175, 176, 183–83, 193
Kunstformen der Natur (Haeckel), xiv, 47
Kyger, Joanne, 77, 159, 168, 179

Lamantia, Philip, xii, 9–10, 15, 23, 37, 38–39, 75–76, 82, 90, 119–20, 162–63, 179, 180, 184, 186, 189, 193

Lane, Jay, 182, 183
Laughlin, J., 83, 87
Laurence, D. H., xii, 72, 104, 156, 158, 177
Leary, Timothy, 122
Life (magazine), 116, 147, 148
Lion, John, 12, 49, 132, 133
Living Theater, 128, 129, 181
Lost Son and Other Poems, The (Roethke), 95

Magic Theatre, 19, 27, 132–33, 183
Mailer, Norman, xvi, 20, 58, 82, 87, 97, 166
Malina, Judith, 128, 129
Manzarek, Ray, xii, xvi, 90, 97, 100–101, 141, 152, 180, 181, 183, 186
Marcuse, Herbert, 71, 89, 159, 170, 179
Margalef, Ramon, 64
Martin, Fred, 52
Martin, Tony, 28
Mayakovsky, Vladimir, 73, 158, 177
McClure, Amy (wife), 183, 192, 194–95
McClure, Michael: and abstract expressionism, 45, 52, 53–54, 57, 60–61, 62, 70–71, 92–93, 102, 115, 117, 121, 165, 188; and anarchy, 9, 38, 42, 69, 71, 76, 77, 78, 80–81, 88, 92, 104, 129, 133, 153, 163, 167, 176–77; on assemblage, xiii, 56–59, 107, 115, 116; and "Beast Language," xiii, 17–18, 25, 26–27, 29–31, 74, 109, 137–39, 149–50, 157, 171, 174, 182, 186, 187–88; and the Beat generation, xi, xiv, xvii, 10–11, 37, 40, 51, 69–72, 78–79, 80, 106, 109, 116, 117, 120–21, 123, 127, 152, 154, 161, 162, 163–64, 165, 166, 171, 175–76, 182, 184, 189, 192, 193; and Buddhism, xvii, 35, 50, 62, 76, 114, 136, 149, 157–58, 159, 163, 164, 165, 176, 190, 193; on Cambodia, crop poisons in, 167–68; and censorship, xvii, 71–72, 83–84, 85, 129, 130, 176; on consciousness, 96–97; and "drive words," 93–94; and drug use, xv, 11, 16, 68, 82, 97, 122, 129, 140, 180, 181, 187; early years, xi, 7–8, 37–38, 53–54, 109–10, 111–12, 123–24; and environmentalism, xii–xiii, xvii, 9, 11–12, 15, 58, 70–71, 78–79, 100, 101, 104, 105, 122, 129, 136, 154, 161, 162–63, 176, 184; and film, xiii, xv–xvi, 8, 14, 20, 21, 28, 57, 68, 87, 92, 115, 116, 117, 122, 128, 131–32, 144–51, 157, 187, 189; on fine printing, 37–38; and Haight-Ashbury, xvi, 27, 57, 114–15, 129, 130, 133, 134, 140, 142–43n2, 169, 192–93; on interview as art form, 88; on jazz, 15, 54, 56, 90, 120, 146, 148, 179, 181; on the McCarthy era, 10; and "meat," 18–19, 31–32, 62, 89, 101, 128, 156, 157, 178; nature/biology, influences of, 7, 8–9, 43, 89, 104–5, 123–25, 156, 157, 158, 159, 161; poetry, evolution of, 13, 15–16, 107; on poetry and form, 32–33, 46–47, 60, 90, 106–7, 117, 174; on poetry and music, 90–91, 100–101; on poetry and plays, 43–44, 45, 48; on poetry being physical, 89–90, 96–97, 100; and politics, 10, 11–12, 42, 69–70, 71–72, 76, 92, 99–100, 104–5, 119, 124, 125, 129, 133, 159, 161–67, 168–69, 170, 171, 177, 181, 184, 189; and projective verse, xii, xvii, 16, 35, 59, 60, 93, 101–2, 106–7, 118–19, 123, 127, 155, 156, 168, 177, 179; on San Francisco, 9–10, 15, 42–43, 91–92; on soulmaking, xvi, 88–89, 109; and surrealism, 8, 10, 22–23, 53,

56; and theater, xv–xvi, 12, 13–14, 19–20, 23, 29, 43–45, 48, 49, 57, 58, 71–72, 85–87, 119, 126, 127–29, 130–34, 137–38, 141, 178; on transrational language, 73–74; on Verticalists, 74; on Vietnam, xiii, 23, 109, 129–30, 161–62, 164, 167, 168–69, 171; and visual artists, 51–53, 92–93; on writing process, 8, 14, 98–99

Works by: *Adept, The*, xvi, 21, 68, 141–42, 180; *Antechamber*, 37, 46, 47; *Beard, The* (play), xvi, 12–13, 24, 29, 71–72, 128–29, 130–33; "Beat Surface, The" (essay), 175, 179; *Blossom, The* (play), 56, 57, 59, 127, 129, 155, 169, 174; *Button, The* (play), 12, 19; "Dallas Poem," 135; *Dark Brown*, 40, 72, 82, 113; "Dark Brown," 179, 180; "Dolphin Skull," 179, 180; *!Feast, The!* (play), xiii, 59, 66, 113, 137, 187; "Fields," 177–78; "For the Death of 100 Whales," xii, 123, 125–26, 162, 167, 175, 182, 190, 193; *Freewheelin Frank, Secretary of the Angels, as Told to Michael McClure*, 21–22, 91, 98, 102–3, 134, 135, 137, 139; *Gargoyle Cartoons* (play), xvi, 14, 49, 126, 132; *General Gorgeous* (play), 37, 49; *Ghost Tantras*, xiii–xiv, 3, 4, 30–31, 60, 66, 73, 137, 149, 156–57, 174, 182, 183, 184, 186, 187–88, 195; *Goethe: Ein Fragment* (play), 50; *Gorf* (play), 37, 126; *Grabbing of the Fairy, The* (play), 44, 48; *Hymns to St. Geryon and Other Poems*, 18, 38–39, 50–51, 46, 82, 109, 119–20, 125; *Jaguar Skies*, 32, 37; *Josephine the Mouse Singer* (play), 152, 174; *Lighting the Corners* (memoir), 103–4; *Mammals, The*, 19, 42; *Meat Science Essays*, xv, 18, 66, 82, 119, 166, 187; "Mephisto 20," 189–91; "Mercedes Benz" (song), 139–40, 152, 182–83; "My mother said to me tonight," 34; *Mysteriosos and Other Poems*, 175; "Nature Poem Written in I. Magnin," 35; *New Book/A Book of Torture, The*, xv, 41, 175, 180; *Of Indigo and Saffron*, 173, 174, 195; *Organism*, 64–65; *Passage*, 38, 39, 69, 186; "Peyote Poem," xv, 55, 119, 120, 175; "Poisoned Wheat," xiii, 109, 110, 124, 161–62, 168, 169, 170, 171, 174; *Pussy, The* (play), 19; "Rant Block," 61, 109, 175; "Rare Angel," 13, 55, 61, 179–80; *Rebel Lions*, 99, 101–2, 111; *Red Snake, The* (play), 133–34; "Revolucion," 33–34; *Scratching the Beat Surface*, 129, 175, 184; *September Blackberries*, 18, 23, 37, 65, 69; *Sermons of Jean Harlow and Curses of Billy the Kid*, 41; "Souls," 108–9; *Surge, The*, 47, 64; "Up Beat," 35; "What strange odors in this room," 34–35; *Wild 90* (film), 87; "Wolf Net" (essay), 156

McClure, Thomas (father), xi, 7
McIntosh, Graham, 41, 47
Meltzer, David, 5, 41, 56, 137, 165, 166
Melville, Herman, 81, 159
Mexico City Blues (Kerouac), 76, 81, 159, 164
Michaux, Henri, xv, 11, 82, 156, 187
Miller, Arthur, 48, 49
Miller, Henry, 39, 72, 92
Miller, Joaquin, 43, 186
Mime Troupe of San Francisco, 133, 142

"Miserable Miracle" (Michaux), xv, 11, 82, 187–88
Monk, Thelonius, 54, 81, 156
Morrison, Jim, xvi, 21, 90, 97, 103, 152, 178, 180
Motherwell, Robert, 8, 23, 53, 54–55, 92, 116

Neruda, Pablo, 159, 184

Odum, H. T., xv, 63, 64
Olson, Charles, xii, xvii, 35, 38, 39, 41, 59, 60, 62, 69, 81, 82, 94–95, 101–2, 103, 109, 118, 119, 144, 155, 156, 168, 175, 177
Oyez Press, 5, 168, 169

Patchen, Kenneth, 9, 15, 39
Perspectives in Ecological Theory (Margalef), 64
Pieces (Creeley), 32
Pinter, Harold, 84
Podhoretz, Norman, 163–64
Pollack, Jackson, 8, 10, 23, 35, 45, 52, 54, 59–61, 63, 64, 68, 89–90, 92, 102, 116, 146, 147–48, 156, 175, 177, 179, 180, 194
Poltroon Press, 41
Pound, Ezra, 66, 83, 106, 121, 158–59, 177

Rare Angel Productions, 86–87, 131
Rexroth, Kenneth, xii, 9, 27, 37, 40, 76–77, 80, 92, 119, 121–22, 128, 163, 176, 193
Richards, Mary Caroline, xi–xii
Rimbaud, Arthur, 113–14, 116, 165, 169, 180
Rossett, Barney, 81, 82, 83–84, 85, 86–87
Rothenberg, Jerome, 141, 179
Rothko, Mark, 52, 60, 116, 117, 188

Sabina, Maria, 122–23
San Francisco Oracle (newspaper), 169
San Francisco State, 28, 77, 117, 145, 183, 192–93
Scalapino, Leslie, 173
Schwitters, Kurt, 74, 107, 156
Semina (magazine), 55–56, 109, 125, 186
Shelley, Percy Bysshe, xvii, 15, 40, 58, 66, 98, 140–41, 157, 158, 166, 174, 175, 183
Six Gallery, xii, 10, 37, 52–53, 58, 69, 75, 77–78, 80–81, 90, 104, 123, 153, 154, 161, 162, 163, 164, 167, 176, 181, 182, 183, 184, 186, 189, 192–93
Snyder, Gary, xii, xvii, 9, 10, 14, 15, 18, 23, 37, 40, 43, 60, 72, 78–79, 80, 81, 82, 90, 109, 115, 154, 159, 162–63, 164, 165, 170, 176, 183, 184, 186, 189, 193
Spicer, Jack, 41, 77, 92, 103
Still, Clyfford, 35, 45, 59, 116–17, 179, 194

Theatre and Its Double, The (Artaud), xii, 88
Thomas, Dylan, 45–46
Thoreau, Henry David, 104–5, 145, 189, 191
To Have Done with the Judgement of God (Artaud), 119, 157, 165
Torn, Rip, 86–87, 139

Ubu Roi (Jarry), 132

Van Newkirk, Allen, 170
Villiers Press, 39
Voznesensky, Andrei, 71

Wagner, Richard, xiii, xvi
Walden (Thoreau), 189
Walter Cronkite Show, The, 130
Wasserman, Rob, 182, 183
Watts, Alan, 85, 117, 122, 131

Welch, Lew, 41, 109
White Rabbit, 77
Whitehead, Alfred North, xiv, 48, 102, 107, 125, 171, 175
Whitman, Walt, 159, 183, 189
Wieners, John, 38, 82

Williams, Jonathan, 37, 38, 39, 177
Wilson, Adrian, 38, 39
Wilson, Bill, 4

Yevtushenko, Yevgeny, 71, 73
Yugen (magazine), 82, 94, 109

About the Editor

Photo courtesy of Eastern
Michigan University Division
of Communications

David Stephen Calonne is the author of *William Saroyan: My Real Work Is Being*; *The Spiritual Imagination of the Beats*; *Diane di Prima: Visionary Poetics and the Hidden Religions*; *R. Crumb: Literature, Autobiography and the Quest for Self*; *The Beats in Mexico*; and has written biographies of Charles Bukowski and Henry Miller. He has edited five volumes of the uncollected prose of Bukowski for City Lights and interviews with Gary Snyder, Allen Ginsberg, and Diane di Prima for University Press of Mississippi. He has taught at the University of Texas at Austin, the University of Michigan, and the University of Chicago, and presently teaches at Eastern Michigan University.

www.ingramcontent.com/pod-product-compliance
Lightning Source LLC
Chambersburg PA
CBHW030106170426
43198CB00009B/518